REVISED & EXPANDED THIRD EDITION

# Marine Aquarium Handbook

## Beginner to Breeder

**TFH Publications**®
One TFH Plaza
Third and Union Avenues
Neptune City, NJ 07753
www.tfh.com

ISBN-13: 978-0-9820262-1-2
ISBN-10: 0-9820262-1-8
UPC-A: 6-81290-02621-7

Library of Congress Cataloging-in-Publication Data

Moe, Jr., Martin A., 1937–
Marine aquarium handbook : beginner to breeder /
Martin A. Moe, Jr. -- Revised and updated 3rd ed. / with a foreword by Julian Sprung ;
photography by Matthew L. Wittenrich.
    p. cm.
Includes bibliographical references and index.
ISBN 0-9820262-1-8
1. Marine aquariums.  I. Wittenrich, Matthew L. (Matthew Lynn).  II. Title.
SF457.1.M63 2009
639.34'2--dc22                       2009028668

First printing, April 1982
Third Edition, first printing, August 2009
Printed and bound in China
11 12 13 14 15   5 7 9 8 6 4

Designed by Linda Provost
All cover photography by Matthew L. Wittenrich

Co-published by

**T.F.H. Publications, Inc.**
Neptune City, NJ 07753
www.tfh.com

MICROCOSM

PROFESSIONAL
SERIES™

**Microcosm, Ltd.**
P.O. Box 550
Charlotte, VT 05445
www.MicrocosmAquariumExplorer.com

**CENTRAL**
Garden & Pet

REVISED & EXPANDED THIRD EDITION

# Marine Aquarium Handbook

## Beginner to Breeder

# Martin A. Moe, Jr.

*with a Foreword by* **Julian Sprung**

*Principal photographer*
**Matthew L. Wittenrich**

with
*Scott W. Michael, Alf Jacob Nilsen,*
*Denise Nielsen Tackett,* and *Larry Tackett*

*To my wife, Barbara,*
*whose support and encouragement*
*are never-failing,*
*and to the memory of my parents,*
*Martin and Clara*

# Acknowledgements

My first efforts on this book began in the mid 1970s. There are so many people I want to thank—for directly contributing to the book and adding to my base of knowledge and experience—that there just isn't enough space to list them. However, I want you all to know that I have greatly appreciated your help and advice over these past 35 years. For this third edition, there are some people who must be acknowledged by name.

First and foremost is James Lawrence, editor and publisher at Microcosm, Ltd. Without his interest, effort, and hard work, the third edition would probably never have happened and the old *Handbook* would languish in the musty, dusty back rooms of secondhand bookstores. But he has given it new life, inspiring me to update the content, commissioning a fresh design by Linda Provost, and making it relevant, once again, to one of the most interesting and exciting hobbies on the planet. Julian Sprung, a good friend for many years and a trailblazer in the development of the coral reef aquarium, contributed the Foreword—which was an interesting turnabout, since I did the Foreword for his first book. And Matt Wittenrich, *wunderkind* of marine fish breeding—an accomplished breeder, photographer, and writer at an early age—generously contributed most of the brilliant new photographs. Images were also contributed by a number of other noteworthy photographers, including Scott Michael, Denise Nielsen Tackett, Larry Tackett, Alf Jacob Nilsen, and Matt Pedersen, and Jeff Turner's marine aquarium designs are featured in many of the photos. To them and many others, I extend my gratitude.

Blue-ring Angelfish
*Pomacanthus annularis*

# Contents

# Foreword

## by Julian Sprung

IN 1977 THERE WERE NO FRAG SWAPS, NO MACNA OR OTHER MAJOR marine aquarium conferences, so it was fortunate for me that I lived in South Florida and was a member of the Florida Marine Aquarium Society (FMAS). That's where I met Martin Moe, Jr. when I was 11 years old.

Martin was the guest speaker at a FMAS monthly meeting at the Miami Museum of Science that year. It was right about the time when I maintained my first marine aquarium, though my brother Elliot already had kept two of them starting when I was just four. Soon after we met Martin, my father planned a trip to take Elliot and me down to Marathon to visit him and see his breeding facility—Dad was a pilot and the trip to Marathon was a good excuse to fly. Martin picked us up at the airport, and during visits like this over a period of several years (most often by car with my family), I saw the results of Martin's fish breeding projects. I vividly remember many things about those visits, but a few things really stand out—tanks with hundreds of baby angelfish swimming like so many guppies, flashing their bright yellow and blue markings in a dense soup of greenwater; a shallow outdoor tank filled with baby jewelfish, their intensely blue polka-dots glowing in the sun; and the amazing Hijack fish, produced by crossing the High Hat and the Jackknife.

The nearest experience one may have today is a visit to the farm at Oceans, Reefs & Aquariums in Fort Pierce, Florida, or C-Quest in Puerto

The author with a Long-spined Sea Urchin, *Diadema antillarum*, his ultimate breeding challenge to date. The wild population of this keystone species has been decimated.

Rico, where one can view great huddling balls of clownfish, brilliantly hued *Pseudochromis*, and other tank-raised ornamental marine fishes, not to mention corals. There are other farms like this now in various business-es around the world, and in many private home settings, like Joe Lichten-bert's basement clownfish hatchery. Several years back, one could see the fantastic home-based setup of Frank Baensch in Hawaii, where he raised *Centropyge* spp. angelfishes. I have been fortunate to see all of these places, and they reminded me of those first visits with Martin more than 30 years ago. It must be so gratifying for him to see these operations, as well as the fantastic work done lately by Matt Wittenrich, Iris Bönig, Matt Pedersen, and others who continue to expand the list of species spawned and raised in captivity and push the bounds of imagination regarding what can be done with aquariums.

Progress in any field occurs when someone manages to accomplish what no one else has ever done. The idea, the goal, the dream can be dis-cussed in colorful imaginary terms, but the barrier remains firm until the first successes give proof that the dream is not an impossible one. Up to that point there is always a seed of doubt in the minds of all who try to accomplish or discover something. (Failure after failure can be pretty convincing!) After the solution is found, and even if it is imperfect, the seed of doubt is removed and the floodgates open for creative minds to improve the methods in ways big and small, so that the hidden path becomes a beaten path and eventually a paved superhighway.

**MOE ADVENTURES:**

Progress in any field occurs when someone manages to accomplish what no one else has ever done...
In so many areas, Martin has revealed the way by developing and widely publicizing his methods for the commercial rearing of clownfish and other ornamental marines.

❧

In so many areas, Martin has re-vealed the way by developing and widely publicizing his methods for the commercial rearing of clownfish and other ornamental marines. Moreover, with this book, first published in 1982, he brought much of the intangibility of successful marine aquar-ium–keeping into a practical, easy-to-comprehend form for beginning hobbyists and experienced aquarists alike. Given the time that has passed since the last edition came out, and the fact that this edition is a joint

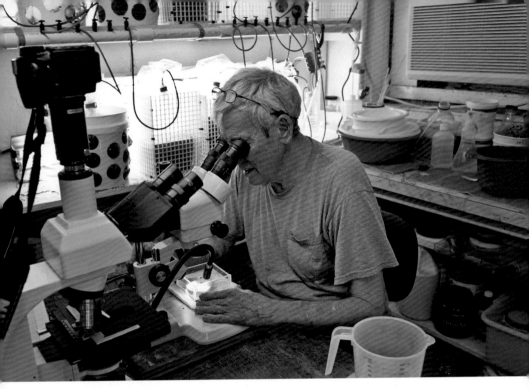

Martin A. Moe, Jr. in his Florida Keys home marine breeding laboratory.

effort that includes Matt Wittenrich's images and James Lawrence's editing, I am sure that it will once again raise our awareness of the possibilities of the aquarium hobby to a new level.

Martin's latest adventure is unraveling the mysteries of the mass cultivation of the Long-spined Sea Urchin *Diadema antillarum*. He is working on propagating this species, not for its potential use as an ornamental aquarium pet, but for its critical function in the coral reef ecosystems of the Florida Keys and the Caribbean. Martin believes, as I do, that the sea urchin's efficacy as a top-down control for algal growth is an important key to the recovery of coral reefs in regions that have lost much of their live coral cover in the past two decades. The decline in coral cover occurred mainly after the sudden mass mortality of *Diadema* as a result of a plague during the 1980s. Preliminary controlled studies by Martin Moe and Ken Nedimyer show that artificially enhancing the population of *Diadema* on patch reefs promotes both coral growth and recruitment of new corals onto the bare, hard substrata cleaned by *Diadema*. This is encouraging news compared to studies by many reef researchers that show a steady decline in coral recruitment and a net loss of coral cover year after

Indomitable marine biologist Moe on the eve of a "Eureka" aquarium breakthrough.

year on the reefs where *Diadema* have been nearly absent. Martin has experienced the discovery phase of many aquaculture challenges, and refers to "Eureka" moments when some small change in technique makes all the difference in the world. The problem of the mass propagation of *Diadema antillarum* has given up its secrets with great reluctance, but on the eve of the publication of this book, Martin has met with success.

Every year I look forward to visiting with "Skip" and his wife, Barbara, though these days it seems we see each other more often at aquarium conferences far away from our homes in South Florida. Once in a while I take my family down to the Florida Keys, and we stop by to catch up, relax, snorkel, and enjoy a long friendship born of a common interest in the sea.

—*Julian Sprung*
*Miami Gardens, Florida*

# Preface

## *to the Third Edition*

ABOUT TWO THOUSAND YEARS AGO, THE GREEK PHILOSOPHER DIOGENES Laërtius was supposedly the first to advance the concept that "the only constant is change." I'm sure he was thinking ahead to the marine aquarium hobby/industry of the late 20th and early 21st centuries. Of course, everything changes constantly: our science, our technology, our religions, our governments, and our environment; maybe only a mother's love, a symbol of the biological laws that underlie our existence, is constant. And within that constant, within the sphere of human experience, lies our fascination with the vast and complex world under the sea. Our experience with the sea encompasses simple spears and fiber nets, wooden sailing boats that brought back tales of faraway lands and great sea monsters, epic seafaring wars, and, finally, revelations of unknown aquatic worlds made possible by the varied devices that allow us to carry our essential atmosphere down into the sea, reaching even the greatest depths of the ocean. But this is not enough. Since the dawn of civilization, we have always wanted to capture the sea and its creatures, holding them in small oceans of our own—making for wonder, enjoyment, achievement, and good eating.

When I wrote the first edition of the *Handbook*, the modern era of marine aquarium–keeping was in its infancy. Few of the intrepid marine aquarists of that time knew that we were recapturing a hobby with beginnings in the last half of the 19th century. It was much more difficult to keep marine tropical fish in those days, but marine aquariums were objects of great interest. Public interest in marine aquariums was captured in

**Young Volitans Lionfish, *Pterois volitans*.**

1861 when William Damon and Albert S. Bickmore, under the direction of P. T. Barnum, sailed from Bermuda in a small fishing boat with over 600 live tropical marine fish for display at the American Museum in New York. Damon was also the first aquarist to have a saltwater aquarium in his home, keeping seahorses quite successfully. And interest in marine aquariums has not waned since that time.

Functional, more modern techniques and knowledge that made keeping small marine aquariums reasonably successful were basically developed in the 1960s, and the biological techniques learned then are still workable today. The hobby has changed dramatically in the last 20 years and is still changing today. Now, many home marine aquariums rival and even eclipse displays at public aquariums, but not at modest cost. One can easily invest

the price of a small (or large) automobile in a spectacular reef tank with living hard and soft corals from around the world and fish of wonderful colors and forms—and expensive rarities as well. But it is also still possible to start out with a marine aquarium that provides much of the wonder of undersea creatures at a very modest cost and without great technical expertise. This third edition of *The Marine Aquarium Handbook* will be very helpful to readers in this endeavor, so I am very happy that Microcosm has undertaken the task of publishing it.

MARTIN A. MOE, JR.
*Islamorada, Florida*
*July 2009*

# Introduction

MOST OF THE EARTH IS OCEAN, AND OF THE AQUATIC ENVIRONMENTS of the world, coral reefs are among the most environmentally stable and biologically dynamic. Coral reefs only occur within about 30 degrees of latitude from the equator. They can only live and grow where average annual water temperatures are approximately 72 to 84°F; salinity is constant and high; sunlight strongly penetrates the shallow, clear oceanic water; and the level of dissolved nutrients is very low. The environment changes little from season to season, year to year; but the animals and plants endlessly war for food and space.

These elements of existence have created a wonderland of form, color, and behavior—a wonderland that we can capture, in small measure, in our home aquariums. The romance and mystery of tropic seas can be reflected in a small simulated coral reef, snug in one's living room, while winter winds pile snow against the door.

Thirty years or so ago, a successful marine aquarist was regarded with awe and wonder as one favored by Neptune himself, and thus privy to the secrets of the deep. Now we know that those pioneering individuals were not specially favored, but only had the courage to persist, despite failures, and the tenacity to stick with methods that worked for them. Now we know why certain methods and techniques work and others fail, and although maintaining a marine aquarium is not as easy as keeping a freshwater tank, most of the questions now have answers—and with a little effort, the average fish fancier can be a successful marine aquarist.

Rock Beauty Angelfish, *Holacanthus tricolor*

Once only a dream, bringing the wonders and diverse animals of a coral reef into a home aquarium is now within the reach of dedicated marine aquarists.

Some of us can recall a time when a would-be marine aquarist had to build his own all-glass aquarium, mix his own salt, and ponder the mysterious death of fishes in a new aquarium. Several very important, relatively recent developments that have put a marine aquarium within reach of most aquarists are the commercial availability of better aquariums and well-formulated synthetic sea salts, and the understanding of how to establish biological filtration in the aquarium. Since the first edition of this book appeared, the marine sector of the aquarium hobby has grown great-

ly and there have been major advances in home aquarium technology. New approaches to filtration, new concepts in lighting, new books, more widely dispersed working knowledge, new livestock and natural "live" substrates, and, most important, new hardware and equipment are now available and allow the novice marine enthusiast to achieve beautiful displays with almost certain success. One still has to do one's homework, but there is now far less uncertainty in the wonderful world of keeping marine aquariums. A good aquarium shop and your local aquarium society are excellent sources of help and information. An aquarium shop will usually know of the nearest aquarium society with a marine interest and steer you in the right direction. Society members will be glad to help you avoid major errors and support you in your efforts to become a successful marine aquarist.

## What does a marine aquarium do?

In essence, a marine aquarium provides an adequate substitute for the natural conditions that a marine organism needs to maintain life.

But what may be an adequate substitute for the natural environment for one species may be woefully inadequate for another. A rock-boring sea urchin may do quite well in the same tank where an anemone withers and dies. In nature there are many different marine environments (microhabitats), often within one small area. If one sets up an aquarium with the main purpose of keeping marine fish, then the habitat in the marine environment that is most important will be the open spaces in the reef structure and the few feet of open water above the bottom. Most fish suitable for a marine aquarium live in this environment, and as long as they have the proper food, light, and water quality, the composition and structure of the tank bottom is not critical, although it must meet their basic requirements.

**THE INSPIRATION:**
Dissecting the marine environment is not a simple task. It is easy to be overwhelmed by a coral reef...

❖

However, a marine invertebrate aquarium, i.e., a reef tank, may include creatures from all marine habitats. These creatures may live under, through, on top of, and/or below the substrate; they may feed on plankton, microscopic algae, tiny animals, mud, detritus, sunlight, worms and other burrowing animals, or a combination of these. They may crawl about, swim rapidly, or remain attached to one spot for life. Thus many factors, such as type and depth of substrate, intensity and spectrum of lighting, presence or absence of algae and detritus, water quality, and patterns of water movement, become very important in the invertebrate aquarium.

Perhaps the best way to get a good idea of what we are trying to create in a marine aquarium is to look at all the different elements of the natural marine environment. Dissecting the marine environment is not a simple task. It is easy to be overwhelmed by a coral reef. The experience of floating in warm, calm, crystal-clear tropical seas under a sky so wide and so blue, of gliding over and through coral formations so massive and yet so intricate, and of viewing life in such a vast array of forms and colors can stir one's soul and make it seem impossible to understand such complex beauty.

## Saltwater symphony

To draw an analogy, think of a symphony orchestra. It creates a glory that is more than the sum of its parts. Everything works together so intricately that one can't separate its component parts and still produce the same result. Individual instruments, however—a violin, a cello, a trumpet, and a piano—can still make beautiful music even if they can't create a symphony.

The goal of most new marine aquarists: a thriving, vibrant, trouble-free aquarium.

A marine aquarium is also a thing of beauty, even though it is only a pale shadow of a coral reef. A symphony orchestra has major sections—the strings, the brass, the percussion—and all are made up of many different instruments. The coral reef environment has different sections also—water chemistry, physical structure, and the biological environment (life)—each of which are made up of many elements. Just as the symphony orchestra has a "center of power"—the conductor—so does the coral reef, and this is the sun. The sun provides the energy that powers the coral reef environment, as it does in almost all other earthly environments. (An exception is the deep sea vent community, which is powered by the chemosynthetic activity of bacteria that feed on sulfur compounds.) Now if you're into rock and roll rather than symphony orchestras, you may want to think of the sun as the lead singer…okay, okay, so this analogy is beginning to break down, but I'm sure you get the basic idea.

### Three basic elements

Let's take a brief look at the major natural elements that compose or affect a coral reef and nearby habitats—what they are, what they do, and how they are measured. Then we will see what happens to each of these elements when we try to capture a coral reef in a marine aquarium. Certain components of marine aquarium systems and methods of maintenance substitute for the elements of the natural environment and provide life support for the various inhabitants of marine aquariums. What they are and how they work are the topics that make up much of the substance of this handbook.

The essence of a marine aquarium is composed of three basic elements. The chemical environment within a marine aquarium includes factors associated with water, such as salinity and the water quality that must be maintained to provide basic life support. The physical environment includes factors that pertain to the physical structure of the habitat, its size and depth, the non-chemical characteristics of the water (such as temperature and movement), light, and physical parameters such as substrate composition and structure. These are created and maintained by the aquarist to serve the vision developed for the aquarium. And, very importantly, the biological environment—the other species of fish and invertebrates, some good, some bad, and the interactions of all life forms that the aquarist has placed, intentionally or unintentionally, in

Captive-bred Ocellaris Clownfish, developed by Bill and Katy Addison's C-Quest hatchery and known in the aquarium trade as "Wyoming Whites."

the aquarium—is the aesthetic focal point of the aquarium. I hope that this third edition of the *Handbook* will serve as an introduction and/or a useful tool in your exploration of the world of the sea and the denizens of the coral reefs, and assist you in creating an aquarium that replicates this natural environment.

My companion book, *The Marine Aquarium Reference: Systems and Invertebrates*, currently being revised and updated, is more advanced and describes modern marine aquarium technology in great detail. It will be useful to any aquarist interested in keeping marine invertebrates or in establishing a reef tank or other type of advanced marine system.

The major innovation now flowering, after long waiting in the wings, is the commercial propagation of many species of marine tropical fish, corals, and ornamental invertebrates. As this occurs, the marine aquarium hobby, and control and preservation of the tropical fish resources of coral reefs, will truly come of age. It is now possible for the home aquarist to

Captive spawning behavior in a pair of Green Mandarinfish being bred by marine biologist Matthew Wittenrich in Melbourne, Florida.

spawn and rear many species of marine fish. Certainly it is more difficult to breed marine fish than it is to rear guppies and goldfish, but the knowledgeable and determined home hobbyist can achieve considerable success in this area, and I write here from actual experience.

Significant captive breeding facilities are now operating in my home state of Florida, as well as in Puerto Rico, Hawaii, and even such unlikely places as Wisconsin, Michigan, and Indiana, with many more appearing on the map each year. Captive-bred clownfishes, Banggai Cardinals, and other species are starting to show up in local aquarium shops, courtesy of home breeders. Small coral farms are proliferating in home basements, garages, and greenhouses everywhere, and there is a thriving cottage industry in "fragging" mother colonies of coral, or taking cuttings of soft corals and producing countless cloned daughter colonies that are eagerly bought up by a growing market of reef aquarists. Even live rock is being "planted and matured," and sometimes even hand crafted, in open-ocean mariculture projects in a number of countries.

A trouble-free, entertaining, and rewarding marine aquarium is the goal of most beginning aquarists, and I hope this new, "mature" edition of the *Handbook* will continue to contribute to that end. I have directed it toward those who need an accurate, easily understood guide to the basics of marine aquarium–keeping. The emphasis is on simple, low-cost techniques that work and the hows and whys of marine aquarium setup and operation. It discusses topics as basic as setting up a tank and as advanced as breeding, and thus should be useful to the old hand as well as the beginning marine aquarist.

# The Aquarium

*Size, Shape, Style, and Construction*

THE FIRST CHOICE YOU MAKE AFTER DECIDING TO BECOME A MARINE aquarist usually concerns the container that will house your own private little parcel of ocean bottom. This basic choice of a tank will have a great effect on your future success and on the types and sizes of fish and invertebrates you can maintain.

There is much more to the selection of an aquarium than its size and cost. Factors affecting the decision include lighting, type of filtration, and, perhaps most important of all, serious consideration about the kinds of marine organisms one wishes to keep. Although expense is still a major factor, the same dollars can purchase systems quite different in design, function, and purpose.

## Before you start

If this is your first marine aquarium, ask yourself some basic questions before you buy or build a tank. Here are a few good ones to start with:

What species do I want to keep? Do I want to keep exotic tropical marine fish or local marine life? Do I want to start with fishes only, or do I want to be able to include corals or other invertebrates? See Chapter 7 for some commendable, hardy choices for a new marine aquarium.

How much money do I want to spend? Do I want to start with a large tank (because large tanks are more biologically stable) and work with it until I know what I'm doing?

Dream reef system with semicircular view glass and flourishing soft corals.

Or do I want to start with a small tank of 30 gallons or less (because the investment is smaller), and then get a large tank when I do know what I'm doing?

Should I try to customize my own system or buy a complete "starter package" (which local marine shops often offer) to simplify the decision-making? (This may be the most economical approach, but you will usually need to add a few items to complete the package to fit your plans.)

Should I build my own tank and filtration gear to save money, or should I buy commercially made equipment? (Determined do-it-your-selfers who are handy working with glass, acrylic, plumbing parts, and wood can construct many aquarium system components.)

What sort of filtration do I want for the type of livestock I plan to keep? Will I start right in with live rock as the natural approach to biological filtration? Will I consider a hang-on-the-tank power filter, perhaps with a built-in protein skimmer? Is a basic undergravel filter something I should consider? Will I have a sump-based system to handle filtration, skimming, and other functions outside the display tank? (This provides a much better aquatic environment for fish and invertebrates, but is neither the easiest nor the cheapest solution.)

**YOUR FIRST TANK:**

I recommend a 20-gallon tank to a beginner, because this is large enough to keep an interesting number and variety of fish and is still small enough to be manageable and economical.

❖

What sort of lighting will I need? Will simple fluorescent light be sufficient, or will I want to have higher intensity reef-type lighting?

What other equipment will I need? A powerhead or other pump to create water movement? Heater? Water testing kit? A hydrometer to measure the salt content in the water?

How much space, money, and time do I have to devote to a marine aquarium?

These are all good questions, and you're the only one who has the answers. But before you make these decisions, it makes sense to get as much information as possible. Read everything you can find and talk to good dealers and successful aquarists. Don't automatically believe everything you read and hear or find online, because there is more inaccurate information around these days than ever before. Good marine hobbyists

Proof that great things can happen in small aquariums: Harlequin Filefish in a 24-gallon reef tank, where they have been successfully kept and spawned by Matt Pedersen.

always think and experiment to find the techniques that work best for them. Seek out advice from those who have experimentally verified facts. The choices of equipment available can be both exciting and bewildering, but most new aquarists soon find someone whose advice they trust when putting together their first system.

## Aquarium size

Contrary to some opinions, a marine aquarium can be maintained in a 10-gallon tank, a 5-gallon tank, or even a 1-gallon jar, if one so desires. The same biological systems will work in one gallon as well as in 300 gallons, but the smaller the system, the easier it is to overfeed and overcrowd, and there is less "reserve" filtration capacity.

I would recommend a 20-gallon tank to a beginner, because this is large enough to keep an interesting number and variety of fish and is still small enough to be manageable and economical. Keep in mind that, as the size of the aquarium goes up, so do the costs of filtration, lighting, aquascaping materials, salt mix, and most other items on your list. Also, if you do graduate to a larger tank, the 20-gallon makes a good second tank for treatment or quarantine.

Another thing to consider when choosing a tank size is weight. This may seem curious, but if you overlook it you could be in a peck of trouble. One gallon of seawater weighs 8.5 pounds, which isn't an awful lot, but 50 of them together weigh 425 pounds, and 100 gallons weigh 850 pounds. It may be a little disquieting to come home after a rough day at work and find your new 100-gallon marine tank in the apartment underneath yours, which, I have heard, has happened. Even a 20-gallon tank can collapse a cheaply made desk, table, or shelf. Be sure not to underestimate the weight of a box of water.

The shape of a marine tank is also important because it can affect the filtering capacity of the tank: the more bottom space for live rock and sand, the greater the number of fish the tank can safely support. A low, flat tank also has a greater water surface area for gas exchange than a high-sided or "tall" tank of the same gallonage. If you really want a high-sided tank because the fish have deeper water to swim in, or because it fits the planned placement of the tank, or just because you like that style better, go ahead and get it. It will likely require a more powerful water circulation pump to ensure a healthy oxygen content, but few marine aquarists will notice any difference in filtering capacity between well-maintained high and low tanks. A marine tank can be any shape you wish, provided that the filter is large enough to support the biological load in the tank. You can even have an inverted pyramid if you wish, but you should plan on a filter outside the tank in this case. With an external sump, a tank can have any configuration one wishes, as long as an appropriate outside location can be found. The typical low and wide configuration, however, still provides the best ratio of surface area to volume for good gas exchange and ease of maintenance. Tall tanks require long-handled tools for cleaning.

## Materials and construction

Unless you want an exceptionally large tank or a very unusual shape, you will likely be faced with two choices of readily available aquariums: acrylic and glass. Both types have their advocates, and your success or failure as a marine aquarist is not likely to depend on whether you choose one material over the other.

**Glass aquariums** have these advantages: they are more affordable, less prone to scratching (although not impervious), and easier to keep clean. Stubborn algae growth of all kinds on the walls of a glass tank can be quickly and effortlessly removed with a razor blade.

There are many companies that manufacture all-glass tanks, and one should shop for price and quality as with any other purchase. Because of the fragile nature of a glass box, it is always wise to inspect it carefully before you truck it home. Watch for cracks, of course, but also be aware of more subtle defects. Are the frame or edges of the tank chipped, and if so, did the chips break through or damage the silicone seals? If it is a large tank, is the bottom piece made from glass a size thicker than the sides? Is the reinforcement about the top and bottom well made, firmly attached, and totally plastic? (There are still metal-frame aquariums from decades ago cycling through the garage-sale world. These are unsuitable for saltwater systems—salt corrodes metal.) Is the silicone seal evenly distributed along all seams? Check for disruptions of the seal by viewing each edge through the overlapping side. Numerous air bubbles and channels through the seal may indicate potential leaks and glass cuts that are not perfectly square. If the glass is not cut square, cracks and leaks will probably occur, especially in large tanks. Buy your tank from a good dealer, one recommended by other aquarists, and you will get a good tank and good advice.

**Acrylic tanks** are lighter and, in the eyes of some beholders, more aesthetically pleasing than the typical glass tank with a plastic frame and silicone seams at the corners.

Nowadays, acrylic tanks can be truly spectacular. A large acrylic reef tank in a custom cabinet, with all the right lighting and filtration, is a marvel to behold—an expensive marvel, but a marvel nonetheless. Acrylic tanks are often more expensive because they are a bit difficult to build, since the plastic must be worked with great precision, especially for large

Architecturally pleasing retro-style marine system has a 1970s look, with bleached coral skeletons, artificial aquascaping elements, and a very light bioload.

tanks, so that all edges are exactly right and will weld together perfectly. Holes must be drilled with special bits and cuts made with special saws to prevent the plastic from melting and chipping. Even though the plastic is more easily worked than glass (once you know how), one still needs special skills to work with acrylic.

Acrylic tanks are more prone to scratching and marring than glass, and one must be very careful when cleaning the inside and outside surfaces. The standard metal-edge scrapers and abrasive pads used to clean glass aquariums must never be used on acrylic. Heavily encrusted coralline algae can be difficult to remove with the plastic scraping tools that you must use (no razors here). Grains of sand caught between a cleaning pad and the interior wall of an acrylic aquarium can cause scratches, and tumbling live rock can leave scars. If acrylic surfaces do get marred, it is possible to polish out shallow scratches and restore acrylic to a perfect luster, but this can be a major project. Note that acrylic tanks also endure space travel very well, especially the bubble-formed tanks. Captain Picard has one aboard the Enterprise, and as far as I know, he hasn't had a speck of trouble with it. He has noted, however, that lionfish sometimes lose their appetite at warp speed.

### Types of marine aquarium systems

When I wrote the first edition of this book in the late 1970s and early 1980s, there was only one basic type of home marine aquarium system. Sure, there were hobbyists who experimented with various types of external filter systems, and there were some multi-tank systems with trickle filters, sumps, and UV filters around; but basically, a marine aquarium system consisted of an undergravel filter, bleached white coral, often some type of auxiliary "hang on the back of the tank" filter, and air lift tubes that moved water through the undergravel filter.

Lighting usually mimicked that used in freshwater tanks and typically consisted of one or two 20- to 40-watt incandescent or fluorescent bulbs with a red or orange tint. This was the basic setup for tanks of all sizes, and the aquatic world of most marine aquarists was limited by available equipment and by the basic concept of a marine aquarium that almost everyone held.

Then, in the mid-'80s, everything began to open up. Aquatic biologists and marine aquaculturists had been talking and writing for some years about the importance of natural spectrum, high-intensity lighting, which suddenly began appearing in marine tanks. Powerhead pumps also became available, water flows were increased, and strong water movement inside the tank was found to be very beneficial to fish and invertebrates. Aquarists also became interested in the ecological relationships between fish, algae, invertebrates, and bacteria, and this led to the wide use of natural substrates in both fish and reef tanks. Aquarium manufacturers began producing new equipment and, with the dawning of the light (full spectrum with a blue peak, high-intensity light, of course), many marine aquarists were satisfied with nothing less than real coral reefs in their living rooms.

### The age of live substrates

Now, in the 21st century, the Golden Age of undergravel filters has passed, as has the Golden Age of trickle or wet/dry filters. We are now in the Age of Live Rock. Live rock, it has been discovered, not only provides a natural environment but also functions as a very efficient biological filter, and tanks without undergravel filters are no longer unusual. Adequate biological filtration can be provided for most marine aquariums with live rock and a sand bottom without water flow through the sand or artificial biomedia, which was once the traditional approach to supporting a large population of nitrifying bacteria.

External sump tanks that can house various forms of remote filtration, such as protein skimming and mechanical filtration, and can also function as refugiums, have reduced the need for confining all biological filtration to the display tank, even in tanks with high biological loading.

One factor that has guided the evolution of biological filtration away from the early systems is that extensive and active aerobic filtration substrates (bacterial activity in an oxygenated environment), such as undergravel and wet-dry filters, enhance the first part of full biological processing of animal waste, the production of nitrate. Thus, these filters may be great at handling heavy bioloads, but they produce a lot of nitrate, which requires more frequent water changes and stimulates the growth of macro- and microalgae. Delicate corals do poorly in high-nitrate environments, losing color and often falling victim to overgrowth by algae. Additionally, if not scrupulously maintained, undergravel and wet/dry filters tend to accumulate detritus that can lower water quality. The Berlin Method of reef aquarium–keeping emphasizes getting all detritus out of a system as quickly and efficiently as possible, and this has become the mantra of most modern-day marine aquarists.

Biological filtration with live rock and/or deep live sand provides an anaerobic (greatly reduced oxygen) environment for some bacteria that allows the transformation of nitrate to nitrogen gas, and this leaves the water through natural gas exchange. Actually, all porous rock and sand in an aquarium eventually develops various species and metabolic states of nitrifying bacteria and becomes "live" rock or sand over time.

### Simplified marine aquariums

Today, a beginning marine aquarist can use a simple formula for establishing a healthy new saltwater tank. Although a world of extremely sophisticated reefkeeping gear awaits while your skills grow more advanced, an intelligently planned starter system has just a few easily understood components.

Typical small reef aquarium, with a mixed "garden" of corals, giant clams, and reef fishes in an aquascape constructed of live rock, which is slowly being covered by coral growth.

**Live rock** is at the core of most marine systems today. Once considered expensive and for experts only, live rock has proved easy to use and highly reliable, even in the hands of neophytes. Many newcomers to marine aquarium–keeping today start with what has come to be known as a **FOWLR** (Fish Only With Live Rock) aquarium. Such systems allow a smooth transition to a reef-type aquarium if your attention is drawn to the colorful and sometimes bizarre invertebrates now readily available to marine enthusiasts.

Live rock is typically harvested from rubble zones near tropical coral reefs, and it consists of porous, usually calcareous pieces of hard substrate, mostly long-dead coral skeletons, that have been taken from the sea with their microscopic life—and often some of the larger invertebrate and algal growths—still alive and functioning. It comes in all sizes and shapes and may be encrusted with handsome pink or red coralline algae. Most important, it can provide effective biological filtration in the marine aquarium.

Once all the mud, silt, and excess organic growth is removed from

Typical Gulf of Mexico live rock, with coralline algae, sponge growth, and various attached live mollusks. Porous rock offers a large surface area colonized by beneficial bacteria.

the rock (a process known as seeding and/or curing), the natural aerobic bacteria on and near the surface of the rock and the anaerobic bacteria deep within it function in the aquarium system to, respectively, oxidize nitrogenous wastes to nitrate and reduce nitrate to nitrogen gas, which then passes out of the system into the atmosphere.

Live rock, then, is the physical base for a captive reef, a functional biofilter system, and the support for (and often the source of) the living organisms of the coral reef community. **Live sand** may also be used to cover the bottom of the aquarium, providing significant additional surface area for biological filtration and a natural substrate for burrowing animals. Some aquarists, in fact, use a deep sand bed as the primary biological filter, with or without live rock. Live sand may be collected from the wild and is usually labeled with its source of origin, such as Fiji Live Sand. Packaged live sand that has been inoculated with beneficial bacterial cultures is now sold by most marine suppliers. Dry calcium carbonate sand and crushed coral gravel are the least expensive and will eventually be colonized by the right bacteria and by many burrowing organisms, especially if they are used to "seed" the system. Advocates of deep sand beds prefer finer substrate, often sold as "sugar-fine" aragonite.

A **power filter** is often employed to trap particulate matter and to house chemical filtration media, such as activated carbon. The goal is to extract excess food, wastes, and detritus to prevent it from accumulating in the aquarium. In simple systems, affordable hang-on-the-tank models can perform this function. Such a filter will have plates or chambers that are easy to remove and clean. It may also include foam blocks or other media to provide additional biological filtration. Hang-on-the-tank models used in the freshwater aquarium hobby are perfectly acceptable for small marine systems, as long as the pump is sufficiently powerful and the filter has an adequate flow rating.

A **powerhead** is a submersible pump designed to create currents in the aquarium. When combined with an automatic timing switch, it can be turned on and off to simulate waves and provide the sort of chaotic water motion that will help most marine organisms thrive. Even a small, inexpensive powerhead will help with oxygenation and gas exchange and stir up detritus so that it can be filtered out of the tank, and will assist in keeping live rock and the sand bed free of settling wastes. Many reef aquarists graduate to having two or more powerheads to ensure that all areas of the tank have active water movement.

A **protein skimmer** is a very important part of this and most other modern marine aquarium systems. A protein skimmer mixes fine air bubbles and saltwater in a tubular container and creates a foam that rises to the top and is trapped in a cup. The dissolved organic compounds attach themselves to the bubbles and are then carried out of the system with the foam. It is an effective and efficient way to remove dissolved organics from the system before they break down into basic nutrient compounds. An efficient, properly sized protein skimmer also helps keep oxygen levels in the aquarium near saturation, as they are on a coral reef. Combination power filters and skimmers are available in many price ranges and sizes and offer great convenience in maintaining long-term water quality.

**SKIMMING PLUS:**

An efficient protein skimmer removes dissolved organic compounds while keeping oxygen levels near saturation in the aquarium.

❖

The **lighting** on a lower-tech system is usually based on fluorescent light tubes or compact fluorescents. Inexpensive strip light fixtures and

A simple beginner's aquarium
with two small islands of live
rock and minimal use
of technology.

hoods can be purchased for all standard aquarium sizes. Many upgrades are available to deliver higher intensity lighting, including power compact fluorescent and T5 fluorescent fixtures. For the most demanding of corals and other photosynthetic invertebrate life, metal halide bulbs pack an unmatched intensity, but at a price and with considerable use of energy and production of heat.

Other basic components include a thermostatically controlled **heater**, a **thermometer**, a **lighting timer**, a **net**, and a **gravel vacuum** or **siphon hose**. Every marine aquarist also needs equipment to measure water quality, including a **marine test kit** and a **hydrometer** to monitor the salinity of the system.

With a basic marine system, it is relatively easy to run a spectacular and healthy fish tank or a fantastic macroalgae tank, and even to start keeping hardy and undemanding corals, such as mushroom polyps and colonial zoanthids. As you gain confidence in your aquarium skill set, such a system can be provided with better filtration and water flow and stronger lighting to meet the needs of more delicate and challenging livestock. At the beginning of the modern marine aquarium era, we often had to build our own tanks, invent our own equipment, and even venture out to collect our own fishes. We had little or nothing to guide us, and had to learn things the hard way as we made up our own rules.

Today, the new aquarist has easy access to aquariums, gear, fishes, and other livestock we couldn't have imagined a few decades ago. The ultimate motivation and rewards, however, are exactly the same: turning a box of water into a vibrant, living underwater scene that can be an endlessly fascinating window on the life and beauty of the coral reef.

# The Water

*Composition, Collection, Mixing, and Preparation*

EARLY MARINE AQUARISTS, BY NECESSITY, OFTEN LIVED BY THE SEA, going to the shore or nearest bay for their water supplies. Some coastal hobbyists continue to take advantage of the ocean to fill their tanks and do water changes, but the great majority of marine enthusiasts now rely on synthetic salt mixes or even the bulk bottled seawater sold throughout the aquarium trade.

Should one use natural or synthetic seawater in a marine aquarium? Traditionally, this question has been sure to spark a lively discussion. Cries of *Pollution! Bacteria!* and *Organic overload!* would arise from the crowd that was suspicious of self-collected water, while shouts of *Natural composition! Complete trace elements!* and *Essential organic compounds!* reverberated from those who believed in using the real thing.

There is much less contention these days about the relative merits of synthetic seawater and natural seawater. The better brands of synthetic seawater have proven to be every bit as capable as natural seawater of supporting life (including delicate invertebrates) in large and small marine aquarium systems. Assuming a pollution- and parasite-free source of natural seawater, cost and convenience are now the most important factors in the choice between natural and artificial seawater.

## Composition of natural seawater
Let's take a look at the composition of natural seawater, and this will give us some clues on how to use it in a marine aquarium. Seawater is

**Shallow inshore water of Indian River Lagoon near Sebastian Inlet, Florida.**

an extremely complex and dynamic fluid when all of its inorganic and organic constituents are considered. Fortunately, you don't have to have a degree in marine chemistry to be able to set up and maintain a saltwater aquarium, but it is helpful to know what kinds of things make up natural seawater, especially if you plan to use Mother Nature's formula. The components of natural seawater can be put into four broad classifications.

The first of these is pure water, the ultimate solvent. Water represents about 96% of all the stuff in a bucket of seawater. This is the part that evaporates, makes rain, and leaves everything else behind in the form of a white, crusty residue. Obviously, it is the stuff left behind in the bucket that makes seawater so different from freshwater.

The second component of seawater falls under the broad term of inorganic solids and gases. All the dissolved salts, trace elements, inorganic pollutants, and dissolved gases belong in this category, which, except for the gases, usually make up over 99% of the crusty white stuff at the bottom of the bucket. Only seven kinds of salts (sodium chloride, magnesium chloride, magnesium sulphate, calcium sulfate, potassium sulfate, calcium carbonate, and potassium or sodium bromide) make up over 99.5% of all the conservative elements in seawater. The conservative elements are the ones that do not change in proportion to each other regardless of the total amount of dissolved matter. In other words, the percentage of sodium chloride, for example, in the total salt content is always the same, whether the seawater is half strength or full strength. This is very important, for this is why the properties of seawater vary so little all over the world, and why it is such a stable, life-supporting environment in all climates.

The remaining .5% percent of the inorganic solids is made up of at least 60 elements, found in such tiny amounts that they are called trace elements, and a variable amount (depending on where the water is taken) of pollutants, such as mercury, pesticides, petroleum, and many other compounds that are released by human activities. Even though the trace elements are present in extremely tiny amounts, some of them (especially zinc, copper, iodine, strontium, vanadium, cobalt, molybdenum, and arsenic) are essential to many living organisms. Some animals and plants can accumulate some of these trace elements, such as mercury, in their own bodies in concentrations thousands of times greater than the concentration in the surrounding waters, and some of these elements may even be depleted in areas of the sea due to the activity of marine life.

If this can happen in the open sea, it can certainly occur in a marine aquarium, where the ratio of organisms to water is much greater. These elements are not always released back into the water when a microorganism dies, and if you remove algae from your tank, you are also removing accumulated trace elements. Therefore, it is wise to replenish the trace elements in your tank every month or so, especially if you do not make a water change with natural seawater or a complete salt mix.

The third basic classification of the stuff of seawater is dissolved organic substances. These are compounds such as amino acids, proteins, enzymes, vitamins, and pigments. Inshore waters carry a greater load of dissolved organics than clear offshore waters. Natural toxins are sometimes found in seawater, especially during reproductive "blooms" of minute marine algae. These blooms are usually called "red tides" and can be very destructive to fish life. Some dissolved organic substances are given off by animals, plants, and bacteria during the normal process of living and are also liberated when the organisms die. Runoff water from the land adds greatly to the organic content of inshore waters, and man contributes ever increasingly to this category through the discharge of petroleum products, sewage, and agricultural and industrial wastes. These effluents add a number of toxins, such as PCBs, which can accumulate in the tissues of marine animals, as well as basic nutrients from sewage that enrich inshore waters and cause heavy growths of planktonic algae.

Life is the fourth category of things to be found in that bucket of natural seawater. No matter how clear the water, it contains an astonishing number and variety of living things. Bacteria and microscopic plants and animals can be found in each drop of inshore water. Some of these, such as larval fish and crabs, have the potential for great growth, while others, such as one-celled algae and copepods, remain as tiny planktonic creatures throughout their brief existence. Living things are always gathering and assimilating the elements of the sea, containing them, using

Remote dive resort on the Wakatobi Penisula in the Banda Sea, Indonesia.

them, and liberating them through death and excretion. Thus, the sea is a dynamic fluid, filled with life, accepting nutrients from the land and energy from the sun and balancing the existence of life on earth upon the complex interactions of the organisms within its waters.

I hope the above discussion makes it easier to understand that a marine aquarium is not a tiny slice of a coral reef or ocean bottom, and that a bucket of seawater and a bucket of marine aquarium water are two entirely different things. How do they differ? Water from a marine aquarium has the same four basic categories of constituents: water, dissolved inorganics, dissolved organics, and life. Water and the conservative constituents (basic salts) are the same in both buckets, but the other, nonconservative constituents differ greatly. Trace element composition changes rapidly because captive life forms use them and they are not replenished by the vast volume of the sea. Dissolved organics are not diffused and reused as extensively in a marine aquarium as they are in the sea, so to a great degree they accumulate from the wastes of animals. These wastes are converted to basic nutrients with proper biological filtration, but the concentrations

of these nutrients can be much, much greater in the bucket of aquarium water than they are in the bucket of raw seawater.

Living things are also found in both buckets, but the infinite variety of tiny plants and animals found in oceanic seawater do not exist in aquarium water. Bacteria are the primary life forms in typical aquarium water. The number of bacteria in one cubic centimeter of seawater ranges from less than 10 in offshore waters to several hundred or more in clear inshore waters. In contrast, marine aquarium water may contain several hundred thousand bacteria, or much more, in each cubic centimeter. All bacteria are not bad, however, and their presence does not necessarily make aquarium water worse for marine life than raw seawater, just different.

## Collection of natural seawater

If seawater were composed of just pure water, dissolved salts, and trace elements, its collection and use in an aquarium would pose few problems. It is the dissolved organics and planktonic life forms that make things complicated for the aquarist. As soon as the seawater is contained, and is no longer part and parcel of the world's oceans, most of the planktonic plants and animals die, and bacteria proliferate mightily. Eventually, all the remains of planktonic creatures are decayed (mineralized) by bacteria, which also utilize some of the dissolved organics.

Most bacteria need a surface of some sort (a substrate) on which to form a colony and grow, and together, the sides of the container, precipitated organics (detritus), and dead plankton provide much more surface area than an equal volume of open seawater does. These and other factors can result in a fantastic proliferation of bacteria in captive seawater, which is why many authors suggest that newly collected seawater be kept in the dark for two weeks or more before use; after that period, most of the organic matter has been utilized, oxidized, and precipitated, and all the dead plankton has been consumed by bacteria. Bacteria levels then drop to 10 to 100,000 per cubic centimeter. A brownish flocculent material accumulates at the bottom of the container, and one is instructed to remove the clear seawater without stirring up the sediment on the bottom.

Here I describe three ways to process collected natural seawater. The first is the classic, sure way, and the second is the lazy man's somewhat risky method. The third is an experimental method that I have had good success with, but I cannot unconditionally recommend it because I don't really know exactly what it does to the water, and I don't know what effect it might have on many species that have not experienced water treated in this way.

The first thing to do is decide where the water is to be obtained. Of course, the very best water would be clear, offshore water, but collecting it requires a boat and your aquarium will operate just as well on carefully collected inshore water. Take your water from an area that has good tidal flushing and no obvious nearby sources of pollution. Avoid sewer outlets, industrial plants, and freshwater creeks and rivers. Don't collect water from areas that show an oil or chemical slick on the surface. Also, look for live fish, crabs, and other life in the area, and if native fish are present and appear healthy, your water should be good. Anyone who lives near the coast should be able to collect good seawater for an aquarium. When you have found the right site, time, and tide, you are ready to collect.

One thing you don't want is 50 gallons of saltwater sloshing around in your car. A good, inexpensive way to transport saltwater is to use those lowly, but versatile, 20-gallon plastic garbage cans. Obviously, the more plankton and particulate material that can be removed when the water is collected, the better the water will be for your aquarium. I use two buckets, a big plastic funnel, and some fine filtering material. Several folds of clean cloth, a one-inch-thick piece of pure polyurethane foam, or, best of all, several layers of filtering floss packed into the funnel do a good job.

Perhaps the very best all-time filtering material I have used over the years is micron filter bags. These are heavy, felt-like bags that will filter water to levels of 10, 5, and even 1 or 2 microns. A lot of water can pass through the bags before they clog and they can also be easily cleaned and re-used many times. These filter bags are usually used in the manufacture of beer and other basic liquid foods, and are now also available from some aquatic supply houses.

Line the plastic garbage can with a polyethylene bag and fill it with filtered water. Leave some room to twist off and secure the bag with a rubber band or wire twist tie, and you have a spill-proof container to carry home your water. It is far better to use two or three small cans that can be handled easily than one large can that is really heavy—but, of course, you already knew that.

After you get the water home, it is generally recommended that you store it in the dark for two or three weeks prior to using it in the aquarium. Then remove the water carefully so that the sediment on the bottom of the container is not disturbed. The lazy man's way is to use the water immediately, not bothering with storage or treatment. Sometimes you can get away with this approach with no problems at all if the water is well filtered. However, small parasites may be introduced in this way and can cause hair-pulling, breast-beating frustration. It is best to avoid using freshly collected, unprocessed water, especially from questionable inshore locations.

The third way of treating the water is the experimental one; I have routinely used water treated in this way for decades to culture marine tropical fish, and it seems acceptable to most marine organisms. You will need some granular dry chlorine, the type used in swimming pools (65% calcium hypochlorite with no additional algaecide) or pure chlorine bleach, an OTO test kit for chlorine (available where swimming pool supplies are sold), and chlorine neutralizer. Sodium thiosulfate is the base for most commercial dechlorinators and is also sold in camera shops as hypo; however, if you use hypo, be sure to get pure hypo without film hardeners.

Add a small measure of chlorine to newly collected water until your test kit measures at least 5 parts per million (ppm) chlorine; up to 10 ppm is OK. Let the water sit with light aeration for 12 to 24 hours and test once again for chlorine. If no chlorine is indicated, this means that you have water with a high organic load that has used up the chlorine without removing all the organics, and you should treat it once again with chlorine. It also means that the dose of chlorine should be doubled if water is collected from the same location again. Chlorine kills all life in the collected water, including bacteria, and oxidizes the organic matter dissolved in natural seawater, including natural toxins. After the water has been chlorinated for 12 to 24 hours, it will be very clear and smell a little like a swimming pool.

Now add the sodium thiosulfate in small measure until your test kit indicates that no chlorine remains. It is best to dissolve the sodium thiosulfate in water before adding it to the chlorinated seawater. It won't take much, so just add a little at a time, no more than a teaspoon, until you can estimate how much is required.

The residue of the calcium from calcium hypochlorite and the particles in the seawater will accumulate on the bottom of the container, and it is a good idea to carefully siphon off the clear water before dechlorination so it won't have to settle out a second time. Now your water is sterile and may have a slightly cloudy appearance. This will clear by itself if the water is left to settle for a day or two under light aeration, or it can be filtered through floss and activated charcoal for a few hours to clear it even faster. In emergencies, I have used water immediately after neutralization with no ill effects, but I don't recommend it as a general practice. We have collected water heavily contaminated with oil waste, decaying fish, red tide organisms, toxins, silt, and organic matter, treated it with this method, and then used

**CHLORINATING SEAWATER:**
Beware of newer swimming pool chlorination products with stabilizing additives that can lower pH in treated water.

❖

it 24 hours later to rear clownfish and Neon Gobies. Old aquarium water can also be rejuvenated with this treatment, but repeated treatments will lower the pH of the water.

We used this method for many years to prepare water for rearing marine tropical fish—clownfish, gobies, Atlantic angelfish, Royal Grammas, porkfish, hogfish, and other species—and in the maintenance and rearing of Spiny Lobsters and other invertebrates.

After 36 years of using natural seawater processed with chlorine and dechlorinated with sodium thiosulfate one to ten days after initial chlorination, and using water so treated with many different species of fish and invertebrates, as well as some of the most sensitive invertebrate larvae of all, those of the Long-Spined Sea Urchin *Diadema antillarum*, without any detrimental effect that I can observe, I have few reservations in recommending this treatment for collected natural seawater. One precaution, however, is that there are now many chlorination products for swimming pools available. I recently tried a stabilized chlorinator product, Sodium Dichloro-s-Triazinetrione Dihydrate, because it delivered a great deal of free chlorine with no residue. However, it also contained cyanuric acid as the stabilizer, and this lowered the pH considerably both before and after dechlorination. So be sure that there are no additives in the chlorine product you used.

As a footnote, I should mention that some collectors of natural seawater treat it with ozone and/or ultraviolet sterilization, followed by mechanical filtration to remove dead microorganisms and detritus.

### Synthetic seawater

If you happen to live in Omaha, Nebraska, you may have a tough time deciding whether to go to the Pacific, the Atlantic, or the Gulf of Mexico to get your saltwater. Even if you live only a few miles from a saltwater source, however, you may not want the hassle of cans, buckets, filters, and hauling water in the back seat of your Mini Cooper. Fortunately, there is a solution for your problem. You can buy a package of synthetic sea salts from your aquarium dealer and carry home the equivalent of 50 or 100 gallons of saltwater in a neat little package on the seat of your car. Synthetic seawater may not be the same thing as natural seawater, but the major brands available today will support marine life in your aquarium almost as well as the real thing, perhaps even better in some circumstances.

Inland coral farm using synthetic saltwater with obvious good results.

Synthetic seawater differs from nature's own in that the concentrations of the major inorganic salts are not exactly the same, the inorganic trace elements are not the same in number or concentration, there are no dissolved organics, and—a very important consideration—all impurities present in the makeup water become part of the aquarium's watery environment. This last point could easily be overlooked. One might figure, "Well, I've got this fine grade of expensive sea salt mix manufactured under exacting conditions from carefully tested, time-proven formulas. I mix it with the water I drink, so what could possibly be wrong?" I hope that at least 99% of the time this is a totally correct assumption; however, remember that the freshwater supply in some areas of the country may be plagued with bacterial contamination (probably not a problem in a marine tank), industrial waste contamination, concentrations of heavy metals (copper, zinc), extreme hardness, nutrients such as phosphate, nitrate, and silicic acid, and detergent contamination—all of which can have marked effects on aquatic life.

## Freshwater preparation

If there is a suspicion about the purity of your water supply, or if you drink and cook with bottled water rather than tap water, then it's a good idea to filter the tap water through activated carbon before making up the saltwater mix. This will take out most of the impurities and get you closer to the final solution that the manufacturer of the salt mix intended.

Reef tank aquarists often use reverse osmosis (RO) to purify their tap water. Many run the tap water through a deionizer to remove excess salts, which makes the RO membrane last a lot longer, and then through the reverse osmosis unit to remove residual nutrients before adding freshwater to replace evaporation in a reef tank. Reverse osmosis and combination RO/DI filters are available from most aquarium retailers and many hardware shops.

Follow the manufacturer's instructions when you mix the salts; after all, they ought to know the best way to handle their own product. If you are just setting up a new tank, you can mix the first batch right in the tank, but if you are changing water in an established tank, it is best to mix the salts in a plastic garbage can or other inert container. Never use a metal can or bucket to mix the saltwater. It is also good to let the newly mixed saltwater age a day or so to let the pH stabilize before adding it to the tank. Always wait until the solution clears and all the elements are dissolved before adding the newly mixed water to your tank. Some of the elements may not dissolve, even after 24 hours of aeration or circulation with a small powerhead pump, and will form a white precipitate on the container bottom. Don't worry about this residue unless it is excessive; just go ahead and use the water, and if some of the sediment gets into the tank it's nothing to be concerned about.

## Chlorine and chloramine

The small amount of chlorine in tap water usually disappears when the salt mix is added, and is of no concern as long as the mix is aerated or actively circulated for at least several hours before use. If there is a question of residual chlorine, a few drops of sodium thiosulfate or of a commercial dechlorinator will set your mind at ease. Unfortunately, in many areas of the country it is no longer possible to dismiss chlorine in tap water with a few drops of a dechlorinator. Due to the recent implementation of Environmental Protection Agency regulations on organics in water supplies, municipal water companies are changing the way they treat our tap water. Ammonia is being added to eliminate trihalomethane, a suspected cancer-causing agent. In the past, tap water received only a charge of free chlorine to keep it pure and free of bacteria until it reached our kitchens and bathrooms. Free chlorine is volatile and soon disappears from standing or aerated water, and it can be quickly eliminated with a little sodium thiosulfate. When ammonia and chlorine are both present in freshwater, however, they form a stable chloramine compound that is toxic to fish, just as free chlorine and ammonia are toxic. In fact, chloramine is even more toxic since it can pass through the gills and into the blood more easily than chlorine alone.

**CHLORAMINE WARNING:** Municipal water containing chloramine is highly toxic to marine life and it must be treated before use in the aquarium.

❖

Chloramine, unfortunately, does not readily escape from standing water and cannot be removed by a standard application of sodium thiosulfate. When ammonia is already present in the water and the amount of chlorine added is below the "break point reaction" level, then chloramine is formed. As long as chlorine levels are maintained under the break point reaction level, chlorine and ammonia are present as the stable chloramine compound. If enough chlorine is added to exceed the break point reaction level, the chlorine becomes free chlorine and the ammonia is no longer bonded. Both chlorine and ammonia can then escape as gases over a period of time. If ammonia levels are not sufficient in the raw water supply, it is added by exposing the water to pellets of ammonium sulphate or adding liquid anhydrous ammonia before it is chlorinated.

Hatcheries, shops, and hobbyists in Texas and Florida have reported considerable loss of livestock due to this development in water treatment technology. If the chloramine levels in your water supply exceed 2 ppm, it may be necessary to remove it from the water before setting up an aquarium. There are ways that the hobbyist can clear freshwater of chloramine before making up a synthetic seawater mix. One of the two basic methods described below should work, depending on the particular problems presented by the local water supply. The first and easiest method is to add twice the amount of sodium thiosulfate (or a commercial dechlorinator) than would ordinarily be necessary to dechlorinate the water. This should break the chlorine bond and chemically remove the chlorine after a working time of two to three hours.

Aeration of the water will allow the ammonia to escape as a gas over a period of several hours (longer if the concentration of ammonia is high). The freshwater can also be filtered through an ammonia-absorbent material, such as the clay clinoptiolite (zeolite), or a similar commercial product for more positive ammonia removal. It is more important to remove ammonia when preparing water for a partial water change in an established tank than it is when setting up a new tank, since the run-in period for a new tank will eliminate any ammonia in the water.

The second method is more involved but may be necessary under some local conditions. First, enough chlorine must be added to break the stable chloramine bond and put all chlorine present into the free state. Addition of 1 cc (about $^1\!/_5$ tsp.) of laundry bleach (no additives) to one gallon of water (or 1 tsp. Clorox, 5.25% sodium hypochlorite, per five gallons) usually accomplishes this after one hour of aeration. Once all the chlorine is in a free state, it can be removed by traditional methods. The addition of sodium thiosulfate until no chlorine registers on an OTO swimming pool test kit is the standard method of chlorine removal. Mix about 4 oz. of sodium thiosulfate to one quart of water to make the treatment solution. Start with five drops for each 10 gallons of water to be

Synthetic salt mix brands abound. Ask someone you trust for a recommendation.

dechlorinated. Re-treat if the OTO test shows that chlorine is still present 5 to 10 minutes after the initial treatment. Activated carbon filtration after chlorine removal is also a good idea, for although it won't remove ammonia, it will take out any residual chlorine. A final filtration of the freshwater through an ammonia-absorbent material will remove the ammonia if this is desired. Don't just soak a bag of ammonia-absorbent material or activated carbon in the water, as this is most inefficient. Set up a flow-through filter to recirculate the water through the filter material.

### Synthetic sea salts

Which brand of synthetic sea salt should you use? I've tried several, and they all seem to do a good job. You should rely on your dealer's recommendation or the recommendations of experienced fellow hobbyists in your area. Advanced hobbyists with rare fishes and priceless corals wrangle endlessly over the merits or suspected deficiencies of salt brands, but the beginner keeping hardy animals need not give this much thought. Unless your region has special water problems, any of the major brands of synthetic sea salts, mixed with clean freshwater, will provide a good life-supporting medium for marine animals and should be the most stable and trouble-free element in the whole system. A local aquarium shop that sells healthy marine livestock can easily recommend a reliable salt brand for your system.

Synthetic sea salts are easy to keep and store. One can keep them in the package in a dry, cool place ready for mixing and use whenever necessary, or if emergency use is anticipated, they can be mixed up and stored in dark containers ready for instant use. Be sure to label the container carefully if you do this, so you will know the date, brand, concentration, and any other pertinent information about the mix.

The concept and practice of mixing various salts to support marine life in an artificial environment is far older than the marine aquarium hobby. During the last 50 years, many formulas have been published for scientists and advanced aquarists to use in formulating their own experimental synthetic sea salt mixes. In fact, in 1884, H. E. Hoffman published a formula for artificial seawater in *Volume 9* of the *Bulletin of the U.S. Fish Commission*. It consisted of 13.25 gallons of well water, 46.5 oz. of sodium chloride, 3.5 oz. of magnesium sulphate, 5.25 oz. of magnesium chloride, and 2.0 oz. of potassium sulphate. Each salt is dissolved separately and then all solutions are mixed and allowed to rest before use. This formula, simple compared with those available today, which contain 70 or more trace elements, supported marine life but produced, at best, inconsistent results.

If you really want to mix up your own synthetic sea salts, you might try the formula published by Lyman and Fleming in 1940 in their article, "The Composition of Sea Water," which appeared in the *Journal of Marine Research*, No. 3, Vol. 134.

**Formula for a simple artificial seawater**

| | |
|---|---|
| Sodium chloride | 23.477 grams |
| Magnesium chloride | 4.981 |
| Sodium sulphate | 3.917 |
| Calcium chloride | 1.102 |
| Potassium chloride | 0.664 |
| Sodium bicarbonate | 0.192 |
| Potassium bromide | 0.096 |
| Boric acid | 0.026 |
| Strontium chloride | 0.024 |
| Sodium fluoride | 0.003 |

**Add water to a total of 1000 grams**

The above formula makes up only 1000 grams, or one liter (0.9 quarts) of solution. Multiplying each ingredient by 100 will make up close to 25 gallons of solution, and it will be much easier to weigh out the chemicals. Adding some natural seawater or commercially available trace elements should round out the solution and make an acceptable grade of synthetic seawater. Mixing your own really isn't worth it today because of the availability of commercial brands, but it's good to know that you could do it—if you had to.

Good water quality is very important in rearing marine tropical fish, but it may not be as critical as one would suppose. The larval fish has membranes that protect its internal environment from the great concentrations of bacteria and inorganic and organic molecules that surround it, and this

barrier is effective from the moment of hatch. So although water quality must be good, it need not be a sterile laboratory medium or even duplicate the clear offshore waters that are the natural environment of most larval fish. The water quality of a balanced, well-maintained marine aquarium is quite adequate for the survival of most larval marine fish if all other factors, such as food, light, temperature, and freedom from predators, are also adequate. Marine fish have been easily reared in many types of synthetic seawater mixes as well as natural seawater from different sources. The rearing tank can be set up with natural seawater processed as usual for a marine aquarium, synthetic seawater aged a few days, or even water taken from a disease-free, uncrowded aquarium. In fact, water from a marine aquarium carries an initial load of the "good" bacteria that will aid the chemical balance in the rearing tank. Perhaps most important to water quality in rearing marine tropicals at home is to make sure that chemical pollutants, such as insecticides, paint fumes, tobacco, cleaning solutions, other household contaminants, and even airborne agricultural sprays, do not get into the water. Such contaminants can create problems that are devastating in effect but extremely difficult to discover and eliminate.

The reef tanks of today, early in the 21st century, require much better water quality than the old undergravel-filtered fish and very hardy invertebrate tanks of decades ago. Corals and many other invertebrates make seawater part and parcel of their being and are quite sensitive to high levels of nutrients and other chemicals that passed under the bar in a hardy fish tank in the old days. Recognizing this was an important part of the discovery process that resulted in the modern reef tank. So a good reef tank aquarist pays close attention to water quality and maintains a high standard when it comes to the purity of the water in the tank.

# Filtration

## *Mechanical, Chemical, Biological, and Sterilization*

THERE ARE A LOT OF DIFFERENT THINGS THAT CAN BE DONE TO AQUARIUM water in the name of filtration, but they all fall under one of the four basic categories listed above.

Your success as a marine aquarist will depend in great measure on how well you understand and work with these and the basic principles of biological filtration. The other types of filtration are important and helpful, but **biological filtration** is where all the action is. Without it you have a chemical time bomb, an engineer's nightmare, and a pit of fishy despair sitting in your living room.

The following discussions provide basic information on the four categories of filtration. More detailed information is available in *The Marine Aquarium Reference* and other books and articles.

There are two basic types of contaminants in aquarium water: suspended physical particles and dissolved chemical compounds. The physical particles may be as big as a baseball dropped into the tank by the kid next door or as small as a microscopic free-floating bacterium. The dissolved chemical compounds may originate outside the tank from things such as insect spray or soap and perfume on the hands of an unwary aquarist, but except for these rare instances, dissolved contaminants are produced by the tank's inhabitants. They are created from the metabolic waste materials of fish, invertebrates, and plants, and also develop from the activity of bacteria on the waste organic matter produced in the tank.

**Mammoth protein skimmer demonstrates one filtration extreme at an aquarium show.**

These dissolved chemical compounds include ammonia, nitrite, nitrate, urea, proteins, amines, fatty acids, phenols, dyes, and many other less abundant compounds. Briefly, the following explains what each type of filtration accomplishes in your aquarium.

## Biological filtration

Simply put, biological filtration is the breakdown of toxic nitrogen compounds, such as ammonia, by populations of beneficial, or nitrifying, bacteria. Biological filtration is a natural process, but if it is not established and properly managed in a marine aquarium, the system water can quickly become a toxic brew capable of killing fishes and invertebrates.

When the first edition of this book was written, back in the 1970s, biological filtration was a relatively new concept. The intrepid marine aquarists of the 1950s and 1960s were very aware of "new tank syndrome," the phenomenon where a newly set up marine aquarium with an undergravel filter, or a even a small pump-powered filter, was initially unable to support much marine life except for perhaps a hardy fish or two. Almost any ornamental marine fish or invertebrate placed in a new tank would sicken and die within a few days. It was known to most, but not all, marine aquarists of the time that if a hardy fish was kept in a filtered aquarium for a few weeks to a month, then, and only then, could the tank support the life of many fish and quite a few invertebrates. But why this was so remained a mystery to marine aquarists in those early days.

One of the best-known marine aquarists at the dawn of the modern marine aquarium age was Helen Simkatis, who wrote *Salt-Water Fishes for the Home Aquarium*, published in 1958. She mentions and describes "biological filtration," but dismisses it with the comment, "We feel that any system that allows quantities of waste material to accumulate is dangerous." Robert P. L. Straughan, undoubtedly the most prolific writer on marine aquariums in the 1960s, did not mention the concept of biological filtration in his 1959 book, *The Salt Water Aquarium in the Home* (Third Edition, 1970), the bible of marine aquarists of that day. Not even Bill Braker, then director of the John G. Shedd Aquarium in Chicago, mentioned biological filtration in his 1966 book, *Marine Tropicals*.

During the 1960s and most of the 1970s, undergravel filtration was generally considered to be a rather ineffective form of mechanical filtration that did little more than capture waste that should be removed from

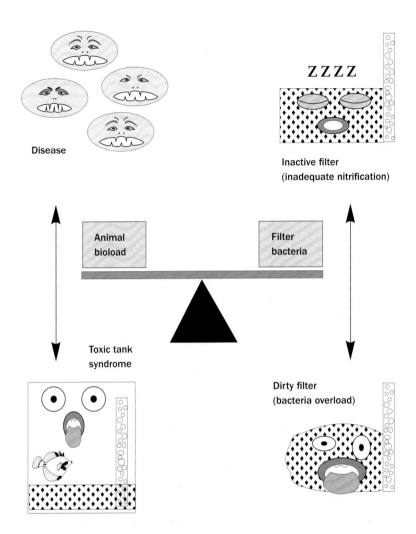

**One key to a healthy aquarium is keeping animal bioload and biological filter in balance.**

the aquarium rather than feeding the function of biological filtration. That concept changed in the late 1970s, as marine aquariums became increasingly popular and more aquarists began having success in maintaining marine fish in small aquariums. One of the most influential writers in the 1970s was Stephen Spotte. His books, *Marine Aquarium Keeping* (1973) and *Fish and Invertebrate Culture: Water Management in Closed Systems* (1979), really laid out the scientific foundation of biological filtration for marine aquarists, professionals, and hobbyists. Ammonia, nitrite, nitrate, and "run-in" or "cycling" quickly became common terms in the lexicon of marine aquaristics.

We began to understand that the elevated levels of ammonia and nitrite in new aquariums could be deadly, and only when healthy populations of the right bacteria developed was it safe to stock a tank with anything other than one or two extremely hardy fish.

Thus the stage was set in the early 1980s for the flowering of the modern marine aquarium age, and I like to think that the 1982 first edition of my *Marine Aquarium Handbook*, the third edition of which you are reading right now, helped the bud of that flower to open. In the 1970s and 1980s, undergravel filters were the foundation of successful marine aquarium–keeping, so the topic of filtration in my first book dealt extensively with the form, function, and maintenance of undergravel filters. By circulating the aquarium water through a bed of gravel, an undergravel filter encourages the rapid proliferation of nitrifying bacteria and, hence, biological filtration. Although the marine aquarium hobby has advanced far beyond the old undergravel filter technology, it is still a viable method

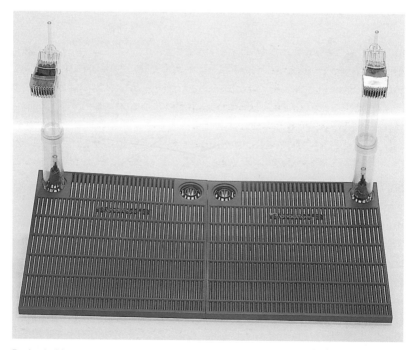

Basic air-driven undergravel filter with plates to create a watery void beneath the sand.

Live rock, heavily colonized by beneficial nitrifying and denitrifying bacteria, is now the mainstay of the marine aquarium world, offering natural, low maintenance biofiltration.

for establishing a successful and inexpensive, if limited, marine aquarium. And for a young aquarist, a novice, or even just for an auxiliary or quarantine aquarium, it is still a valuable technique—so I believe there is good reason for keeping this information available. (See Chapter 4.)

Interestingly, with the ascent in the 1990s of the reef tank concept, a form of the old "natural marine aquarium system," biological filtration took a back seat to what used to be auxiliary forms of marine aquarium filtration. Various types and applications of mechanical and chemical filtration have become the bases of advanced filtration, while the workhorse role of biological filtration, both aerobic and anaerobic, has been relegated to a chunk of bacteria-laden limestone rock that needs very little technology in its application.

## Mechanical filtration

Mechanical filtration removes suspended particulate matter from the aquarium system water. It extracts detritus, uneaten food, feces, and other waste from the display aquarium and concentrates it where the aquarist

**Affordable external power filters, available in many types, some with biofilter features, can be a useful adjunct for a basic small-to-medium-size marine aquarium.**

can easily remove and dispose of it frequently. The efficiency of the filter depends on how fast water moves through the straining surfaces, the surface area of the filter, and the size of the trap for the particles. A mechanical filter can use sand, gravel, fiber pads, floss, metal or plastic screens, or diatomaceous earth to strain particles from the water. Obviously, a filter for baseballs and tree trunks is designed differently and operates differently than a filter designed to sieve microscopic plankton and bacteria.

A mechanical filter also becomes a biological filter if it is not cleaned or changed frequently. A good mechanical filter that removes very small particles with a rapid water flow is an excellent auxiliary to the basic biological filter because it maintains high water clarity, removes free-swimming parasites, and traps accumulated dirt and detritus from the aquarium when it is kept clean. If the media is not cleaned or exchanged frequently, however, the filter clogs and slows water flow, harbors bacteria, and eventually becomes a biological filter. In order to effectively remove organic particles from the aquarium system, the particles must be removed from the filter before they are broken down into dissolved nutrients, thus the filter must be cleaned every few days, or at least once a week, or its efficiency as a mechanical filter is diminished.

For smaller aquariums, a good auxiliary mechanical filter, such a "hang on the back" power filter or a canister filter, will help reduce some of the organic load and keep the water free of small particulate matter. In reef-type systems equipped with a sump, mechanical filtration is usually incorporated, using fiber pads, filter cones, and/or blocks of foam.

## Chemical filtration

Chemical filtration removes dissolved compounds and elements from solution in the aquarium water. There are four basic chemical filtration methods commonly applied to marine aquariums:

1. Activated carbon
2. Ion-exchange resins and polymeric adsorbents
3. Protein foam skimming or foam fractionation
4. Oxidation through ozonation

**Activated carbon** resembles nuggets or pellets of black charcoal and is able to remove dissolved solids from the water because each carbon grain contains uncountable microscopic pores throughout its entire mass. These tiny pores adsorb the molecules of various organic and inorganic substances from the solution so that they are no longer present in the solution. Of course the complete technical explanation is more complicated, but this gives you some idea how activated carbon works. When all the pores are filled or coated with organics and bacterial slime, the carbon is deactivated and then functions only as a biological filter, but this takes quite some time, depending on the filtering load. The home hobbyist really can't reactivate the carbon by baking it in an ordinary oven, except to drive off some adsorbed gases, but if the carbon is not exhausted, it can be cleaned of accumulated organic dirt and reused, although its effectiveness will be limited.

The adsorptive properties of activated carbon change as the carbon is used. New carbon has a greater ability to adsorb gases than old carbon and, in general, will pick up more molecules at a faster rate. Some of the things that activated carbon will remove to some extent from your aquarium water, depending on the type, amount, and age, are oxygen and carbon dioxide (but not enough to affect a well-aerated aquarium), copper, ozone, chlorine, antibiotics, some dissolved proteins and carbohydrates, iodine, mercury, vanadium, chromium, cobalt, iron, molybdenum, methylene blue, malachite green, sulfa drugs, organic dyes, and many other elements and compounds. Some of these, such as organic dyes, are removed very quickly and efficiently, others more slowly. Most compounds are not completely removed by activated carbon, but are reduced in concentration to a variable extent.

Thus, activated carbon is a mixed blessing to us aquarists because it pulls out some good things as well as many of the nasties. It does not effectively remove ammonia, nitrite, or nitrate and cannot substitute for a biological filter. Activated carbon is usually changed on a monthly basis, although it may be in effect longer in some situations, and it may be that older carbon is better than new carbon, because older carbon may retain the capacity to remove large organic molecules after its affinity for simpler compounds has diminished. Perhaps the greatest danger in using activated carbon is that it is so efficient in clearing and cleaning the water that it hides the need for occasional partial water changes.

Properly used, activated carbon can be one of the most useful tools of the marine aquarist. My opinions and recommendations on the general use of activated carbon are as follows: Set up the carbon filter as an outside power filter that can be turned off, removed, and cleaned without disturbing the tank. Use it sparingly on invertebrate tanks because invertebrates seem to be more dependent on trace elements in the water than fish are. Carbon can be used constantly or with great frequency on fish tanks, but give the tank a rest from carbon filtration once in a while, especially immediately after water changes or renewal of trace elements. Never use carbon filtration on treatment tanks or any tank where medication is being used. Activated carbon should be given a long rinse in running cold water before use to remove all possible dust. There is some suspicion, yet unproved, that fine particles of carbon dust may be related to the onset of Head and Lateral Line Erosion (HLLE), a disfiguring condition in fishes. Remember that no one really knows exactly what activated carbon does or doesn't do to aquarium water, so use it cautiously and let your own experience be your best guide.

Today, it is a rare marine system that does not utilize some carbon filtration. Most aquarists renew the carbon regularly and keep the system water crystal-clear. Many serious reefkeepers use two mesh sacks of car-

Canister filters, residing behind or below the aquarium, can house multiple types of filtration media, including activated carbon and phosphate.

bon, changing one each month. Fish and most invertebrates don't seem to suffer, but heavy carbon filtration does remove some important trace elements, such as iodine. If heavy carbon filtration is used, it is wise to regularly supplement trace elements. Some reef tank aquarists simply drop a bag of activated carbon in the sump tank and replace it every six months or so, but this is not the best way to use carbon filtration. The water flow should be directed through the carbon filter media and not just allowed to flow around it; as one well-known aquarium expert has said, "You might as well soak a potato in the tank if you just lay a bag of carbon in the sump." A bag of carbon in the sump tank does do some good, of course: it can effectively keep the water from turning yellow, but it is not nearly as effective as flow-through carbon filtration.

Most carbon filtration in small tanks takes place in special chambers in power filters that hang on the back of the tank, and this works very well. Change the carbon every month or two, or when you begin to notice a bit of yellow color in the water. If the tank has a heavy bioload, more frequent changes may be warranted.

## Ion-exchange resins

Ion-exchange resins and polymeric adsorbents are more of an unknown than activated carbon. They are available to marine aquarists as small, dull-surfaced beads, alone or in a mix with activated carbon, and as fibers in pads and sheets of filter material. Opinions range from advocacy of certain resins as total substitutes for biological filtration to complete dismissal of the value of ion-exchange resins to marine aquarists. As in most instances where two great extremes exist, the truth is somewhere in the middle. Some resins are used to remove ammonia or nitrate in freshwater sewage treatment and others are effective in removing dissolved organics.

The use of ion-exchange and polymeric adsorbent resins in home marine systems has greatly increased in recent years. They are now manufactured for greater specificity in the removal of particular types of molecules, and many can be easily regenerated. Some aquarists feel that activated carbon is all the chemical filtration that is needed, and others say that ion-exchange and polymeric resins are very valuable chemical filtration tools, especially for reef tanks. My opinion is that resins can be beneficial, but the individual aquarist must determine how useful they are in any particular system, and whether the benefits of their use justify the expenditure.

## Phosphate binders

Phosphates have a tendency to accumulate in a marine aquarium and can fuel the growth of nuisance algae and also inhibit calcification, negatively affecting the growth of stony corals, tridacnid clams, and coralline algae. Phosphates enter the aquarium via foods, makeup water, and sometimes salt mixes and activated carbon.

Two primary types of chemical binders are used by aquarists to keep phosphate levels within bounds: iron oxide hydroxide (a reddish, rust-colored powder) and aluminum oxide materials (usually white granules). The binders are usually contained in a fine-mesh sack placed in the filter system where water flows through or in a fluidized bed reactor. Some hobbyists have reported negative impacts on corals, including failure of polyps to expand, with the use of aluminum-containing compounds, and most advanced reefkeepers today seem to prefer iron oxide hydroxide (also known as granular ferric oxide or GFO) as a phosphate-binding medium. However, GFO has been implicated in the recession and bleaching of coral tissues, especially when large doses are used to drop phosphate levels suddenly and dramatically. Any phosphate binder should be used with care and introduced to a system gradually. The primary non-chemical approach to removing phosphate involves cultivating macroalgae in the system or in a lighted refugium. Periodic removal of part of the macroalgae mass is an effective means of exporting nutrients, including phosphate.

**PHOSPHATE CONTROL:**

One of the most effective ways of exporting phosphate from a system is cultivating macroalgae in the tank or in a connected refugium.

❖

## Protein skimming

Protein skimming, airstripping, and foam fractionation are all terms for the same basic process, which has revolutionized water cleansing for marine aquariums. The technique is old, but its application to marine aquariums was a radical development when first introduced. Protein skimming operates on the principle that many of the compounds dissolved in saltwater are attracted (adsorbed) to the interface between a gas and a liquid. Therefore, if you mix extremely tiny and abundant bubbles of air or other gas into a solution, many of the dissolved organic and some inorganic compounds "stick" to the surface of the molecules and ride them until they burst.

When the organics are heavy, they coat the bubbles and create a surface foam sort of like soap suds, but not as stable. If you can scoop up these suds and discard them, you can remove the compounds that stuck to the bubbles when they formed in the aquarium water. And this is just what the protein skimmer does. It collects the foam created in the foam generation chamber in a small cup, where the foam breaks down into a nasty liquid containing all the compounds that stuck to the bubbles. This cup is emptied periodically, or drained continuously, and the aquarium is rid of many things like proteins, amino acids, some organic dyes, fatty acids, albumin compounds, other complex organic compounds, and some inorganic compounds that tend to hook up with some organic molecules.

There are unknowns, however. As with activated carbon, no one knows exactly what, and how much of it, is removed by an efficient protein skimmer, and it is possible that valuable trace elements and nutrients are removed along with waste compounds. Also, protein skimmers have to be carefully adjusted for peak efficiency in small marine systems, and

A hang-on-the-tank external protein skimmer is an excellent addition to a small-to-medium-size marine aquarium, helping ensure better water quality and gas exchange.

if the air discharge is not at just the right volume and bubble size, the effectiveness of the unit declines greatly. Wooden air releasers or wooden airstones, still used in some protein skimmers because of the tiny bubbles they create, should be changed often, for the wood decays and fills with organics and air release is restricted. *The Marine Aquarium Reference* has an extensive section on types and operation of protein skimmers, including directions on making a homemade protein skimmer from PVC pipe.

A protein skimmer can be a very useful tool—some say essential, especially for heavily loaded fish tanks and coral reef tanks—but you have to be sure that it is operating properly, and remember that it may remove important trace elements and nutrients. The primary value of protein skimming and carbon filtration is that when properly employed, they significantly aid water clarity and cleanliness, and decrease, but do not eliminate, the need for periodic water changes. Protein skimming is most valuable, because when properly set up and operated, this method of chemical filtration removes dissolved organics before they are broken down into basic nutrients.

Collection cup above a protein skimmer filling with complex organic waste compounds.

Finally, a properly sized and maintained protein skimmer also offers the beneficial side effect of providing aggressive oxygenation of the system water, bringing a captive system closer to the natural ideal of the oxygen-saturated water found around coral reefs in the wild.

### Ozone

The last method of chemical filtration I'll discuss is the oxidation of dissolved organics through the application of ozone. Ozone is the triatomic form ($O_3$) of oxygen and is a very unstable compound. It is formed just before introduction into the water by air passing through an electric discharge. As the ozone breaks down in the water, it oxidizes or "burns" dissolved organics and kills bacteria and parasites.

Ozone functions as a "chemical filter" in that it changes the structure of many complex dissolved organic compounds if it is abundant enough and in contact with the water for a long enough period of time. Although ozone can oxidize some ammonia and nitrite to nitrate, it cannot substitute for a biological filter. The best method of mixing ozone into the water is to use a reactor tube. This is a filter tube or container that trickles water over a filter media with a large surface area in a pressurized (only 2–3 psi above ambient) atmosphere. This is also a good way to oxygenate water, and when used with just air it is termed an oxygen reactor.

**OZONE CAUTIONS:**

Best left to advanced aquarists, ozone is a potentially dangerous filtration aid that can harm livestock and humans.

❖

The ozone contact tube should be of a counterflow design for maximum efficiency. This means that the water flow and the flow of ozonated air must go in opposite directions in the reactor or contact chamber (air up and water down) to ensure that the ozone and water are in contact for as long as possible.

It must be pointed out that ozonation is a delicate and potentially dangerous filtration aid. Too much ozone escaping into the aquarium can burn the gills of fish and the delicate tissues of invertebrates and cause death and distress, and too little ozone mixing with the water will not effectively oxidize the dissolved organics. Ozone escaping into the atmosphere can also cause headaches and stomach distress in humans, although such symptoms would not appear unless there were large and constant releases. If you always smell ozone in the vicinity of the aquarium, then there may be excessive release of this gas into the atmosphere.

Because each aquarium carries a different organic load and therefore requires a different amount of ozone, it is difficult to maintain maximum efficiency without delicate chemical adjustment. Activated carbon will remove ozone and can be used to prevent a buildup of ozone in the aquarium. A carbon filter should be present in the water line that returns water from the ozone reactor to the aquarium or sump tank. *A caution: never pass ozone through dry activated carbon, as a fire might result.*

Ozone is frequently used in protein skimmers, and the efficiency of each is enhanced when they work together and both are optimally adjusted. Ozone treatment devices are best left to the advanced aquarist, since they can create problems for the casual or unknowing hobbyist.

### UV sterilization

Sterilization can be considered a filtering method in that it removes life from the aquarium water. The most common sterilization device for marine aquariums is the ultraviolet light sterilizer, in which the aquarium water is passed through a filter tube that contains a short-wave, germicidal ultraviolet bulb. Some chemical filtration is also affected since the device also oxidizes some dissolved organics. (Other sterilizing devices release ozone into a contained tube of aquarium water and an ozone and air mixture. The ozone dissolves in the water and oxidizes the protoplasm of the target organisms. See "Ozone," above.) The primary use of sterilization devices is to decrease the abundance of free-floating bacteria and control parasitic infections by killing the organisms during the free-swimming stages of their life cycles.

**Note:** It is important to realize that UV sterilization cannot completely remove free-swimming parasites from the aquarium water because a UV sterilizer cannot treat all the water in the system at the same time. The degree of reduction depends on the flow rate and efficacy of the UV device. Sometimes this is enough and the reduction in numbers is great enough to keep the parasite in check. But as the efficiency of the bulb diminishes, or as an organic film coats the bulb, the parasite load increases. This is not to say that UV treatment is not useful. It can be very helpful in reducing bacterial and parasite loads in many systems, mostly systems with heavy bioloading.

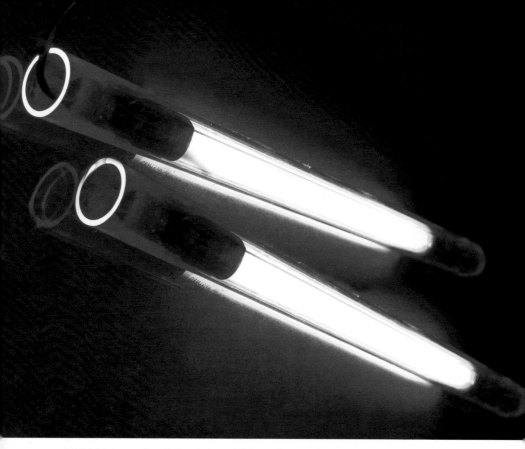

UV light tubes emit radiation that can kill bacteria, parasites, and algal spores.

Ultraviolet light is a good sterilizing agent when the water is clear, the bulb is new, the UV has to penetrate less than an inch of water, and the exposure time of the water to the UV light is longer than one second. UV works by affecting the function of the living cell through alteration of the structure of the cell's nuclear material and through some production of ozone in the treated water. The usual structure of a UV unit designed for marine aquarium use consists of a 4- to 8-watt UV germicidal bulb sealed in a watertight jacket that allows the aquarium water to circulate in a thin layer past the bulb. Both UV irradiation and ozonation have the capability to alter the structure of some dissolved chemical compounds. Therefore, neither ozonation nor ultraviolet sterilization should be used in conjunction with any drug or chemical medication.

Sterilization of aquarium water is not necessary for the maintenance of a successful marine tank. The most effective application for these devices is reducing the number of free-floating bacteria, and such bacteria are usually not a problem in a well-maintained, uncrowded tank. However, if you feel that UV treatment helps you to maintain a cleaner, more stable, and trouble-free tank, then by all means go ahead and use it, but remember that the glass in the UV bulb will gradually lose its ability to transmit UV germicidal radiation, and the bulb should be replaced every 8 to 10 months in order for the unit to retain its effectiveness.

There are two very important human safety considerations to be aware of when operating a UV unit:

1. Never look directly at the lighted germicidal UV bulb. UV light in a germicidal wavelength can injure the delicate tissues of the human eye.

2. A UV bulb designed to operate within a flow of water should not be operated without the water in the filter. The bulb will heat up when operated in air and may then break if it is immersed in water while hot, and, of course, this can electrically charge the tank (a shocking situation!).

## Biological filtration

Biological filtration is the transformation of toxic waste substances, primarily ammonia, into relatively nontoxic nutrients through the activity of living organisms, primarily nitrifying bacteria. Algae also utilize the basic nutrients produced by nitrifying bacteria, thus can function as a type of biological filter under the right conditions. Note that the phrase "removes from the system" is not mentioned in the definition of biological filtration, as it is in the definitions of other types of filtration. The only drawback to biological filtration is that the process does not remove waste products from the aquarium; it only transforms the waste into compounds with limited toxicity. These compounds accumulate in the aquarium and eventually have to be removed, through either filtration, algae growth, or the simple process of periodic partial water changes. Marine aquariums can be maintained for years with low-maintenance live rock and live sand biological filtration; monthly 10–20% water changes; and regular filter cleanings.

Tremendous volumes of words have been written in the aquarium literature about the nitrogen cycle, "new tank syndrome," and nitrification and bacterial decomposition—and rightly so, for they all refer to the basic process that allows life to exist in your aquarium. Just as human communities need septic tanks or sewage plants, aquariums require biological filtration. All animals, including fish, crabs, anemones, butterflies, snakes, and parakeets, consume food and oxygen in order to grow new tissues and produce energy for living. Waste products—carbon dioxide, undigested food and intestinal bacteria, and nitrogen wastes from the utilization of protein and the normal breakdown of body cells—are produced by every animal and must be excreted. The solid wastes of fish and invertebrates, uneaten food, and an occasional dead fish all suffer the same degenerative fate in a marine aquarium. The aerobic bacteria of decay attack this dead matter and produce, among other things, a lot of **ammonia** from the decomposed protein. This process of decay is termed ammonification or mineralization.

The major sources of ammonia in a well-run aquarium, however, are the nitrogenous wastes of the aquarium inhabitants. The way an animal rids itself of waste nitrogen depends greatly upon its relationship to water. Ammonia is rapidly formed in the blood of animals from the breakdown of protein, and it has the characteristics of being very toxic and very soluble. It must be either immediately excreted or rapidly transformed to a less toxic substance. Fish, living as they do in a watery environment, are able to excrete ammonia directly through their gills into the surrounding water. Land animals cannot afford the water loss that would be the price of direct ammonia excretion and thus, through a clever biochemical mechanism known as the ornithine cycle, they convert ammonia to less toxic urea and excrete it in a concentrated solution whenever the mood strikes them. Some animals that live where there is very little free water, such as desert rats, are so conserving of water that they transform their nitrogenous waste to nontoxic crystals of uric acid that can be stored in the body or excreted in dry form.

**NEUTRALIZING AMMONIA:**
Ammonia excreted by fishes and from the breakdown of wastes is highly toxic and must be quickly and constantly neutralized.

❖

So now we have a tank full of highly toxic, soluble ammonia derived from animal excretion and the activity of decay bacteria. Whatever shall we do? Fortunately, Mother Nature comes on like the U.S. Cavalry at this point with her nitrifying bacteria. These bacteria are found throughout the world and have the capacity to oxidize toxic ammonia to nitrite, and less toxic nitrite to the relatively non toxic nitrate. All we need to provide is a large surface area for the bacteria to colonize and a source of ammonia. Even if we avoid employing an external biological filter, which is only a device that provides a lot of surface

A failing reef tank smothered in cyanobacteria, a sure sign of poor water quality.

area for colonial bacterial growth, the bacteria colonize every available internal surface in the system to do their oxidative work.

The intermediate product, **nitrite** ($NO_2$), is also toxic, but less so than ammonia. Levels of up to 15 ppm can be tolerated by most species of marine fish for a limited period. A well-established marine aquarium should always show zero levels of nitrite.

The end product of bacterial action on nitrite, **nitrate** ($NO_3$), is relatively nontoxic and can be allowed to accumulate in the fish-only marine aquarium without much concern. However, if the tank is allowed to develop pockets of low oxygen or anaerobic conditions, uncontrolled bacterial reduction of nitrate can produce hydrogen sulfide and other toxic compounds. In a reef aquarium, nitrate can foster the growth of troublesome hair algae that can overgrow corals, and most advanced aquarists try to keep it under 10 ppm in fish-only systems and often under 2 ppm in reef tanks.

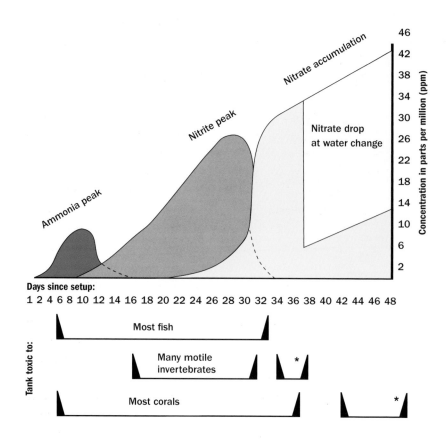

Typical pattern of tank toxicity and relative levels of poison waste nitrogen compounds during the run-in of a new marine aquarium with a traditional undergravel filter or new biomedia such as dry rock and sand. Note that all aquariums do not cycle exactly the same.

* Tank toxicity after water change is very variable.

Ammonia occurs in two states depending on pH: the un-ionized state ($NH_3$) and the ionized state ($NH_4^+$). The un-ionized state is more toxic than the ionized state because it can invade body tissues more readily but, fortunately, almost all free ammonia is in the ionized state at the normal pH of seawater. As pH increases, the nontoxic form of ammonia rapidly decreases and the toxic form rapidly increases. Thus, a lethal level of toxic ammonia may be present at a pH of 8.4, while the same total amount of ammonia may be tolerable at 7.8. Fish that are susceptible to ammonia poisoning may suddenly suffer symptoms if the pH increases rapidly and significant levels of ammonia are present. At any rate, levels of ammonia and nitrite are always very near zero in the established and balanced marine aquarium.

Ammonia is very toxic to marine and other organisms, but fortunately, ammonia is quickly oxidized into nitrite (NO2) and then into nitrate (NO3) by two genera of nitrifying bacteria. "*Nitrosomonas* oxidizes ammonia into nitrite, and *Nitrobacter* oxidizes nitrite into nitrate." This statement was considered gospel when the first edition of this book was written. Almost every aquarium book written in the latter half of the 20th century has described this fundamental process and identified these two species of chemolithotrophic bacteria as the species that provide this activity. However, as more and more research is done on the entire process of mineralization, nitrification, and denitrification, using the cutting-edge tools of molecular phylogenetic methodologies and environmental science that are now available, it has become apparent that many species of chemolithic and heterotrophic bacteria contribute to this process. Numerous species of chemoautotrophic nitrifying bacteria, including the genera *Nitrosomonas, Nitrobacter, Nitrospira, Nitrocystis, Nitrosococcus,* and *Nitrococcus,* are commonly found in natural and enriched marine and freshwater environments. Environmental variations, such as salinity, temperature, substrate or absence of substrate, and type and amount of organic material and microscopic and macroscopic life present, all seem to affect the species mix of bacteria that process nitrogen in the natural ocean world. In much the same way, the species types and mix, and population densities, of nitrifying and heterotrophic bacteria in a marine or freshwater aquarium vary according to the maintenance procedures and lifespan of the aquarium.

It is not important that the average aquarist know which species of bacteria accomplish the transformation of nitrogen in an aquarium; it is enough to know that bacterial colonies are the sewerage treatment plant of the aquarium system, that provisions must be made for their existence and well-being, and that they make it possible for fish and invertebrates to survive in a small glass box.

Nitrification happens. It will occur in a marine aquarium sooner or later, even if sterile sand and rock are used in the initial setup; it will just take a longer time for nitrifying bacteria to colonize filter and tank substrates and build to population levels that will offset the waste generated by the living organisms in the aquarium. As discussed in other areas of this book, an aquarist can enhance this process by adding a bacterial seed from an active marine aquarium, by the ancient method of using a small amount of compost and/or garden soil (not recommended), by using live rock or live sand (which both provide a complete and almost immediate nitrification and denitrification biological filter), and/or by using a commercial product that provides a large amount of seed of a specific species or mix of species of bacteria, which will help to quickly establish effective nitrifying biological filtration. This last option may or may not be helpful: its efficacy depends on the quality and age of the product and on its suitability for the task at hand. Ask a knowledgeable person at your local aquarium shop to recommend a reliable brand, if you choose to use bacterial supplements.

**NATURAL INOCULANTS:**

Live rock and live sand deliver huge populations of beneficial bacteria that can help jump-start the biological filtration in a new system.

❖

In a relatively sterile new biological filter, it takes some time for adequate populations of bacteria to develop, especially if only a few bacteria are present at the start. Bacteria usually reproduce by division, one individual splitting into two; thus, the last phase of population growth proceeds much more rapidly than the first phase. This is why ammonia and nitrite levels climb so high so slowly and then drop so rapidly to less than 1–2 ppm. The nitrite drop usually occurs within a day or two, even though it had been building to levels as high as 20–40 ppm over a period of weeks.

After the populations of nitrifying bacteria have become well established, the oxidization of ammonia and nitrite occurs almost as soon as these compounds are formed. Because of this, they do not have a chance to accumulate in the system, and only the end product, nitrate, can build to high levels. Accumulated nitrate can be removed by dilution through partial water changes; also, because nitrate is a basic plant nutrient, a lot of this compound is taken up by algae as they grow. Harvest of the excess algae then removes this nutrient and others, including phosphates, from the system.

The accompanying graph illustrates the typical "run-in" pattern of a classic biological filter, including the times that a system can be toxic. Ammonia ($NH_3$), nitrite ($NO_2$), and nitrate ($NO_3$) are variably toxic at different concentrations, and this chart provides an indication of when the filter is most toxic to different organisms during the period of typical establishment of bacterial colonies in a biological filter.

As discussed elsewhere, live rock has the ability to act as both a nitrifying filter (with aerobic activity on its exposed surfaces) and a denitrifying filter (through anaerobic activity deep in the porous structure of the rock). Similarly, a deep bed of fine sand can also perform both functions: aerobic in the top inch, anaerobic further down in the bed. See Chapter 4 for more detailed information on live rock and live sand beds.

## Natural systems

A so-called "natural system"—a tank established without manmade filters, only an airstone or powerhead to gently turn over the water, and containing a limited number of fish, invertebrates, and algae—still depends on the same biological process of nitrification that the biological filter is designed to support and enhance. Nitrifying bacteria are still present and working hard, but their populations are restricted to tank sides, rock, sand beds, and most other surface areas present in the aquarium. Such sites for bacterial activity are sufficient if the tank is well maintained and the biological load is kept well within the range of natural balance. Invertebrates that consume waste matter, and algae that utilize nutrients, greatly aid tank balance in a "natural system" aquarium, and their biological interaction is important in this system where there are no adjuncts, such as particulate filters and skimmers. Algae can, and usually do, play an important role in the marine aquarium. They serve as a diet supplement for many fish and invertebrates, enhance the beauty of a natural tank, and can perform as a biological and chemical filter. The types of algae under discussion are the mixtures of single-celled and filamentous green, brown, and red algae that form on the sides and rocks of well-lit aquariums. Brown algae are usually the first to appear and are really diatoms or golden brown algae. Heavy growths of these diatoms mixed with other algae go by the esoteric name of "lab-lab" and are used in the culture of some marine food fish. Also included are the filamentous green algae in the genera *Entromorpha*, *Derbesia*, and *Chaetomorpha*. These al-

Live sand used to inoculate a new system with bacteria and sand-dwelling organisms.

gae form the thin, green, hair-like filaments that grow on rocks and glass and provide browse for many aquarium fishes and grazing invertebrates. Growth of the algae is dependent on the intensity and quality of light and the amount and type of dissolved nutrients. Good growths of green filamentous algae may be welcome in a fish-only marine system or one with motile invertebrates, but reef aquarists work very hard to keep such algae under tight control by maintaining nutrient-poor conditions and employing herbivorous fishes, snails, and hermit crabs.

### Live rock

There is no doubt that the arrival of live rock as a medium to support biological filtration was a major turning point in marine aquarium–keeping. Imagine a product that, when placed in a new marine system, simultaneously introduces billions of beneficial bacteria, provides a permanent, maintenance-free filter medium, and offers authentic decorative effects and hiding places for fishes.

Good quality, porous live rock is now an aquarist's best friend, serving to kick-start the nitrogen cycle in a new system and provide a realistic substrate for natural-looking aquascapes. The term "live rock" covers a huge diversity of types, shapes, and sizes from many points of origin. Live rock is pieces of calcium carbonate rubble, typically created over many, many decades by storm damage to wild reefs. It is primarily composed of old stony coral skeletons, but may also incorporate material from other calcareous organisms such as mollusks, tube worms, and encrusting algae.

Live rock that has been well handled between its collection and its arrival in the home aquarium brings with it complex cultures of nitrifying bacteria, algae, cryptic sponges, and myriad tiny invertebrates, all of which can contribute to maintaining water quality. When combined with healthy water movement, live rock and its community of organisms can quickly work to neutralize ammonia and nitrite, while also working over the long term to help control levels of nitrate and phosphate. As long as detritus is not allowed to build up on the surfaces, in the interstices, and beneath the rock, this is a material that can provide a lifetime of service without replacement.

A captive reef built of porous live rock (as opposed to solid boulder-like stones sometimes sold as "base rock") can provide ample biological filtration, both nitrification (end product, nitrate) and denitrification (end product, nitrogen gas), and can usually eliminate the need for other mechanically assisted biological filtration devices, such as trickle or undergravel filters, which require periodic cleaning. Exceptions may be so-called Fish-Only-With-Live-Rock (FOWLR) systems with heavy bioloads, but these are now generally managed with live rock combined with aggressive protein skimming and possibly ozone and UV sterilization.

### Live sand

Live sand serves the same functions as live rock and may be either collected from the wild or cultured with the inoculation of beneficial bacteria. It offers a huge surface area for colonization by bacteria, and a bed 3.5–4 inches deep, or more, can also develop deep anaerobic areas where nitrate is converted to nitrogen gas. So advocates say it is as good as, or superior to, live rock.

Once a specialty item, cultured live sand is now available pre-packaged at most marine aquarium shops and can be used to help establish a thriving population of beneficial bacteria very quickly in a new system. Wild-collected sand will bring with it a much greater diversity of life forms, but it may need to be special-ordered. Either way, a bed of live sand will eventually become populated with burrowing organisms, including many

A hybrid refugium provides one chamber for live sand and algae, another for a skimmer.

types of (harmless) worms, crustaceans, snails, brittle stars, and others that feed on detritus, feces, and food wastes. See Chapter 4 for more detailed information on live sand beds.

## Macroalgae

Live rock, in the presence of dissolved nutrients, may sprout unexpected and seemingly spontaneous growths of macroalgae. A moderate growth of filamentous green algae is usually useful and desirable in a traditional marine aquarium with moderately intense lighting and a full load of marine fish, but not in a reef tank with a focus on hard and soft corals. Macroalgae in the genus *Halimeda* and red coralline algae are now much more highly desired than green filamentous algae. *Derbesia* and other types can reach plague proportions if not controlled by grazing animals and reducing nutrient levels.

Algae aid bacterial nitrification only by providing some sites for growth of nitrifying bacteria and some detritus for heterotrophic (decay) bacteria. It is as a "chemical filter," however, that algae really have potential. During photosynthesis (the process plants use to make food and energy from sunlight, water, $CO_2$, and nutrients), algae take up $CO_2$, which keeps the pH of the aquarium high, and utilize nutrients such as nitrate that are made available by bacteria in the biological filter. Thus, algae can clean the water of accumulated nitrates, take up ammonia and nitrite, release oxygen, and remove $CO_2$, all good things to do for your aquarium. They are also exceptionally good at scavenging phosphates from aquarium water.

Abundant algal growth, however, will also remove trace elements, and this can be a potential disaster. As algal activity raises the pH, any ammonia present becomes more and more toxic as the amount of un-ionized ammonia increases. Usually ammonia levels are so low and algal activity so limited that no problems develop. Many algae also use ammonia as a nutrient, so ammonia seldom gets a chance to accumulate in systems with heavy algal activity. It is possible, however, for algal activity in closed systems without $CO_2$ injection, under sunlight or intense artificial light, to raise pH levels to 8.5 and 9.0, so it's worthwhile to at least be aware of this possibility.

There are delicate balances in a closed system aquarium between type and quality of algal growth, total animal load, quality and intensity of lighting, frequency and amount of water change, and degree of organic pollution (possibly from overfeeding). It is possible, especially in smaller, overcrowded tanks, to stimulate a luxuriant algal growth for several weeks or months only to have it suddenly die and pollute the tank. Many species of *Caulerpa*, for example, occasionally go through a reproductive phase where the algae disintegrates to release reproductive spores, and if the growth is heavy, this can cause problems in a marine aquarium system. If heavy algal growths develop in the tank, the excess algae must be harvested and the remaining growth closely watched for changes in type and amount of algae.

Moderate algal growth in the tank is beneficial to the contained marine environment, but it cannot properly be termed an algal filter. An external unit with algal growth controlled by harvesting and special illumination effectively serves to remove phosphates, nitrates, and $CO_2$ and performs a real filtering function. *Caulerpa* spp. had their heyday in

Although once popular in marine aquariums and refugiums, the various species of *Caulerpa* macroalgae are now widely banned because of their potential to become invasive weeds if released into local waters. Note cryptic frogfish.

algae filters, but today are frowned upon and even banned in many areas because the genus contains several species regarded as potentially invasive plants. *Caulerpa taxifolia* accidentally released into the Mediterranean by the Monaco Aquarium has smothered huge areas of ocean bed, and releases off southern California have been stopped only with rapid, very expensive intervention. *C. taxifolia* is a federally banned noxious weed in the United States, and there are stiff fines for anyone caught transporting, selling, or possessing it. A total of nine *Caulerpa* species are banned in California.

The algal filter species of choice today are *Chaetomorpha linum* or Spaghetti Algae, Red *Gracilaria*, and *Ulva lactuca*, or Sea Lettuce. All can grow rampantly in a simple box hanging on or housed under the display tank, with a constant flow of nutrient-rich water and moderately bright illumination 12 hours per day. Both *Gracilaria* and *Ulva* can be fed to herbivorous fishes, while the tough *Chaetomorpha* can be distributed to other aquarists, sold to the local fish store, or added to the compost heap. As an added benefit, these plants can harbor large populations of small crustaceans, such as amphipods, that are washed back into the display tank where they are greedily eaten by many fishes.

The effects of algal filtration are reversed in darkness (oxygen and pH levels drop), so the aquarist must also be aware of the potential problems. Many aquarists have developed a reverse type of algal filter that is illuminated during the night when the main tank is dark, and this mitigates the chemical effect—the changes in pH that considerable algae growth has on the system water.

# The Biological Filter

*Live Rock, Live Sand, and External Options*

IN THE PAST, A MOTHER AT THE BEACH MIGHT HAVE SAID TO HER YOUNG son, "Oh, yuck! Joey, put that rock down. It's full of bugs and worms." That same mother may now say, "Oh, great, Joey. You found a live rock. Uncle Mike will pay you $50 for it!"

Times change, and live rock has changed the face of the marine aquarium hobby forever. Interest in reef tanks is booming, and marine aquarium systems are getting a whole new look. Fewer and fewer hobbyists are content to keep fish-only aquariums. Marine aquarists are developing a new appreciation for invertebrates and the physical and biological structure of the marine environment; and live rock is the substrate on which this is built. Live rock can be one of the neatest and most interesting things that one can put in a marine aquarium, when done right. It can also bring one of the most costly disasters a marine aquarist can suffer. Let me explain.

First of all, live rock is not alive, it simply contains life. Secondly, there is nothing magic about live rock. Live rock is just coral rubble, calcareous or other porous rock taken from the waters of a tropical or subtropical area and transported to a marine aquarium system with some or most of the natural microscopic and macroscopic life forms still viable. Most importantly, it contains a constellation of bacteria that can efficiently perform biologicial filtration in the aquarium. These bacteria will both nitrify

**The new Smithsonian Institution reef exhibit designed by Jeffrey Turner in its first year of operation, with biological filtration dependent on a massive live-rock aquascape.**

(aerobically convert toxic ammonia to less toxic nitrite and then break down nitrite to relatively harmless nitrate), and denitrify (anaerobically turn nitrate into nitrogen gas, which will exit the system). It does this without prompting, care, or feeding, although it will need good water circulation within the tank to prevent stagnant water layers from developing around the rockwork.

Used properly, good live rock can provide your new marine aquarium with excellent biological filtration almost overnight. Purchased blindly and used without caution, live rock can also produce extreme ammonia spikes and lead to whole-tank wipeouts, leaving every fish and invertebrate dead or dying.

### Live rock origins and collection

Hurricanes, typhoons, and storm surges take a constant toll on coral reefs, breaking down stony coral colonies and tumbling pieces of all sizes into rubble zones. Over periods of years and decades, chunks that have died are colonized by microscopic and macroscopic marine life of all types. Collectors have different handling techniques depending on equipment, environment, and their own work habits; but, generally, they select the individual rocks based on current orders, the type of life attached, and the size and composition that experience has taught them are most suitable. Rocks with particularly desirable species of anemones and algae are usually given special treatment. The rocks are picked up from the bottom and placed on a boat, usually in old milk crates or other containers. The rocks are usually covered and kept wet while on the boat.

Most of the small motile invertebrates, such as crustaceans and echinoderms, leave the rock during this period and are flushed off the boat. Some of these small invertebrates are undesirable in reef systems. The post-larval and juvenile stages of the mantis shrimp, *Squilla*, for example, are common in the deep holes and crevices of the rocks, and the mantis grows up to be an efficient predator of other invertebrates and small fish. Small stone crabs also ride along with live rock and can cause problems in reef systems. Some collectors may keep all the rocks (or at least those with special algal or invertebrate attachments) in holding cages, under saltwater sprays, or in tanks of circulating water. The rocks are then transported to a wholesaler who may keep the rocks in a tank of filtered water, stacked under a constant or occasional spray of saltwater, or just stacked up un-

Dry base rock: inexpensive and useful for building reef structure.

der wet newspaper until shipment time. The rocks are usually shipped "dry," which means damp, but without water, to lower the shipping cost. Importers may put incoming rock into holding facilities or simply reship the boxes directly to customers. Rocks with special invertebrate or algal growths are, or should be, kept in water except during actual shipment, and some organisms should even be shipped in water.

At some point during the early collection and shipment process, the collector or wholesaler may put the rock through a process known as seeding or grooming. Seeded live rock has been through two processes. First it has been carefully cleaned of all macroscopic (large enough to see with the naked eye) growths of undesirable or dying invertebrates, such as sponges, mollusks, and certain algae. Brushes and picks may be used to clean the rock. Some growths may be left if they are interesting to the aquarist. The cleaned rock still contains a great deal of dead and decomposing organic matter in the pores and crevices; a "sniff test" usually gives one a rough idea of how much and how dead. The stage at which the end consumer receives a piece of live rock can make all the difference in how difficult it is to prepare and use.

Base rock: cheaper than premium rock, but already colonized with bacteria.

## Rocky disasters

The next paragraph is very important to any aquarist who is planning to set up a marine aquarium system using live rock as the biological filter. Placing 25 or 50 pounds of fully cured—that is, cleaned ("seeded") and completely stabilized—live rock in a marine system is the equivalent of transplanting a fully functional biological filter into a new system.

Placing uncured rock, that is, uncleaned rock that has not developed a population of nitrifying bacteria and still has a high concentration of dead organic matter, into a new or existing marine system is the equivalent of dumping several pounds of dead fish and shrimp into an aquarium with an unprepared and unconditioned biological filter. In the case of the former, the system is functional and is ready to receive fish and invertebrates. In the latter case, however, extensive decay occurs; fish and invertebrates die; ammonia, nitrite, and eventually, nitrate levels shoot to the sky; and in most instances, the rock is useless as live rock and the aquarist has created an organic disaster. At this point it may be difficult to know what, if anything, is still alive on or in the rock that is worthwhile.

## Types of rock

Important considerations and categorizations for live rock are methods of collection and treatment, composition, structure, and the microscopic and macroscopic life forms still alive on the rock. The best live rock is colorful, complex in shape, and porous. Dense, solid, boulder-like pieces with smooth surfaces are much less desirable. Calcareous pieces formed by stony corals are perhaps the best.

**Premium** or **fancy rock** is the interesting and often very beautiful rock used to top off a new aquascape. Some of the very best rock consists of pieces of old *Acropora* tables and branches, *Porites* heads, and other distinctive coral skeletons. Premium rock has been properly handled between collection and final sale to the aquarist, and it will usually display colorful red or pink coralline algae growth—and often other desirable organisms.

Rock that has particular invertebrates or algae attached is often named for the organism. Mushroom anemones, colonial polyps, and *Caulerpa, Halimeda, Hypnea,* and *Bryopsis* spp. algae are organisms frequently sold attached to live rock. Pink and red coralline algae often coat the rock, and tiny growths of filamentous algae such as *Cladophora, Chaetomorpha, Enteromorpha, Boodleopsis,* and *Derbesia* are hidden deep in crevices and pores. They bloom when good conditions are established and may even become a problem if nutrient levels in the system are too high.

**Base rock** is a term usually applied to dry pieces of rock, often mined or gathered from ancient reef formations on tropical islands or coastal areas. So-called "Bahamian Reef Rock" is typical base rock. Although it may have been high and dry for thousands of years, it will inevitably become colonized by bacteria, coralline algae, crustaceans, and other life forms over a period of months in the aquarium. It is much cheaper than live rock and can be used to form the first layer of an aquascape, where it may be almost entirely hidden by more pleasing-looking live rock used to dress the top of the reef.

**ROCK-SOLID REEFSCAPE:**
When assembling a large reef, the hidden foundation layers can be laid down with economical dry coral rock or cured base rock.

✤

It is important to use some rock that has been colonized by bacteria and invertebrates in the sea, but it is not necessary that every rock in the tank come from the bed of the ocean (although this is strongly advised for a dedicated stony coral system). The main trade-off in using some economical base rock to build a reef is the time it takes to develop the tank's reef versus the initial expense of live rock. Of course, the more live rock, the greater the kind and quantity of marine life you can introduce to the tank without waiting a period of months. The reef in a system set up with only 10% live rock will take longer to develop than a reef in a system set up with 50–75% or 100% live rock; but within a few months, or perhaps a year or so, the system with less live rock will catch up with the totally transplanted live rock reef system. Another consideration, however, is that nutrients on the surface of terrestrial rock are not stabilized by bacterial colonies or coralline algae, and hair algae are much more likely to grow on uncured rock. These are options that the reef tank aquarist should consider.

**Foundation rock** is live rock that has been kept submerged, usually in storage, but is less shapely and more drably colored than better-grade rock without desirable attached organisms and is usually used to form the basic hidden structure of the reef in the tank. It lacks the attractive colors of coralline algae, but comes at a discounted price and is useful in building the hidden bottom layer of a reefscape. In time it will become indistinguishable from other rock in the aquarium.

### Wild sources
Live rock for the marine aquarium trade is collected from many Indo-Pacific island groups, notably Fiji, Tonga, the Marshall Islands, Vanuatu, Indonesia, Bali, Timpora, Irian Jaya, the Solomon Islands, and others. Florida has banned wild live rock collection, but maricultured rock is being produced in the Florida Keys and the Gulf of Mexico. Caribbean live rock is available at times, particularly a distinctive platelike type from Haiti consisting of coralline-encrusted blades of old Lettuce Coral skeletons.

Hawaii prohibits live rock collection, and other places have placed limits on its harvest, but many observers believe that the collection of live rock need not harm the environment. Some restrictions on and management of the collection of live rock have been instituted in heavily harvested locations, but rock is very abundant in nature, and there will always be a way to provide active live rock for marine aquarists.

Reef formations and live coral should not be broken up, of course, and all the rock should not be removed from localized, specific areas. Terrestrial rock, usually formed by ancient coral reefs, can be mined from tropical islands and coastal areas, usually from dry inland quarries. Those of appropriate size and composition are placed in the sea and later har-

Cured premium-grade live rock, in this case from Fiji, can be used with or without base rock to provide an almost immediate biological filter for a new marine aquarium.

vested by collectors, a practice that has proved successful in the Florida Keys and on tracts in the Gulf of Mexico, and perhaps other areas as well. Hand-formed "rock" composed of crushed coral gravel and sand, coral rubble, and cement, which has been placed in the ocean to age and attract bacteria, calcareous algae, and many other organisms, is now available and can be difficult to distinguish from the real thing.

### Beginner's rock

For someone new to marine aquariums who is setting up a system of modest size, easily the best advice is this: buy your rock from a local aquarium shop and hand-pick the pieces that catch your eye. Buy only "fully cured" rock—that is, live rock that is cleaned of all dead and dying organisms and that is no longer a source of decay and toxic ammonia. Be sure to ask how long it has been in the dealer's tanks and look for rock that has been on site for at least three to four weeks. It will smell clean and of the sea and be free of white or black patches, ready to start performing biological filter duties immediately. If in doubt, pick up and smell the rock. (If there is any hint of foul odor or rotten egg smell, it is not cured.) Fully cured rock will not be the cheapest rock you can buy, but it will be the safest. You can take it home, put it directly into your new tank, and very likely be stocking a few fish within a matter of days.

How much to buy? The usual recommendations for live rock call for approximately one to two pounds per gallon of tank volume, but as little as one pound per 5 gallons can be sufficient to start a 20- to 30-gallon tank. At one pound per gallon, the rock will offer a rather sparsely filled, open aquascape. Two pounds per gallon gives more opportunity to create interesting reef topography. Some aquascapers recommend buying an odd number of pieces for a small tank. Start with three and you have the makings of a cave or small island, with two foundation rocks and a capstone placed atop. Live rock makes the most effective biological filter when water currents can swirl around the rock and through the reef. Try not to stack your rock tightly. The "stone wall" look is both unnatural and less than optimal for the biological filter and the fishes, who appreciate all manner of holes, crevices, and niches for shelter.

### Uncured rock

Starting with uncured rock makes a whole different set of demands on the aquarist. You can easily find a source of "cheap" live rock by the boxful, but you will likely find that the time and expense of curing it yourself can add considerably to the cost.

First, never add just-shipped rock directly to an established aquarium. Dry shipping, even of cured rock, usually requires a period of transition to be sure that the incoming rock is not a source of ammonia. Uncured rock placed in an established home aquarium can fill a house with the unmistakable odor of rotting animal flesh. Family members will be up in arms, but the inhabitants of the tank will be gasping at the surface, lying on the bottom, showing red streaks indicative of internal bleeding, and almost surely dying.

When the aquarist gets it, every live rock has a particular ratio of living organisms to dead organic matter. The more living organisms and the less dead organic matter, the better the live rock is for the aquarium system. Dead organic matter brought into the system with the rock must be mineralized by heterotrophic bacteria and oxidized by nitrifying bacteria, and this results in increased nitrate levels that have to be handled by the system or by water changes. Live organisms, if they survive, grow and reproduce and aid the function of the system. The ratio of living to dead material depends on the amount of dead organic matter in the rock when it was collected, how the process of collection and transportation affected life on and in the rock (this includes time out of water, exposure to heat and cold, and degree of desiccation), and whether or not, and how carefully, the rock was cleaned. All these considerations determine how soon the rock will add to the biological balance of the tank, and whether it will contribute algal and invertebrate growths to the tank's inhabitants.

The best approach when starting with freshly imported rock is to cure the rock in a separate container isolated from your living space. Most home-cured rock is processed in 30-gallon plastic garbage cans or Rubbermaid cattle watering troughs. Here are the steps for curing live rock. The process can take from two weeks to a month or longer, depending on the initial condition of the rock, the process used, and the water temperature.

**CURING FRESH ROCK:**
Newly imported live rock is somewhat less expensive than cured rock, but it must be given several weeks of special handling in a process that can be too smelly to be done in an indoor living space. During this time decay and ammonia generation gradually stop.

❖

1. Rinse each incoming piece of rock in clean saltwater mixed to a specific gravity reading of 1.021–1.025. (It can be a bit dilute compared to full-strength seawater, to save money.) This can also be old aquarium water removed during water changes, or new saltwater that has been aged for at least eight hours and brought to 75–82°F.

2. Place rinsed pieces in a new plastic garbage can dedicated to aquarium use. Do not pack rock tightly, but rather create a loose stack of rock.

3. Cover the rock with saltwater and add a powerhead to create constant water movement and a heater to keep the temperature at 80–82°F. (Curing will take longer at lower temperatures.) Leave the container uncovered for gas exchange.

4. Perform 33% water changes daily or 100% water changes every three days.

5. When doing water changes, brush away any white or black decaying material and rinse each piece in a bucket of clean saltwater.

6. Keep the vat of water out of direct sunlight and do not use any artificial light, which can trigger an algae bloom.

7. When the vat passes a "sniff test" with no odor and nitrite readings of zero, the rock can be given a final rinse and moved to an aquarium.

The more you can control ammonia and nitrite in the curing water, the greater will be the survival rate of desirable organisms on and within the rock. An adequately sized protein skimmer will help mitigate the polluting effects of decaying sponges and other matter. A power filter containing a phosphate binder, activated carbon, or a Poly-Filter pad can reduce the toxic effects of ammonia, nitrite, and phosphate.

For a beginning aquarist, all this may be more than a bit overwhelming. It can also dramatically increase the cost of that "cheap" rock. An advanced aquarist needing to build a large reefscape with many pounds of rock is much more likely to have the time, equipment, and experience to cure specially ordered rock properly and efficiently.

Do not buy rock from an unknown source. Some cheap live rock is actually shipped by boat, rather than air freight, from Fiji and other places, and may have been held in a hot, dry cargo container for three to six weeks. It is sometimes known as "Boat Rock," and it is no bargain. Similarly, beware of free or pass-along rock from someone tearing down a tank. Rock that has been exposed to fast-spreading fish parasites such as *Amyloodinium ocellatum* (sometimes called Marine Ich), *Cryptocaryon irritans*, or *Brooklynella hostilis* may be carrying cysts that can hatch and spread disease to your system. Live rock exposed to copper sulfate and other aquarium drug treatments may be contaminated and could be a future source of trouble for delicate invertebrates. Avoid any live rock that has been through a tank "wipe-out" event unless you are prepared to bleach it, give it a long soak in fresh water, and essentially start with dead, sterile rock.

Many distributors and Internet sellers offer "cured rock" that has been cleaned after collection, but that may still be very capable of going through an active die-off stage when it reaches the local store or hobbyist. Any newly arrived rock should be regarded with suspicion until it proves to be clean, odor-free, and not still producing ammonia and nitrite. If in

Deep bed of live sand, laced with worm burrows, in a well-established refugium.

doubt, find a local store you know and trust and specify only rock that has been in their tanks for a full month and is "completely cured." Buying directly from your livestock retailer allows you to hand-select each piece, looking for attractive shapes, coralline algae growth in shades of pink or red, and sometimes attached small coral colonies, live clams or other mollusks, macroalgae, or colorful sponges. Again, avoid any rock that fails a "sniff test" or that has fungus-like patches of white, indicating active decay of encrusting organisms, often sponges.

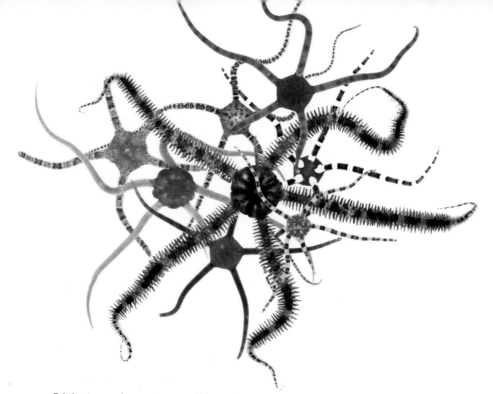

Brittle stars and serpent stars will keep the sand surface groomed and free of uneaten food, although they do most of their work at night, hiding under rock during the day.

### Live sand

This is coral sand or fine gravel of various particle sizes that has been colonized by nitrifying bacteria and usually also by tiny organisms that live in benthic substrates and process the sand and wastes to provide complete biological filtration. It is typically used in conjunction with live rock, but it presents a large surface area and can be relied upon as the primary biological filter medium in a marine aquarium.

True live sand has been collected from tropical waters near coral reefs and will bring with it beneficial bacteria and many types of "infauna"—animals that live, eat, breathe, and reproduce in the protective world of wet sand. These include many different worms, crustaceans, mollusks, burrowing echinoderms (sea stars and sea cucumbers), and others. Many are detritivores, eating uneaten food, feces, and other waste material. All serve to keep the sand bed stirred and active, and without them a sand bed will be less effective as a biological filter.

Cultured live sand is now also commonly available in shelf-stable packaging, and has been inoculated with desirable forms of bacteria to help support biological filtration. It will usually lack any infauna, and you will want to mix in some portions of wild-collected live sand and/or "detritivore kits" from various suppliers that offer cultures of small, desirable sand-dwelling invertebrates.

Any sand or particle substrate becomes "live" after weeks or months in an aquarium with fish and/or invertebrates. However, if tiny sand-dwelling organisms are desired, they must be acquired and added to the sand.

### Curing live sand

Unless it arrives smelling foul, live sand should be rinsed in saltwater to remove any organic matter that may foul the water in the aquarium. To rinse, half-fill a bucket with warm saltwater and pour the live sand in. Swirl by hand and pour off any cloudy water, which should be discarded.

To avoid clouding the aquarium water, place the sand in a plastic bag, lower it to the bottom of the aquarium, and pour it out slowly and gently. Spread and stir lightly into the surface layer of substrate.

If the sand has off odors or black patches, or seems suspect, put it in an auxiliary aquarium or clean container with saltwater and provide some sort of water motion with an airstone or a small powerhead. Remove any dead matter that might be contributing to the putrefaction. Keep the water warm and stir the sand bed daily. Using a small power filter or skimmer will help speed the process. Do a 50% water change every couple of days until the sand smells clean and there is no obvious decay.

**DEEP SAND SECRETS:** Microorganisms that keep a deep sand bed functional cannot thrive in coarse substrate such as crushed coral, which is filled with sharp edges and impedes their free movement.

❖

**Deep sand beds (DSB)** are 3–6-inch deep sand beds without air lifts or filter plates on the bottoms of aquariums. Water is not forced through the beds, as with undergravel filters, but natural sand-dwelling organisms are present, and both aerobic and anaerobic biological filtration occurs in the bed. Most nitrifying activity takes place in the top one inch of the sand bed, while denitrification happens in the deeper substrate.

The key to success with deep sand beds is the use of material mostly composed of fine or very fine particles. These are sold in the aquarium trade as "sugar-fine" or "oolitic" sands, with diameters of .2 to 1.0 mm. The tiny organisms that keep a deep sand bed active are best suited to moving in the watery space between tiny particles in the range of .1 mm in diameter. They won't establish themselves in beds of coarse sand or in crushed coral gravel, which present too many sharp edges and impediments to their movement.

Deep sand beds can be created with or without plenums. A plenum is an open water space about an inch or two high that is established under the sand bed and has no direct interaction with aquarium water. The function of the plenum is to enhance the anaerobic function of the deep sand bed. In most installations the prevailing opinion is that any enhancement of function, if it does occur, is negligible, but also that there is no discernible negative effect from the presence of the plenum.

Natural populations of sand-dwelling organisms work the sand and keep it functioning. Organic material that falls to the surface is attacked by organisms that live in the top layers of the sand bed, and eventually the products from this aerobic digestion move into the lower layers, where anaerobic bacterial action eventually transforms much of it into nitrogen gas. Thus, a deep sand bed can perform both nitrification and denitrification, but it is very important that strong circulation of aquarium water, 10 to 20 times the entire volume of the tank per hour, over the surface of the bed be present for this filtration technique to work properly.

The function of any sand bed can be enhanced by the presence of bottom-dwelling detritivores, including amphipods, copepods, miniature starfish and brittle stars, bristle worms, and small grazing snails such as *Stomatella varia*. Collections of such organisms are sold by a number of suppliers, usually marketed as "detrivore kits." Some reef aquarists add a fresh kit every 6 to 12 months to keep the detrivore populations at full strength.

While a deep sand bed is an interesting option, a good aquarist can set up a successful large or small reef tank using only live rock with a thin layer of coral sand, a modest sump tank, a good protein skimmer, and excellent lighting. There must be strong water flow throughout the tank, and the live rock must be loosely stacked to allow free flow of water around and between the rocks. Strong lighting powers photosynthesis, and the live rock provides biological filtration. A balance is established between plant and animal life forms, and the tank survives very well.

## Other biological filters

Undergravel, wet/dry, compound, hang-on-the-tank, trickle, biowheel, fluidized bed, algae and denitrification filters can also be used for biological filtration, and each of these has different techniques for establishment and maintenance.

**Compound filters:** Although an in-tank biological filter (whether live rock or an undergravel filter) and a monthly partial water change (10–20%) will maintain an uncrowded marine aquarium very nicely, advanced aquarists may decide to set up a separate and/or different water management filter system. Commercially available external power filters and other filter attachments can be used on small as well as large tanks. These offer many advantages: mechanical filtration to extract detritus from the system; chemical filtration, with chambers for activated carbon and other media; and increased oxygenation and water flow.

Larger external water management systems may be set up behind a wall or in a cabinet under the aquarium, and although some work is in-

A gravity fed external sump with skimmer and chambers for various reactors and filtration devices is the heart of most reef aquarium filter systems.

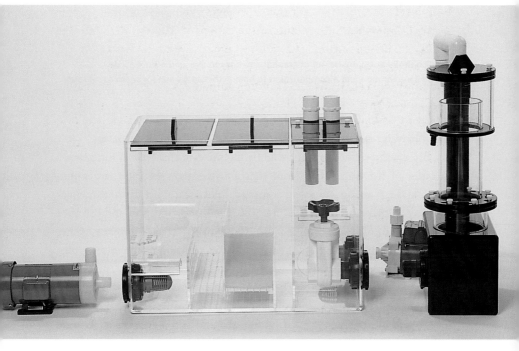

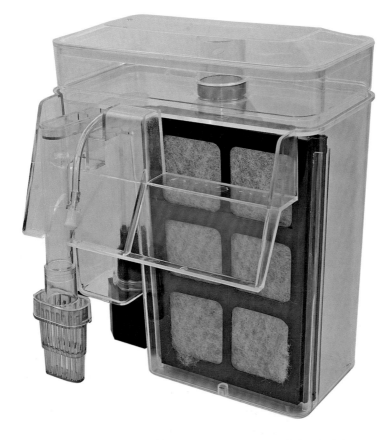

Hang-on-the-tank skimmers are affordable and easy to use, and often include mechanical filtration and a compartment to hold activated carbon for chemical filtration.

volved in planning and plumbing a custom-made filter bank, the best possible water quality and largest fish populations can be achieved.

Briefly, the elements that could be included in this type of filter bank, in order of the water flow from the tank through the filter, are a mechanical filter, an algal filter, an activated charcoal filter, and an ultraviolet sterilizer. A protein skimmer is also a very valuable addition and operates most efficiently on water taken directly from the tank before any other type of filtration. These elements would be in addition to the in-tank biological filtration accomplished by the live rock and sand bed. The system can be pressurized, except for the protein skimmer, and located below the water level of the aquarium. However, this type of unit is more difficult to service and clean, since it must be drained and taken apart first. A more functional design maintains the filter elements in unpressurized compartments at or below the tank water level. Each compartment should have an overflow, so if flow is restricted in one of the filter elements, the flow can bypass it and not pump water out of the system. Also, if you build such a system, make sure the mechanical filter is easy to service; a simple floss replacement or washable foam pad works well. And if an algal filter is part of your system, grow the algae on a surface that can be removed for harvest, and replaced, or use a free-floating species such as *Chaetomorpha linum*, which forms a mass of tangled filaments. Periodic partial harvests are an excellent method of exporting nutrients from the system.

**External hang-on-the-tank filters:** Drilling a hole in the tank bottom to provide internal drainage for a trickle filter is not always desirable, so a number of easy-to-use and relatively inexpensive compound filters that hang on the tank and include mechanical, chemical, and wet/dry biological filtration are now available. These employ biomedia such as plastic plates, foam, Bio-Balls, or Bio-Bale™, where beneficial bacteria populations can easily establish themselves.

**Trickle filters:** Trickle filters are devices that provide a relatively low volume of water from the display tank to flow over and through a container, pad, or tray of filter media. The water can flow from a revolving spray pipe or a perforated tray. The water then trickles through a high–surface area filter media positioned above the sump, allowing maximum water contact with an extensive surface area that is highly oxygenated since it is not immersed in water—thus air, water, and substrate provide the optimum environment for the colonization of nitrifying bacteria. In a marine aquarium sump-based system, this type of biological filtration is extremely efficient. In fact, many aquarists feel that the device is too efficient on the front end of biological filtration, which is aerobic transformation of ammonia to nitrite and then to nitrate, and that this creates a situation where nitrate accumulates too rapidly, requiring extensive water changes and/or a special effort to denitrify. It was because of this drawback that trickle filters gave way to the natural and complete biological filtration found in more extensive use of live rock. Trickle filters also increase evaporation, which requires more frequent salinity adjustment, and increase the humidity within the sump compartment. They are still used in some systems with very heavy bioloads, for example, a large aquarium housing big predatory fishes such as groupers or sharks.

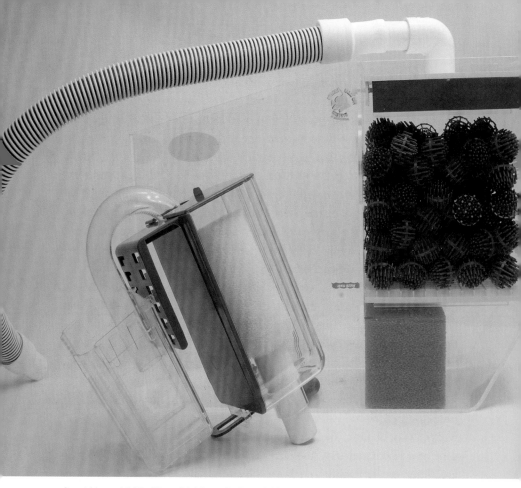

A wet/dry or trickle filter with biomedia is a viable option for fish-only systems.

**Biowheel filters:** Large biowheel filters are widely used in commercial aquaculture. They are a type of trickle filter, but instead of the water trickling through a stationary media, the media is shaped like a wheel and is half immersed in the water. It slowly revolves, allowing water and air to wash through the media as it rotates above the water surface. This does two things: it prevents detritus from building up in the media and it increases the efficiency of biological filtration by increasing exposure of the media to oxygen. Small biowheel filters are available to the marine and freshwater hobby and provide good auxiliary biological filtration.

**Fluidized bed filters:** Commercial aquaculture and the marine aquarium hobby have often exchanged ideas and products. One such product is the fluidized bed filter, basically a vertical tube that contains fine sand or, in some instances, a light plastic bead media. Water flows relatively rapidly into the tube from the bottom, and this upward flow has the effect of suspending the media particles and creating a moving, swirling mass of water and sand particles. All the sand grains in the filter are exposed to oxygenated water and the grinding movement of the sand also breaks up detritus. Fluidized bed filters are extremely efficient. There are some drawbacks for small systems, however. If water flow is not adequate, channelization of the media (compaction of the sand except in a few channels or pathways) may occur and the filter will not function properly. Also, if the supply of electricity to the pump is interrupted, the sand will settle and, depending on the amount of time that the filter is out of commission, the organic material in the filter may cement the sand grains together and the filter may become non-functional. Biological filtration is all aerobic, so nitrate production and the high efficiency of the filter in small systems must be counterbalanced with water changes or denitrification filters. Some marine aquarists have had good success with fluidized bed filters and some have not. In my opinion, these filters are best used in large systems with high bioloading—particularly commercial aquaculture systems.

**Algae filters:** An algae filter is simply a structure on which macroalgae can grow with a light source adequate to power photosynthesis. The algae will remove nutrients in the water as it grows, and when the algae are harvested from the system, the nutrients are also removed. An algae filter is usually a tank or container separate from the display tank, where the algae grows and from which it is periodically removed when necessary. In some instances, algae grow in the display tank and are removed when growth becomes excessive. This is also an algae filter, but it is not typically referred to as a filter. Algae filters usually require more maintenance than typical biological filters and are more unpredictable. They can add to the stability of marine systems, but are generally not utilized on small sytems. A reverse algae filter is one that is kept dark during the day when the display tank is well lighted and illuminated at night, so that photosynthesis in the algae filter will counteract the tendency for the pH of the system to fall at night when photosynthesis in the display tank ceases.

**Denitrification filters:** A denitrification filter can be run as a batch filter. Water from the marine system is captured in a container with or without an open plastic or fiber media, and closed off from water and air flow; then lactose, glucose, or, more commonly, methanol, is added to the now-airtight container to provide food for the bacteria, which will utilize nitrate instead of oxygen in their metabolism. Anaerobic bacteria do their thing in this environment and nitrate is removed from the water. Although it is effective when you know what you are doing and have the need for large-volume denitrification, this is not a technique that a typical marine aquarist will employ. A flow-through denitrification filter is more common. This may be a series of airtight boxes with a very slow flow through the media in each box; the water is cleared of nitrate by the time it has passed through the last chamber. Or it can be a long, coiled tube through which water passes very slowly; nitrate is removed on the long, winding journey. In any case, a methanol drip is added to the flow to provide food for the bacteria. Most aquarists, however, rely on live rock or deep sand beds to provide denitrification activity in the system, supplementing with water changes when necessary.

### Overcrowding and the biofilter

*Don't overcrowd your tank!* Everybody says that…I say that, too, but what does it mean? Essentially, a tank is overcrowded when the capacity of the biofilter and the tank water to maintain the existing animal load in good health is nearly exhausted. If the animal load exceeds the capacity of the system to process their wastes, then the tank balance is destroyed, bacteria populations change drastically, oxygen decreases, toxins appear, and fish die. This can happen suddenly, perhaps due to the introduction of a number of new fish into an already overcrowded tank, or more likely, as a slow breakdown when a well-stocked tank is overfed and not maintained for many months. There should be a margin of safety, a buffer zone, between the maximum carrying capacity of the tank and the total animal load occupying the tank. This safety margin allows for a skipped water change, an unobserved dead fish, or a fish sitter's overfeeding without the danger of a tank breakdown.

So how do you know the safe carrying capacity of your tank? Unfortunately, this is one of those situations where the extremes are easily identified—a few fish in a huge tank or dozens in a small one—but there is no precise line between too much and too little. There are so many variables that each individual aquarium setup has its own optimum carrying capacity, and this capacity changes with age, maintenance schedule, and fish and algal growth.

The filter media (rock, sand, artificial biomedia) is by far the most

Spaghetti Algae, *Chaetomorpha linum*, is a tough, easy-to-keep species for algae filters.

important single determinant of a tank's carrying capacity. Many other factors, however, serve to extend or restrict the maximum animal load that can be supported by the system. The following list will give you an idea of the kinds of things that can limit or reduce the carrying capacity of your aquarium:

1. Not enough live rock, insufficient sand bed substrate
2. Filter clogged with detritus or caked up undergravel bed
3. No algal growth
4. Consistent overfeeding
5. Infrequent or no water changes
6. Poor quality lighting
7. Poor water flow in the aquarium or through the external filter system
8. Inhibition of filter media bacterial action due to medication

A heavily stocked home reef, expertly maintained, employs an aquascape structure of high-quality live rock and aggressive protein skimming to handle the bioload.

The wastes and toxins produced by the animal load of a tank are balanced by the activity of the filter bed, the capacity of the water to retain altered wastes and still maintain life-support quality, and the capacity of algal growth or supplemental filtration to extend the time frame of this balance. Thus, I can't tell you exactly how many fish to put in a certain size aquarium, for a lot depends on how you set up and maintain your tank. However, I can give you a ballpark, maximum figure of 3 to 4 inches of fish for every five gallons, and suggest that you watch for overcrowding when this level of occupancy is attained. Some of the indicators are:

1. Reduction of green algal growth and more rapid growth of red and blue-green algae

2. Development of yellow water coloration before the next scheduled water change

3. Persistent, rapid drop in pH below 7.8

4. Rapid accumulation of nitrates and persistent traces of ammonia or nitrite (perhaps the most important indicator of filter breakdown)

5. Distress behavior in fish, fading colors, loss of appetite, hyperactivity, rapid respiration

Some of these symptoms may have causes other than overcrowding, and if a water change doesn't help, then look for a very dirty filter, poor diet, and/or the presence of disease. Remember, the most trouble-free marine aquariums are those that are not overpopulated with animals and have an efficient mode of nutrient export—protein skimming, macroalgae growing in the display or in a lighted refugium, and mechanical and chemical filtration to get detritus and dissolved organic compounds out of the system.

# The Undergravel Filter
## *Function and Construction*

$A$t one time, little was understood about biological filtration, which is the detoxification of animal waste by beneficial species of bacteria. Early marine aquariums had very high mortality rates, as fish were killed by the effects of ammonia and nitrite. When undergravel filters and then trickle filters came along, aquarists started having success keeping their fishes and even hardy invertebrates alive.

When this book was first written, undergravel filters were basically the only game in town. Live rock has now taken over most of the biological filtration function of marine aquariums, but undergravel filters are still a basic and inexpensive method for providing biological filtration. If you do not run a marine aquarium with an undergravel filter and have no intention of ever doing so, even for an auxiliary or quarantine tank, or of using this technique to teach your 10-year-old niece or nephew the hows and whys of the nitrogen cycle and keeping a marine aquarium, and don't feel the need to better understand the roots of the modern marine aquarium hobby, then you can completely skip this section—but think of what you might be missing!

### Function

A biological filter is a living thing. It consumes oxygen, feeds on the waste products of animals in the system, and excretes wastes of its own. This is as true of a working undergravel filter as it is of a piece of premium live rock. It is very important to understand and remember this, because you must treat the biofilter as a living, breathing creature, which, in a way, it is. The nitrifying bacteria in the filter are dependent on the

The author with *Diadema antillarum* sea urchin broodstock in his laboratory, where he continues to use undergravel filtration in his auxiliary aquariums.

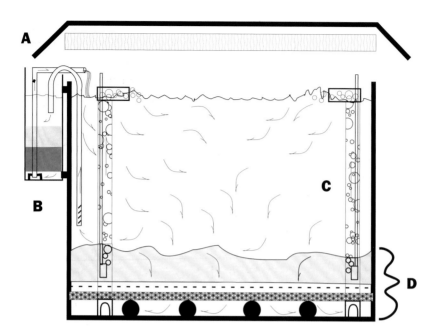

**A. Lighting.** Shop light with two 2- or 4-foot fluorescent bulbs or a standard aquarium light hood.

**B. Auxiliary filter.** A small external filter with pad for mechanical flitration and activated carbon for chemical filtration.

**C. Air lift assembly.** One-inch-diameter lift tube powered by air stone or powerhead pump.

**D. Undergravel filter.** One to two inches of filter media held above the filter plate with a fine screen. The filter plate is held off the bottom with marbles or other solid supports.

oxygen in the water flowing through the filter. If this flow of oxygenated water stops, the good bacteria die, the water fouls, and the entire tank eventually dies. Because of this great demand for oxygen, there must be a rapid flow through the filter at all times. The amount of water flowing through a filter designed for a freshwater tank is not adequate for marine tanks, and the proper populations of nitrifying bacteria will not be established. (Note that freshwater contains more dissolved oxygen than saltwater of the same temperature.) The best general rule for an undergravel, biological filter in a marine aquarium is to get the maximum flow rate that your equipment can deliver.

The object behind establishing a biological filter is to bring the nitrifying capacity of the filter into equilibrium with the waste production of the tank's inhabitants. The more efficient the filter, the more fish the tank can support. Each individual under-gravel filter will have a maximum potential carrying capacity, which depends on many things besides the overall size of the filter. First of all, the extent of the surface area of the filter is more important than the depth of the filter bed. This is because the bacteria need oxygen to function, and as the water flows through the filter bed, oxygen is depleted and nitrification decreases. Thus, the top inch of the filter bed does almost all the work. (In a reverse-flow undergravel filter, in which the water is pumped down under the filter bed to percolate back up through it, both the lower and upper surfaces of the filter bed are exposed to oxygenated water, and biologi-cal filtration is a bit more efficient.)

**GRAVEL DIAMETER:**
Properly sized gravel or crushed coral will allow good water flow and trap some particulate matter without clogging.

❖

Other factors of importance are the size and shape of the particles of filter gravel, the rate of water flow, whether the filter is new and clean or old and dirty, and how the filter was established. The gravel size should be small enough to provide a large amount of surface area for a high bacteria population and to provide some mechanical filtration, yet large enough to allow good water flow with some freedom from particulate clog-ging. Irregular gravel about 1/16 to 3/16 inch (1 to 4 mm) in diameter is a good size for a marine undergravel filter. It allows a lot of water to pass through and keeps the filter bed well oxygenated. Large air lift tubes with at least a 3/4-inch internal diameter, and a strong air flow broken up into small bubbles, are essential to provide the necessary water flow through the filter bed.

A tank with no filter bed, such as a larval rearing tank or a tank set up according to the original "natural method" (a few airstones, a few live rocks, many invertebrates, and a few fish), still develops a healthy community of nitrifying bacteria on every exposed surface inside the tank. Sand grains, shells, decorations, tank sides, algal growths, and especially live rock all harbor colonies of nitrifying bacteria. So even a tank with no "biological filter" does, in fact, have a lot of biological filtering going on—it just isn't contained, isn't controlled, and may not be able to adjust to changes in tank populations, hidden fish deaths, or overfeeding.

In most situations, larval tanks do not need an external biofiltration system. Lar-val tanks do not carry a large biomass and are in operation for only a few weeks, thus wastes do not quickly build up to toxic levels. Therefore, many fish and invertebrate larvae can be reared in a relatively small tank with a few fairly large water changes during a four-week larval period.

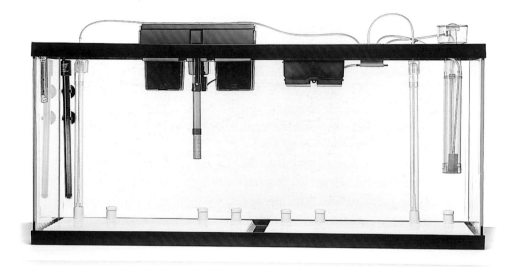

Prudent aquarists set up a new system and fill it with freshwater first, to test for leaks or any equipment problems. This water is then removed or lowered before adding gravel. Running the tank overnight is a good way to be sure the heater is working properly.

### Feeding the new biofilter

A biofilter bed established with an inorganic source of ammonia has a much greater initial carrying capacity than one started with an organic ammonia source such as fish or crabs. The reason for the increased carrying capacity is that all the available sites for bacteria growth are taken by the nitrifying bacteria rather than sharing sites with other types of heterotrophic bacteria that feed on other "foods" such as organic compounds generated from uneaten food and fish waste. This allows large populations of the right bacteria to develop, and the filter bed can operate at its maximum capacity. Ammonium chloride ($NH_4Cl$) is a good compound to use to establish the nitrifying bacteria with an inorganic ammonia source.

Very little is required to develop the proper concentration (1 to 5 ppm) of ammonia in the tank water. You can fly by the seat of your pants and put in about a quarter teaspoonful (2 to 3 grams) of ammonium chloride for each 20 gallons and let it run until nitrite levels drop to near zero, or you can be scientific about it and add 20 drops of a 6% solution per 10 gallons every three days for nine days. The important thing is to test the nitrite ($NO_2$) level in the tank at least every three days until the nitrite level has peaked, probably at about 15 ppm at 18 to 20 days after starting. It should then drop to less than 2 ppm, which should occur in 21 to 25 days.

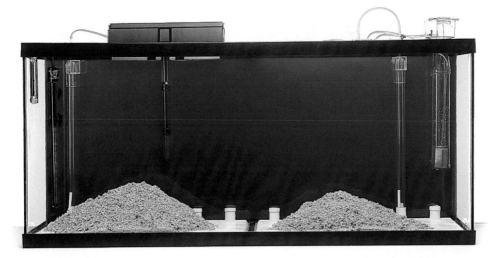

With a background applied, the tank is ready to have washed gravel added to cover the filter plates to a depth of one to two inches. Mixed saltwater is then poured in, using a clean dinner plate to avoid disturbing the gravel and stirring up any gravel dust.

Many variables, such as temperature, salinity, lighting, actual ammonia concentration, size of the initial bacterial colonies, and type of substrate may extend or shorten this time period, whether the tank is cycled with hardy fish or artificially with ammonia. It is not unusual for a marine undergravel or trickle filter to take four to six weeks to complete the growth of bacterial colonies. After the nitrite level has dropped to less than 2 or 3 ppm, the tank is ready for fish and invertebrates. If water changes are no problem, a complete or half change is very beneficial at this time, and an inoculation of marine algae, as a unicellular culture or a macroscopic plant, is also a good idea. Note: Placing a live rock or two in the aquarium along with a hardy fish cycles the tank more rapidly, but still, be careful: test for nitrite, and don't add delicate fish until the biological filter is well cycled.

There are a number of products now on the market that claim to provide a seed of nitrifying bacteria in a preserved form. The bacteria are viable when released into a marine aquarium, according to the directions of the manufacturer. Some aquarists claim excellent results from such products and some do not. There are a great many variables when using these products—production variables, storage, effective dosage, water condition, water temperature, lighting, and type of filter substrate, to mention a few. So if you do use a filter run-in aid, buy a high-quality brand and always test the water for ammonia and nitrite a few days after adding fish, just to be sure that bacterial colonies have actually formed and that toxic levels of ammonia and nitrite have not developed.

### Selecting an undergravel filter

Way back in the dark ages (the 1950s and early '60s), the only biological filters commercially available were designed for freshwater aquariums and had only small diameter, big bubble air lift tubes to provide water flow through the filter bed. Thus, the serious, knowledgeable marine aquarist had to build his own filter plate and air lift tubes to provide the kind of filtration necessary for a good marine tank. Nowadays there are many commercially available biological filters that are designed for marine aquariums and provide the proper construction features.

If you purchase a filter, look for the three basic features a marine undergravel biological filter must have. (We will assume that all commercially available filters are made from non-toxic material.) First, the filter plate must fit snugly over the entire bottom of the tank and be designed to allow water to flow evenly through its entire surface. The plate should be positioned well above the bottom of the tank and allow water to flow evenly toward the bottoms of the lift tubes. The plate should not allow the filter gravel to accumulate underneath and block off portions of the filter or restrict flow through the air lift tubes.

Second, the lift tubes should have an internal diameter of at least 3/4 inch (2 cm), although small tanks, 20 gallons or less, can get by with tubes with only 1/2-inch internal diameter—even so, bigger is better. There should be elbows on the air lift tubes at surface level to contain and direct the streams of water and air bubbles to various areas of the tank.

Third, the filter material—shell hash, oyster shells, silica sand, dolomite, quartz gravel, limestone gravel, or any combination of these—must be of a particle size that allows free circulation of water yet still removes most suspended particulate matter. A particle size of about 1/16- to 3/16-inch diameter (1 to 4 mm) seems best. Particles this size do not easily cake up and prevent water flow, but do filter out most suspended organic matter. Biological filter media of carbonate composition—coral gravel, oyster shells, dolomite, or limestone—also serve to chemically buffer the water.

The buffering effect of these materials under average marine aquarium conditions, however, is slight, and will not prevent a drastic drop in pH in a crowded aquarium overloaded with organic matter. In most situations, a calcareous filter material, such as oyster shells, will prevent the pH from falling below about 7.8, but it may also hasten the fall of the pH from 8.2 to 7.8 through chemical interaction with the buffer

With all systems running, the tank can be inoculated with nitrifying bacteria, using water and/or sand from another healthy, established marine system, and water testing started.

system of seawater. A relatively inert filter material, such as silica sand or small plastic or ceramic structures, does not interact with the natural buffer system of seawater, and the pH usually remains higher for a longer period of time without water change. However, when the pH does drop because the natural buffers are exhausted, and there is no extensive amount of calcareous material to provide a pH "floor" in the system, then the pH can quickly drop to really dangerous levels like 7.5 or even lower. Undergravel filters and trickle filters, too, produce a lot of nitrate and the enhanced nitrification process also contributes to the drop in pH.

### The filter bed

Filter bed material can be obtained at aquarium shops, plant nurseries, and construction supply stores. Whatever the source and whatever the material, be sure to wash it well under running water until all dirt and organic material has been washed out. Be aware that material obtained from sources other than aquarium shops may contain rusty nails, bits of wood, and other contaminants, and must be cleaned and inspected very well. If oyster shells (obtainable from animal feed stores) are used, don't try to wash away all the milky water or the sun will set and rise on your efforts. In fact, even though the filter media is well washed, the tank water will be slightly milky for several hours to a whole day after setup, until the suspended microscopic particles settle. These particles often settle on the glass sides and give the tank a cloudy appearance

A classic undergravel marine system, typical of aquariums in the days prior to the easy availability of live rock. Decor must be easily removed for cleaning sessions.

even though the water is clear. The sides can be easily wiped clean if this occurs; just don't stir up the bottom all over again.

The filter bed also serves as a mechanical filter by removing suspended particles. Depending on their nature and the condition of the filter bed, these particles are trapped between the grains of filter media or become attached to each other and fill the larger spaces between filter grains. Eventually, the entire filter becomes clogged with organic material, and the biological action of the filter declines. This detritus accumulates most rapidly in an overcrowded, overfed aquarium that receives a lot of light. A little detritus in a filter bed is good because it enhances mechanical filtration and provides some additional sites for nitrifying and heterotrophic bacteria and microscopic life, but too much restricts water flow, cakes the filter bed, and enhances too much "bad" bacterial growth.

Thus the filter bed should be cleaned as required, depending on the animal load, type and amount of feeding, and size of filter grains. For a system with invertebrates, that might mean every few weeks; a simple, fish-only tank might go several months between gravel cleaning sessions. The depth of the filter bed is also important. The deeper the filter bed, the greater the mechanical filtration activity, the greater the build-up of detritus, and the greater the risk of developing anaerobic decay in the filter. Anaerobic decay occurs when oxygenated water cannot reach pockets of organic matter, and then the bacteria that do not need oxygen go to work and produce hydrogen sulphide (that rotten egg smell) and other toxins that cause fish great distress. Filter beds composed of fine particles will clog up more rapidly than filter beds composed of more coarse particles.

A filter bed depth of about 2 inches in a 50-gallon (or larger) tank is about right for most aquarium systems. This depth provides enough media for nitrification and mechanical filtration, and gives the fish enough bottom to stir around without piling up all the gravel in one corner. There are many techniques that can be developed for cleaning filter beds of accumulated detritus, and undoubtedly you will develop the one that works best for you as you gain in experience. Aquariums that receive natural sunlight or intense artificial light and carry a heavy load of animals accumulate detritus more rapidly than lightly stocked, sparingly fed tanks that receive minimum lighting.

### Cleaning the filter bed

The basic idea, when cleaning time comes around, is to stir up the gravel to release the trapped detritus particles, and then remove them from the aquarium. Filter cleaning and water changing can go together because the water removed when the bottom is siphoned can be replaced with new water. This is also a good time to give the entire tank a house-cleaning, so I'll describe the whole process. It's not necessary to remove the fish from the tank unless you know from experience that they are hyperactive and will continue to bash themselves about the tank during the cleaning. Exposure to some turmoil and dirty water is usually less traumatic to the fish than capture with a net and removal to a holding tank. After all, this sort of situation often occurs in nature during storms.

The first step is to remove any decorations that require cleaning. Some folks like their coral pieces and little castles totally free of green and brown algal growths, and others prefer the natural growths. If these pieces can be cleaned with an old toothbrush and a little water, so much the better. However, if you must be clinical about it, a chlorine solution will quickly remove all organic growths. Placing any rocks or decorative pieces exposed to chorine in a bucket of water treated with a few drops of dechlorinator (sodium thiosulfate) is also a good idea. The next step is to clean the sides of the aquarium of any heavy mats of algal growth. Unless a little algae interferes with the aesthetics of your ocean world, it is better for the inhabitants if you leave some algal growth on the back and sides that aren't used for viewing. The front glass is best cleaned with a plastic abrasive mat or sponge. Just don't carry the grease from last night's frying pan into your tank.

The water will now be a little stirred up, and the fish will be looking for a safe place. A flower pot or a rock that they can hide in or near gives them some security as their home is being cleaned. This temporary refuge can be moved from one side to the other as necessary. The detritus in the filter bed is mostly lighter than the gravel and will float up into the water as the gravel is stirred. The gravel can be stirred with a small rake or other implement, but fingers are best because you can feel and break up any caking of the filter material and have greater control over the stirring process. Hard clumps of sand are detrimental, as water tends to flow around, not through them.

As your fingers work and stir the gravel, the detritus quickly clouds the water and then begins to settle out on top of the gravel. After the entire filter bed has been worked, the detritus must be removed. Much of it can be taken out by pulling a fine meshed net repeatedly through the water, but probably the best way is to let the dirt settle and then carefully siphon the accumulated detritus from the gravel surface. This removes the major portion of the dirt, and a power filter can quickly pull out the remainder. Any gravel removed by the siphon can be washed and replaced; new saltwater can then be added to replace that lost by siphoning, and the tank decorations can be replaced. The water will clear in an hour or two, as the suspended particles settle on the bottom.

**AUTOMATIC CLEANING:**
A large marine hermit crab can gradually turn a filter bed over completely, consume uneaten food and algae, and keep the sand bed loose.

❖

This process will not kill the nitrifying capacity of the filter, but it will knock it back because some of the bacteria have been removed with the detritus and some have been dislodged from their site. Keep a check on nitrite for a week or so after the cleaning to be sure that the tank adjusts properly, and avoid adding new fish until everything is balanced again.

Filter cleaning is, at best, a time-consuming, messy chore. It is possible to employ a full-time automatic filter cleaner who'll be glad to work for what he can pick up on the tank bottom. A large marine hermit crab, *Pagurus* or *Petrochirus* sp., can gradually turn a filter bed over completely, consume uneaten food and algae, and keep the bed loose for a long time. Detritus will still have to be removed periodically, but Mr. Hermit Crab makes the job a whole lot easier. (He is not, however, "reef safe" and will happily feast on corals and other bottom-dwelling invertebrates.)

**Deep sand beds (DSB):** I regard undergravel filters with some affection, but there are certainly other approaches that require less maintenance and do a better job of biological filtration in the long run. As pointed out in Chapter 4, some aquarists now use deep sand beds (DSB), 3 to 6 inches of sand, that are established without an undergravel filter plate so that water does not actively flow through the filter material. This type of sand filter supports both aerobic (with oxygen) and anaerobic (very low oxygen) conditions in the upper and lower regions of the sand bed. Natural sand organisms, such as many species of worms and tiny crustaceans, work the sand and keep it functioning. Organic material that falls to the surface is worked by organisms that live in the top layers of the sand beds, and eventually the products from this aerobic digestion move into the lower layers, where anaerobic bacterial action eventually transforms much of it into nitrogen gas. Thus, a deep sand bed can perform both nitrification and denitrification; however it is very important that strong circulation of aquarium water over the surface of the bed be present for this filtration technique to work properly. Aim to have the entire water volume of the tank turn over at least 10 times per hour, preferably 20 times or more. Thus, a 20-gallon aquarium will require a pump or pumps rated at 200 to 400 gallons of flow per hour.

To establish a healthy population of sand-burrowing organisms, some wild-collected live sand should be mixed into the bed. So-called "detritivore kits" are also a good way to introduce live sand-dwelling animals (tiny crustaceans, worms, small burrowing sea cucumbers, and the like) into a new sand bed. The table on the following pages details the procedure for setting up and maintaining a marine aquarium using both organic and inorganic methods of biofilter establishment, along with a suggested care schedule for the first year. Remember that not all aquariums will break in or run exactly according to this suggested schedule, but this will give you some idea of the typical maintenance schedule for a marine aquarium with an undergravel filter.

*Ciliopagurus* sp. hermit crab: an interesting, sand-grooming addition to a fish-only system.

## Table 1  Conditioning and maintenance chart for the undergravel filter

| Time | Organic conditioning method | Inorganic conditioning method |
|---|---|---|
| Day 1 | Set up tank and filter. Run undergravel filter and allow tank to settle and clear. Add a cup or two of disease-free, active seed media if available. | Set up tank. Run undergravel filter and allow tank to clear. Add ammonium chloride (NH4Cl) to about 3–5 ppm. (1/4 teaspoon for each 20 gallons, or better yet, 20 drops per 10 gallons of a 6% solution.) Add a cup of disease-free, active seed media if available. |
| Day 2 | Wipe off any sediment that has settled on the sides. Add a source of organic waste matter. A couple of crabs or a few hardy and expendable fish will do fine. Feed sparingly. | Wipe off any sediment that has settled on the sides. Let it run and test ammonia if test kit is available. |
| Day 3 | Feed sparingly twice a day. Satisfy the animals, but do not let uneaten food accumulate. Continue feeding throughout conditioning period. Note if appetite declines and then decrease the amount fed. | Add another dose of ammonium chloride. |
| Day 5 | Continue animal maintenance. Test ammonia if kit is available. | Test ammonia if kit is available. Add another dose of ammonium chloride if ammonia level is below 2 ppm. Skip dose if test is not done. |
| Day 7 | Check ammonia and nitrite levels. Observe fish for signs of stress. | Add another dose of ammonium chloride if ammonia level is below 2 ppm. Add a dose anyway if an ammonia test is not done. Begin to test for nitrite level. |
| Day 10 | Test nitrite level. It should begin to show up at levels of 3 to 10 ppm. Keep an eye on fish for signs of stress. | Nitrite should show up now at level of 5 to 10 ppm. Add a half dose of ammonium chloride and let it run. Check nitrite every other day until it peaks and drops to less than 3 ppm. |
| Day 15 | Nitrite should be rising well above 10 ppm. Watch the fish and remove any dead or very distressed fish. Do not replace dead fish if nitrite levels are higher than 15 ppm. | Nitrite still rising. Should be above 10 ppm. Add a half dose of ammonium chloride. |
| Day 20 | Same procedure as day 15. Nitrite level should be near peak. | Nitrite should be near peak. Test level every day if possible. This shows you when it begins to drop. |
| Day 25 | If your fish aren't stressed yet, you know you have a hardy species. Nitrite level should peak and fall off within the next 5 days, although it's quite possible for high nitrite to run on for another 10 days. | Nitrite level should fall off within the next 5 days, but may remain high for a longer period in some situations. |

| | |
|---|---|
| Day 30 | Most likely nitrite level has peaked and fallen off to less than 2 or 3 ppm by this time for both methods of conditioning. If not, don't worry unless you want to, for nitrite level will surely drop within the next 10 days. If temperature is cold, below 75°F, it may help to warm the tank up to 80°F. |
| Day 30 to 40 | Begin the next phase as soon after the nitrite drop as possible, certainly within 5 days. Make a partial water change, 25% is about right at this time although you can go up to a total change if clean saltwater is available. Now is the time to begin adding the fish and invertebrates you desire. Don't put in a great load all at once, and begin with the specimens recommended as most tolerant of aquarium conditions. Add one or two animals to a 20-gallon tank and up to 5 or more in 50 gallons and up. Allow 7 to 10 days between each introduction of animals to let the tank adjust to each increase in the animal load. |
| Day 60, Month 2 | Time for a water change. Clean the inner surfaces of algae and siphon out any accumulations of detritus on the bottom. First top up the tank with freshwater, then change 10 to 25% of the water and replace with clean, new saltwater. (If mixed from a dry salt mix, let it rest with aeration or circulation overnight before adding it to your display aquarium.) |
| Day 90, Month 3 | Repeat the maintenance performed at month 2. Change 20 to 25% of the water if you feel you have a heavy load of animals in the system. A 10% change is adequate if the tank is lightly populated. Make this procedure a monthly routine and you should have a trouble-free tank. |
| Month 6, 7, or 8 | Time for a filter cleaning (see Chapter 4). It could come as early as month 6 or may drift to month 10 to 12 depending on lighting, animal load, feeding rates, and invertebrate populations. A partial replacement (10%) of the filter bed media may be helpful. |
| Year 1 | Six to 8 months after the first filter cleaning your tank should be ready for another house-cleaning. By now you probably have two or three marine aquariums and enough experience to write your own book, so good luck, and give a helping hand to a fellow marine aquarist whenever you can. Another partial replacement of filter bed media (10 to 20%) may be helpful. |

**Coral Croucher**

# Physics & Chemistry

*The Essential Information for Marine Aquarists*

Physics and chemistry—these are two words that strike terror into the hearts of those who would rather stand in awe of the universe than dissect it. But don't worry, this section is designed to tell you in simple language only what you really need to know, so you can put away your calculator.

## Light

Light—its intensity, quality, and daily duration—has great influence on all life and all environments, and a marine aquarium is no exception. The major constant through ages of evolution has been sunlight. Temperature, water levels, and even continents have changed, but sunlight has always been constant and animals have incorporated it into their essence as they evolved. They make vitamins with it, navigate by it, and among other things, control their reproductive periods by its daily duration. Too often, we take light and its effects for granted, because it is always there at the flick of a switch and does not force our attention as temperature does. (We become very aware of the importance of light in our modern lives, of course, when some idiot gets drunk and runs down the electric pole at the end of the road.) Yet in our aquariums, we must take as much care to provide the right lighting as we do to provide the right temperature.

Sunlight in shallow tropic seas is very intense. The warm, clear water allows some sunlight to penetrate hundreds of feet, although 80% of the

T5 fluorescent bulbs efficiently bring more intense lighting to reef-type aquariums. This fixture includes blue and white tubes and moonlight-simulating LEDs.

sun's radiation is absorbed in the first 33 feet. Red, the low-energy, long wavelength end of the visible spectrum, is 90% absorbed in the first 15 feet, but blue and ultraviolet, with high-energy, short wavelengths, penetrate much deeper. Thus, marine tropical fish from shallow coral reefs do best with relatively high light levels that contain at least the normal amount of blue and ultraviolet radiation. These short wavelength radiations are particularly important for the growth of green algae and healthy fish. In fact, long wavelength ultraviolet (black light) is said to have very beneficial effects on marine aquariums. Under normal conditions, only fluorescent, metal halide, or LED lighting should be used, because incandescent bulbs produce too much heat. About 2–4 watts per gallon of natural spectrum (daylight) fluorescent light with a good reflector should be ample for a fish-only marine aquarium. This is roughly two tubes of the proper size for the length of the tank for a 50-gallon tank, and four tubes for a 100-gallon tank. Many aquarists like to combine white or full-spectrum bulbs with blue or actinic-blue fluorescents for a more pleasing appearance.

It's a good idea to use a timer to control the duration of light on the tank. Fish do best when the duration of light each day remains constant or changes very slowly. They should have 8 to 12 hours of darkness every day. Their periods of activity can also be controlled this way. Most aquarists prefer their fish to be active in the evening hours when they are home to enjoy them, so the timer can be set to turn the lights out at 11:00 PM and turn them on again at 11:00 AM. Fish adjust well to such a schedule

and are less stressed than they are with a highly variable lighting schedule. Also, if the room becomes pitch black at night after all the lights are out, a small night-light above or near the tank provides enough light to keep the fish comfortable. The natural shallow water environment with moon and stars is never absolutely dark, and a marine aquarium should have some dim night light also. Another good thing to do for your fish is to have a

Compact metal halide lamp clamps onto the frame of a nano-reef aquarium.

blue fluorescent light that comes on about 15 to 30 minutes before the main tank lights come on and stays on for about 15 to 30 minutes after the main tank lights go out. These crepuscular (dawn and dusk) lights don't have to remain on all day, but they make for a natural transition between light and dark and reduce stress on the fish. (You know, when you take your fish to the movies in the middle of the day, how they bash around in the bowl when you come out of the theater into the bright light—well, this eliminates that kind of stress.)

Even though there has been a great revolution in lighting for marine aquarium systems over the last few years, some newer aquarium lights may not be appropriate for traditional tanks with undergravel filtration. It is a mistake to put high intensity lighting over a tank with an under-gravel filter that holds a lot of fish and accumulates a lot of nutrients. Good lighting is important, but a couple of 40-watt, full-spectrum fluo-rescent bulbs are fine, as they help the fish do well and grow some good macroalgae. High intensity lighting will create an algae monster in the undergravel filter and greatly increase the need for water changes and maintenance. The kind of lighting I am recommending here is not the little fixture that comes with some commercial freshwater tanks and has

**Well-designed metal halide fixtures have built-in reflectors.**

Combination fixture with
metal halide lamps and T5 thin-tube
fluorescent bulbs, all controlled with built-in timers.

one or two 20-watt red/orange fluorescent tubes. These may be fine for freshwater tanks, but they are inadequate for marine fish. There are good commercially made light hoods available that carry 40 to 80 watts of full-spectrum or blue actinic fluorescent lights, and these are fine for marine fish tanks and low-tech reef type systems. One must be aware of the lighting requirements for the kind of marine system that is planned and be sure that the light hood selected will deliver the necessary light.

High intensity lighting—10,000–15,000 lux at the surface—should be put above reef type systems with skimmers and live rock reefs that are intended for coral and photosynthetic invertebrate culture. A tank for only, or mostly, marine fish can do quite well on lesser lighting, although most marine fish also do very well, if not better, in reef type tanks with high intensity lighting.

Over the last 20 years, lighting a reef tank aquarium has become a science in itself. The marine aquarist can pick from a great selection of various types of lights designed and developed for marine aquarium systems. Many types of the standard 40-watt fluorescent bulbs display various spectral qualities and intensities, and some contain internal reflectors; T5 fluorescent lighting is very popular, partly because it provides high intensity in a small space, and there are High Output (HO) and Very High Output (VHO) fluorescent bulbs that require special ballasts and produce double and triple the lumens of standard bulbs. Other, newer fluorescent technology includes power compact, or compact fluorescent, bulbs. The most intense light available comes from metal halide lamps designed and built expressly for marine aquariums, and these fixtures allow marine aquarists to almost capture the sun and place it above their own little coral reefs. These fixtures generate intense heat and usually require a fan. The latest major advance in aquarium lighting is LED lights. They have many advantages, including low heat output, little or no UV radiation, long-lasting bulbs, energy efficiency, and flexibility. Whether you wish to light a large or small reef tank, you will have to research the possibilities and chose what best fits your prospective system and your budget. *The Marine Aquarium Reference* has an extensive section on light and lighting, and should be consulted if one wishes to build a custom light fixture or needs more information on aquarium lighting.

## Temperature

All animals—with the exception of humans, who can engineer their environment—have a range of temperatures that define the limits of their existence. Internal chemical reactions and external physical characteristics have adapted to particular environments through ages of evolution, thus polar bears aren't found in Florida and Queen Angelfish don't often frequent New York Harbor. Fish, like all other poikilothermic (cold-blooded) animals, are totally dependent on the proper environmental temperature range because they cannot regulate their internal temperature. Lizards and snakes can bask in the sun to raise their body temperature or hide under a log to lower it, but fish can only be the same temperature as the water around them, so we must meet their temperature demands rather precisely. The broad temperature range for most marine tropical fish and invertebrates is 65–90°F. A few species can exist above and below these limits, and a few have somewhat narrower tolerances. Please note that this does not mean that fish can be moved from 65°F to 90°F with one quick kerplunk. Fish can withstand some rapid changes of a few degrees. I've seen such quick changes occur on the reefs due to varying current patterns, but slow changes are much easier on the fish. At the extremes of the temperature range, a fish merely survives.

Optimum temperature for a marine aquarium ranges from 75°F to 82°F (24°C to 28°C). In these days of air conditioning, one seldom has to worry about tank temperatures rising above 85°F, since heat loss from evaporation usually keeps the water a couple of degrees below room temperature. However, metal halide or other lighting that produces very high heat, improper use of powerheads, or insufficient maintenance can all cause overheating of the tank water. Tank temperatures can also easily drop too low, and a good aquarium heater should be used to keep the tank at a comfortable (for the fish) 78–80°F.

A heater can be very dangerous in a saltwater tank because it produces heat through the electrical resistance of a wire coil, and if saltwater gets into the heater, it can be a very shocking experience. Glass immersion heaters with internal thermostats are the most commonly used and are quite adequate, providing they are designed for saltwater use and have safeguards against the intrusion of saltwater and salt spray. An important safety measure is to unplug the heater while working about the tank. This prevents destruction of the heater through inadvertent lowering of the water level or removal of the heater while it is still active, since the glass tube quickly overheats and shatters if it is exposed to the air when the coil is heating. Be sure the heater is of the proper wattage for the gallon-age of the tank. Too small a heater may not do the job when the room is cold, and too large a heater can quickly "cook" a tank if the thermostat malfunctions. Figure the heater at about 2 to 4 watts per gallon or follow

A heater with built-in thermostatic control is essential in most situations, and a digital thermometer allows easy monitoring of water temperature.

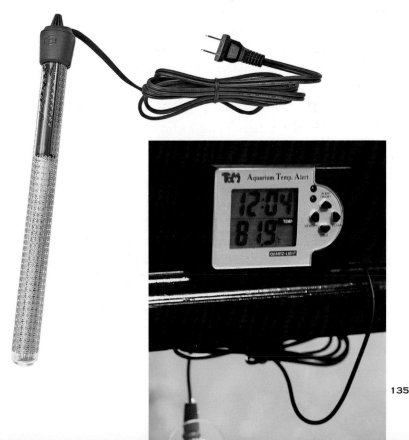

the manufacturer's instructions. If the heater malfunctions, tank temperatures can easily creep up or drop without your notice, so be sure to have a water temperature thermometer always in or near the tank for ready reference.

Cooling water is a bigger deal than heating water. The water must be passed through coils that are being cooled by a thermostatically controlled chiller, and this is usually an expensive addition to a marine aquarium system. The only situation where a chiller is necessary might be when the tank environment in a large reef tank system housing delicate hard and soft corals will not keep the tank below 80°F. Temperature excursions above 84°F can lead to coral bleaching and other problems.

## Salinity

Salinity is a measure of the quantity of inorganic solids (salts) that are dissolved in the water. It is usually measured in parts per thousand (ppt or ‰), and most tropical seas are 34 to 35 ppt (35 grams of salt in one kilogram of water). Coastal waters are often diluted by freshwater runoff and range between 5 and 30 ppt. "That's easy to understand," you might be thinking, "but what's all this 1.025 SG stuff?" Well, this requires a little bit of an explanation. When three pounds of salt are dissolved in 10 gallons of water, the salt is no longer visible, but it hasn't gone away. The atoms of chlorine, sodium, and the other elements that made up the white salt dissociate into their ionic states and slip in between the water molecules—and if the water didn't taste salty, you would never know they were there.

There are other changes, though. One of the most important is that a given volume of saltwater is heavier (more dense) than an equal volume of pure freshwater. A floating object is pushed upward by a force equal to the weight of the water it displaces. This means that an object light enough to float is more buoyant in saltwater than in freshwater (it floats higher), and the more salt in the water, the greater the object's buoyancy and the higher it floats. Specific gravity (SG) is a ratio or comparison of the weight (density) of saltwater, or any other substance, to the weight of an equal volume of pure distilled water. Thus, since 1.0 represents the value for distilled water, a heavier substance (such as lead or saltwater) sinks and has a SG greater than 1.0; and a substance lighter than pure freshwater (such as oil or wood) floats and has a SG less than 1.0.

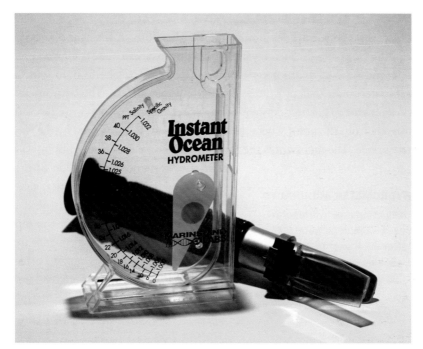

Floating arm hydrometers offer a cheap method for measuring salt content, while refractometers provide more accurate readings if kept properly calibrated.

Now our problem is to find out just how much salt is in the water, and there are four commonly used methods to do this. In the traditional oceanographic research method, the quantity of chlorine ions (chlorinity) is measured by chemical analysis, and the total salt content is calculated from this figure. Two other methods now commonly used are to measure the electrical conductivity of the water, which increases as the salt content increases, or to measure the refractive index (how light is bent by a thin film of water), which also changes with salt content.

These methods are too complicated and expensive for most marine aquarists, so the method of choice is to determine the specific gravity, a measure of density. Since water gets denser as salt is added, we can determine its specific gravity by observing the relative buoyancy of a small glass float, and then determine how much salt is in the water by consulting a graph or table that converts SG to salinity. There is one variable, however, and that is temperature. Molecules of warm water are further apart than molecules of cold water, because they have more energy and move faster. This means that warm water is less dense than cold water; thus a floating object sinks a little deeper in warm water. Therefore, to get an accurate SG reading from a hydrometer, water temperature has to be considered.

One type of hydrometer is a weighted glass or plastic bulb with a calibrated stem that protrudes above the water surface. The hydrometer floats higher as the salt content of the water increases, so SG can be read directly from the point where the calibrated stem is intersected by the water surface. The meniscus is the little upward curve the surface film makes as it tries to climb up the side of the glass stem. For greatest accuracy, take your reading at eye level from the flat surface of the water, not from the top of the meniscus. Some hydrometers are calibrated to give an accurate SG reading at 59°F (15°C), so be sure to look for one made specifically for the marine aquarist; these are calibrated at higher temperatures.

**HYDROMETER ACCURACY:**

A floating-arm hydrometer must be rinsed in fresh water after each use. Be sure no bubbles cling to the arm when taking a reading.

❖

The most popular and economical design has an arm that floats in a plastic case, with an indicator line that points at a specific gravity reading printed on the outside of the case. This is a quick and easy method for a marine aquarist to get an approximate specific gravity reading, but one must be sure that all air bubbles that might be stuck on the indicator arm are knocked off, since these air bubbles make the arm lighter and will cause a false reading.

There is much more to be said about specific gravity and salinity, but in actual practice, you needn't get all in a dither about salinity for a beginner's aquarium housing hardy fishes. I don't think that the salinity of a fish-only marine aquarium must be any one particular value within a range of 28 to 35 ppt (1.020 to 1.026). With the possible exception of certain invertebrates, marine animals and biological filters do better at salinities a bit lower than that of oceanic seawater. Lower salinities keep more oxygen in the water, allow the nitrifying bacteria to work more efficiently, and reduce the metabolic work load of the fish. It is entirely possible to maintain a beautiful tropical marine aquarium at salinities of 20 to 25 ppt instead of 30 to 35 ppt. The only difficulty is the gradual acclimation of new fish to the lower salinities. Some fish are euryhaline and can easily move between saltwater and freshwater, adjusting their osmoregulatory systems to deal with abrupt salinity changes. Most coral reef fish are stenohaline, and must remain in seawater—although they can adjust to somewhat lower salinities than those found on coral reefs.

When this book was first written, reef tanks with live coral and other sessile invertebrates were nothing more than a gleam in the eyes of a few 10-year-old kids. Marine fish are more forgiving of lower salinities than are invertebrates that incorporate seawater into their very being. Echinoderms, for example, move seawater through their bodies and use it to circulate fluids, and even to power their water vascular systems, which they use to move their tube feet. So it is important to maintain a stable salinity in a reef tank, and keeping a reef tank constantly as close to 35 ppt (1.026 SG) as possible is a good idea. Some delicate invertebrates, such as ornamental shrimps, will expire within minutes if subjected to rapid salinity changes.

All fish, freshwater or marine, carry salt levels in their blood and tissue of about 12 ppt, roughly equal to those of land animals. Freshwater fish do metabolic work to prevent loss of salt to the surrounding freshwater, and marine fish work even harder to prevent loss of freshwater from their bodies. Marine fish even drink seawater to increase their water content and excrete excess salt through special cells in their gills. Theoretically, lower salinities ease this metabolic work load and allow the fish to put this energy elsewhere. However, unless you want to do a lot of salinity response experimentation on fish and invertebrates, it is best to maintain your aquarium at a salinity between 30 and 32 ppt (a specific gravity range of 1.022 to 1.024). This slightly lower salinity does not seem to increase acclimation stress on the fish, and allows a comfortable evaporation margin.

Unless you have a very small tank, the evaporation of .5–1 inch of water will not push salinity up past the normal range. Be sure to put a mark on the outside of the tank at the water surface right after filling it to the proper level. This allows you to add freshwater to replace evaporation loss without concern for salinity. You know, of course, that only the water molecules evaporate off into the atmosphere. The salt molecules stay behind, and the solution becomes more concentrated. If you must add a great deal of freshwater to make up for evaporation loss, do so gradually and avoid adding tap water heavy with chlorine or with a large temperature differential. Some salt may be lost through spray encrusta-

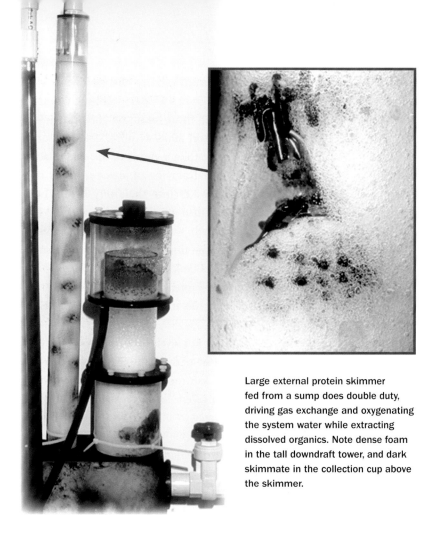

Large external protein skimmer fed from a sump does double duty, driving gas exchange and oxygenating the system water while extracting dissolved organics. Note dense foam in the tall downdraft tower, and dark skimmate in the collection cup above the skimmer.

tion on the outer surface of the tank, but this is seldom enough to even detect through salinity measurements.

It is possible to inadvertently increase the salt concentration in marine systems by adding saltwater when freshwater should be added. One may notice that a lot of water has been lost to evaporation and think, "Oh, this is a good time for a water change." A 10–20% water change made at this point replaces the freshwater lost to evaporation with saltwater and tends to increase salinity. Salinity may also be increased if specimens and the saltwater in their bag are added to the tank when replacement of evaporated water is needed, as this replaces some freshwater with saltwater. Even with adequate water changes and a mark on the tank to indicate the proper level, it is important to occasionally measure the salinity to make sure that it has not crept up or down when you weren't watching. Over time, if one is not aware of the potential to increase or reduce salinity in these ways, it can change to abnormal levels. This can result in the gradual decline, or even death, of sensitive corals and other invertebrate life.

## Oxygen

The two things most essential for life in a marine aquarium are water and dissolved oxygen gas ($O_2$). Fish can live a short while without the other things, but without water and oxygen they die immediately. Dissolved oxygen is used by all the animals, including the biological filter, and is replenished almost entirely by oxygen entering through the air/water interface at the surface of the tank. Algae produce oxygen during lighted hours, sometimes a considerable amount if growth is heavy, but these same algae use oxygen during dark hours, so the gain is not completely positive, and oxygen levels quickly drop to normal saturation or below when algal photosynthesis stops. Some additional oxygen enters the water from air bubbles in air lifts, but this amount is quite small compared to that entering through the surface. The tank water must be well circulated to maintain proper oxygen levels, and this is one of the most important functions of the air lift system. Oxygen cannot diffuse through water rapidly enough to replace that used by animals and filter bacteria, so without good circulation, oxygen is quickly lost in the lower levels of the tank. Colonies of nitrifying bacteria in an undergravel filter can die after only a few hours without oxygenated water circulating through the filter.

Water does not hold a lot of dissolved oxygen, and the amount it can hold decreases as temperature and salt content increase. Warm saltwater contains only about 4 to 6 ppm dissolved oxygen at saturation levels. Under unusual conditions, algal activity can supersaturate the water with oxygen and push it up to 8 to 12 ppm. Most fish suffer severe stress when dissolved oxygen drops below 3.5 ppm, and die when the level sinks below 2.5 ppm. So in a tropical marine aquarium, there is only a difference of 2 or 3 ppm oxygen between a living tank and a mass of anaerobic decay.

Though test kits are available for advanced aquarists, it is not necessary for the typical aquarist to measure oxygen levels. But it is important to know that oxygen enters water very quickly and that normal oxygen levels are dependent on active water circulation throughout the tank. The biological filter also has a great need for oxygen, and if circulation stops, the filter will quickly use up most of the oxygen in the lower levels of the tank. Watch out for black discolorations in the filter and/or a "rotten egg" smell from anywhere in the tank. These are both sure signs that circulation is restricted and oxygen is being depleted in certain areas of the tank or filters. Another sure sign of oxygen depletion is all the fish gasping at the surface and even trying to jump from the tank. The latter is an extreme situation and would only occur under very crowded or dirty conditions, when water circulation has completely ceased.

**AIR SUPERSATURATION:**
Low water level in a sump can lead to supersaturation with tiny bubbles of nitrogen gas that can cause "gas bubble disease" in fishes.

❖

There is a type of "filter" that will slightly supersaturate aquarium system water with oxygen and keep oxygen levels at or above saturation in almost all situations. This is an oxygen reactor, which is a sealed, pressurized tube filled with an open filter media. Water trickles over the high-surface-area filter media and is exposed to air at slightly higher-than-normal (by about 2–4 psi) air pressure. Oxygen enters the water at levels above saturation, at normal atmospheric pressure, and returns to the tank with this higher-than-normal dissolved oxygen level. See *The Marine Aquarium Reference* for more information on oxygen reactors.

### Nitrogen

Nitrogen and oxygen occur in the tank water bound up in numerous molecular compounds—nitrate ($NO_3$), for example—or as dissolved gases. Nitrogen in the form of dissolved gas is not a consideration to the average marine aquarist. In some instances, water supersaturated with nitrogen and then compressed can cause "gas bubble disease" in small fish.

Supersaturation with nitrogen gas is now a greater possibility because more aquarists are using powerful pumps to move water around marine systems. An air leak on the intake side of a pump can pull air into the water, and the impeller of the pump may create enough pressure to force considerable air (nitrogen) into the water while it is in the pump. When the water gets into the unpressurized aquarium, it comes out of the water in very tiny bubbles. These tiny bubbles actually make the water look milky, and an aquarist may think that the tank has a bacterial or algal bloom. One can easily check to see if it is tiny bubbles by filling a glass with the milky water and setting it on a table. If so, after about 10 to 30 minutes, tiny bubbles will leave the water and it will be clear. Another source of air into the water line just before the pump in reef systems is a sump tank with a low water level. If water lost to evaporation is not replaced, the sump level may fall so low that air is sucked into the pump intake line, and this can cause air supersaturation in the tank water. This often makes an audible sound, such as "sllllluuuuuurrrppppppp." This is known in some reef-system circles as the scary surreptitious slurper syndrome, but most aquarists need not be concerned about it.

## pH

One can be a successful marine aquarist without ever taking a pH reading, because if you go by the rules of good aquarium management, the pH of the tank water will take care of itself. However, the pH of your water is a good indicator of water quality, and how slowly or rapidly water quality changes occur, and it is well worth knowing. pH is a measure of acidity and alkalinity (acid and base) expressed on a scale of 1 through 14, with 1 being the most acid, 7 neutral, and 14 the most alkaline (basic). The symbol pH stands for the "power of hydrogen" or "weight of hydrogen." The H is capitalized because it is the chemical symbol for the element hydrogen. An acid condition is caused by an excess of the positively charged hydrogen ions (H+), and the alkaline condition is caused by an excess of the negatively charged hydroxyl ions (OH-). When there is an equal number of each, the solution is neutral, neither acidic nor basic. pH is expressed on a logarithmic scale, each point being 10 times more concentrated than the one before. Expressed mathematically, each point is a power of 10 ($10^0$ to $10^{14}$). The chart on page 145 illustrates the pH scale.

Measuring pH is not at all difficult. It can be done with an electronic pH meter, with pH test paper, or with a liquid pH indicator. The latter two depend on color changes to indicate the pH of the solution. Liquid pH indicators are inexpensive and suit the needs of the typical aquarist very well. There are a number of pH tests on the market for freshwater and saltwater aquariums.

The acceptable pH range for a marine aquarium is 7.8 to 8.3, with 8.2 as the ideal point, if such a thing exists. The pH of most well kept home aquariums falls between 7.9 and 8.2. There are a number of problems that can cause a drop in pH, and if the water is filtered with activated carbon, these conditions may remain masked by the clarity of the water until the pH has fallen below 7.6. It is very important to test pH if you do not change a percentage of water regularly and use activated carbon to maintain water clarity. A pH drop to less than 7.6 under these conditions indicates that it is way past time for a water change.

Seawater has a considerable natural buffering capacity, which is the ability to "absorb" excess H+ ions without lowering the pH. The biological activity of the filter and the animals, however, eventually overcomes this built-in buffer and the pH begins to drop. The decline is hastened by overcrowding, heavy detritus accumulation, lack of calcareous material with exposed surfaces, and accumulation of dissolved organics. Regular partial water changes dilute accumulations of dissolved organics and restore natural seawater buffers. Sodium bicarbonate (baking soda) is frequently used to push pH up the alkalinity scale when water changes are not possible, but pH will drop again soon, and water changes must be made eventually. If it becomes necessary to artificially buffer the tank to bring the pH up, it can be done as follows: In a cup of water from the tank, dissolve one teaspoon of sodium bicarbonate for each 20 gallons and slowly add the solution to the tank. Wait for thorough mixing to occur and then test pH. Do this repeatedly to bring the pH up to 8.0, and then test pH frequently until a water change can be accomplished.

The consistent trend in a marine aquarium is always toward a lower pH. Once in a while, however, pH can rise above 8.3, even to 9.0 in some cases. This is a result of $CO_2$ uptake by vigorous algal photosynthesis and is not, in itself, harmful. If such a high rise in pH is noted, it is probably more than evident that the algal crop should be harvested. Note that at night, when photosynthesis is not occurring, algae remove $CO_2$ from the water and pH will drop a bit. Some day/night fluctuations of pH are normal and, in fact, are seldom noticed. However, when $CO_2$ steadily accumulates in the water, excess carbonic acid is formed and pH drops. In many systems, especially those with extensive biological filtration and little aeration (such as the traditional undergravel setup), the accumulation of $CO_2$ is great enough to keep the pH at uncomfortably low levels. Addition of a trickle or wet/dry filter, or considerable increase of internal tank aeration, will help vent excess $CO_2$. To check for accumulation of excess $CO_2$, take a cup or two of water from the tank, check the pH, and

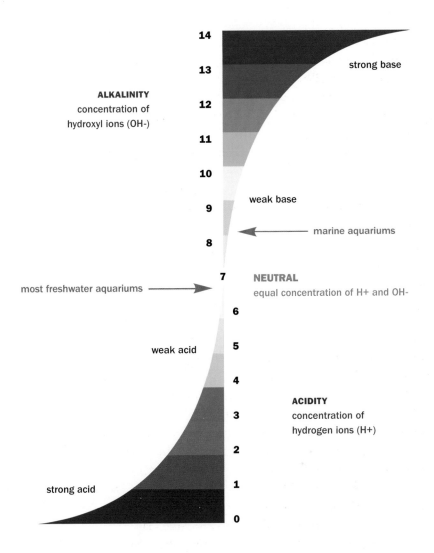

14
13    strong base

ALKALINITY
concentration of    12
hydroxyl ions (OH-)

11

10

weak base

9

&larr;   marine aquariums

8

7    **NEUTRAL**
equal concentration of H+ and OH-

most freshwater aquariums &rarr;

6

weak acid    5

4

**ACIDITY**
3    concentration of
hydrogen ions (H+)

2

strong acid    1

0

**The pH scale (hydrogen ion concentration)**

aerate the sample for a couple of hours. Then check the pH again, and if it has risen a point or two during aeration, the system is accumulating $CO_2$ and additional aeration will be very helpful.

### Dissolved organics

Organic matter is added to the marine aquarium in the form of new animals or plants, as food for fish and invertebrates, and, sometimes, it is

Large predatory fish, such as this Giant Grouper, *Epinephelus lanceolatus*, can produce prodigious amounts of organic wastes and overwhelm inadequate filtration systems.

in the water used for water changes. This organic matter is cycled and recycled by the living organisms in the tank, and eventually accumulates as either detritus or dissolved organics. Many organic compounds, including proteins, amino acids, peptides, fatty acids, urea, ammonia, organic dyes, amines, and phenols, fall into the category of dissolved organics. Unless physically removed from the tank through filter cleaning, algae harvesting, filtration, and water changes, organics continue to accumulate and cause changes in the tank environment detrimental to its inhabitants. Excess organics accumulate slowly in uncrowded, sparsely fed tanks and rather quickly in heavily stocked, well fed tanks, but in either case, they must be controlled by good aquarium management.

There are three sure signs of excess dissolved organics: a heavy, persistent foam on the water surface, a yellowish color in the water, and a drop in the pH. These become most evident if the maintenance routine has been skipped for two or three months, and indicate a need for a filter cleaning and water change. Although partial water changes are the best way of controlling dissolved organics, they can be reduced to some extent by carbon filtration, good protein skimming, and UV irradiation. New filtration products that claim to remove dissolved organics are appearing on the market, and, if effective, should ease the life of a marine aquarist by extending the intervals between partial water changes. As with all new innovations, time will prove or disprove their utility. Some filter media available (polymeric styrene and acrylic polymers) remove some organics from saltwater solutions, and some aquarists use them extensively, but in most systems they will not take the place of good protein skimming.

The surest time-tested way to remove dissolved organics is with a well-designed, efficient protein foam skimmer. A little skimmer that sits inside a big tank and foams away once in a while is helpful, but only marginally so. A tank over 50 gallons really needs a tall (18-inch or so) external skimmer that can really process a lot of water. This is the only way I know to remove a large amount of dissolved organics from a marine aquarium system while oxygenating the water. A mechanical filter that is frequently changed (every two or three days) will also capture and remove some microscopic particles and dissolved organics, but it is not as efficient as a good skimmer.

# Setup & Maintenance

*The First Day, The First Year*

THE BIG DAY! YOU'RE READY TO PUT TOGETHER A MARINE AQUARIUM. This chapter should answer most of your questions and can serve as a basic maintenance guide during the first year of operation. First of all, watch your bottom. Most commercially manufactured tanks have a bottom supported with a plastic frame, but if this is not the case or if it is a large homemade tank, be sure to set it up on a sheet of Styrofoam. This will even the stress on the bottom glass and prevent cracking. Placing a glass-bottomed tank on an uneven surface is a sure way to warp, stress, and crack the bottom piece.

To be prudent and avoid wasting saltwater, fill the tank with cold or room temperature freshwater to test for leaks. Carefully dry any spilled water and check all seams to ensure that there is no slow seepage. At this stage you may also want to connect your filtration equipment and any pumps to test them as well. To be perfectly safe, you may wish to let the system run overnight and inspect everything the next day to be sure nothing is leaking or faulty.

If you do things the right way, you will make up your water in a clean plastic garbage can, and allow it to settle out. Once clear and of the right salinity, it is ready to go into the aquarium. If you plan to add live rock or live sand immediately, the temperature should also be right, in the range of 76°–80°F (24°–27°C).

A beautiful, well-established European aquarium with coral growth filling the reefscape.

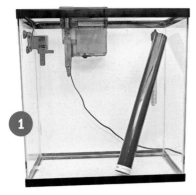

1. Place aquarium on its stand, affix backing material, fill with freshwater and test all filters, pumps, heater, and lights. Empty tank.

2. Carefully place live rock on empty bottom of tank. Be sure to leave clearance for easy cleaning of tank viewing panels.

3. Add live sand or washed crushed coral substrate to a depth of one to two inches.

If you are the casual type, you may be tempted to pour the salt package into the aquarium and just fill it with tap water. Although the latter method will work, it doesn't give you precise control over salinity, because a tank holds less than its listed gallon volume when rocks and filter media take up space. Usually, at least 15% of the volume of a typical aquarium is taken up with rocks, coral, and other structures. Mixing in the tank makes it more difficult to remove chlorine and/or chloramine from the freshwater (see Chapter 2, page 53).

When using dry substrate, this is the time to prewash it in running water to remove as much dust and other foreign matter as possible. Also have the rock you plan to use for the base of your aquascape ready. If it is live rock, it should be kept moist and at room temperature.

Before adding water, the ideal method is to add your live or base rock

**4.** Fill tank with premixed saltwater at the proper salinity and 77 to 80°F, directing stream of water onto a dinner plate to avoid disturbing sediment in the substrate.

**5.** Once tank is filled, turn on filter, pump, skimmer, heater and allow system to run for several days before adding any livestock. Bacterial cultures can be added at this stage.

first, directly on the bottom of the tank, then pour in your coral sand or gravel substrate to a depth of one to two inches. If rockwork is placed on top of a bed of sand, it may later be disrupted by burrowing animals. Most aquarists like to arrange the sand in a slightly downward slope from the rear of the aquarium to the front, to encourage detritus to accumulate where it can be most easily removed. It is much easier to arrange sand, rock, shells, pirate ships, or other decorative elements before the water is in the tank, and they won't be disturbed when the water is added if it is done carefully.

Next place a china dinner plate on the gravel bottom and slowly pour the premixed saltwater onto the plate. This will prevent the water from washing the sand or gravel out of place. Remove the plate when the tank is full. If done properly, the tank should still be relatively clear. Unless the water is full of sediment, hook up your pumps and filters right away, as

Hardy damselfishes are sometimes used as an ammonia source to cycle a tank.

this will help the tank to clear. Otherwise, let it settle overnight before powering up the system.

The air in heated and air-conditioned rooms is dry and will take up substantial quantities of water from an aquarium. The salt, of course, stays behind, and salinity increases as the tank level drops. Be sure the tank has a close fitting, non-metallic cover. The cover should fit inside the edges of the tank to contain drips and condensation and prevent salt encrustation on the tank and table or stand. A good cover will not be airtight, but it will dramatically reduce evaporation from the tank. Besides containing water and salt spray, a good cover prevents fish from jumping out of, and odds and ends from falling into, the tank.

Make a mark on the side of the tank at the original water level, and when the level drops ¼ to ½ inch, refill the tank with freshwater to the original level. Never replace evaporation losses with saltwater, for this just increases the total salt content of the tank water.

### Cycling the tank

Before you add any fish, the tank should run for a few days to a week. Temperature, specific gravity, and pH should all be in their safe zones. Lights should be set to come on and go off at the desired intervals.

The tank is now ready to be "run-in" or "cycled," meaning that the bacterial populations are allowed to proliferate to the point that toxic ammonia and nitrite are no longer measurable.

This is especially important if you are starting with dry sand and mostly dry rock rather than live substrates. The conditioning process can be enhanced by the addition of "seed" bacteria from an already established tank or a commercial bacterial culture. The advantages of seeding a tank with active filter media, sand, or even water from an established system are, first, to introduce the proper kinds of bacteria, and second, to reduce the time required to build sufficient bacteria populations. The disadvantage of this method is the possible introduction of disease organisms, both protozoans and bacteria. However, gravel from a good, trouble-free tank is usually a safe bet. Spread it around your own new sand bed. Seeding the new aquarium shortens the conditioning time by a week to 10 days, depending on the amount of seed media used. Seeding is not worth the risk of disease introduction, so don't attempt it unless you are sure that the source aquarium is healthy and disease-free. Warm water and low salinity are two factors that will reduce the conditioning period.

It is possible to purchase nitrifying bacteria in liquid or freeze dried form that can be added to the aquarium when it is first set up, to provide a large dose of the right kind of bacteria. This does not necessarily give the tank an "instant balance," but if the product is good, it can significantly decrease run-in time. An initial "food" (a source of ammonia and/or nitrite) is usually provided in the product, but it is still wise to start off with a few hardy fish until the nitrifying capacity of the tank is well established. If you would prefer not to use live fish for starting a new tank, one or two table or "cocktail" shrimp from the seafood counter can be dropped in the tank and allowed to decay and provide a source of ammonia.

One can also now buy bottled unicellular green algae cultures to add to new and established tanks to aid the growth of green algae. Some nitrifying bacteria are also introduced into a new tank with these cultures. Neither of these is a substitute for careful run-in and good aquarium maintenance, but they will aid the "balance" of the aquarium within the limits set by the conditions of the individual aquarium.

## Water testing

Chemical testing for ammonia and nitrite are important during the run-in period because it keeps you informed of the changing condition of the tank, and most important, it lets you know when the process is complete and the nitrifying bacteria are established. The ammonia test can

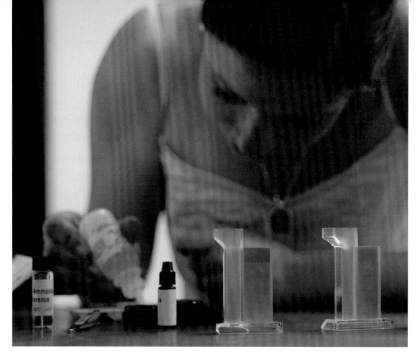

**Water testing is crucial when setting up a tank, and is also part of routine maintenance.**

be skipped if necessary, because when nitrite (NO$_2$) levels rise, you know that ammonia (NH$_3$) is being converted and that ammonia levels in the tank have dropped.

When starting with dry sand and without live rock, measurable nitrite levels typically appear in the tank about day 10, and rise gradually to a peak of 20 to 30 ppm about day 20 to 25. The most toxic period for a new tank is the period from day 15 to day 25, when nitrite levels are highest (see chart, page 80). At some point, usually between day 24 and day 30, nitrite levels drop within a day or two to only 1 or 2 ppm. Testing for nitrite during the conditioning period tells you when the tank is most toxic and when the conditioning period is complete. It is possible to run in a marine system even if you can't test for nitrite, but be sure to allow at least 40 days for run-in before adding delicate and/or expensive species.

An important point to remember is that a tank will not run in by itself. It must have an organic or inorganic source of ammonia to feed the developing bacteria populations. Keep a small notebook near your aquarium, and make it a habit to record test results, water changes, algal growth, new acquisitions, spawnings, and other events. This will take a lot of the guesswork out of maintenance ("Let's see now, did I change the water before or after Aunt Gert's visit?") and provide an interesting history of your aquarium.

When using cured, good quality live rock and live sand, the cycling may be almost immediate. However, depending on the size of the aquarium and the amount and condition of the live rock used to establish biological filtration, the cautions and the schedule developed in Table 1 on page 126 have relevance, especially after day 30 when a newly set up, sterile biological filter will have established a functional bacteria population for biological filtration.

Sometimes the bacteria populations in newly acquired live rock may be compromised because of the way the rock was handled, shipped, and stored before placement in your aquarium. If, for example, a sponge hidden in a crevice of the rock dies in transit, it can create an ammonia spike very quickly. So even with live rock, and a thin sand bottom, it is wise to start off with a few hardy specimens and test for nitrite ($NO_2$) accumulation after a week or two before adding more fish or delicate fish or invertebrates to the tank.

### Routine maintenance

**Daily.** Do a visual check of the systems and a mental roll call of the livestock population. Are all pumps and filters running? Use your senses: does everything sound, look, and smell as it should? Instant alerts include foul odors, silence (pumps not running), and cloudy water (dead fish?).

Is the temperature at a safe level? Is anyone missing? (If yes, you want to be sure it hasn't gotten into a filter or perished where it can cause a pollution problem.) Feeding is a good time to make sure nothing is amiss.

A small or uncovered tank may also need to be checked daily for evaporation and topped up with fresh water if necessary.

**Weekly.** Run your routine water tests, including a pH test and a hydrometer check. (Most aquariums tend to become more acidic over time, and salinity often creeps higher and higher unless measured and corrected. Do the water tests before stirring up the aquarium. Jot down your results in a log or notebook.)

Clean interior and exterior surfaces of the aquarium. Remove any salt creep. Change particulate filter if necessary. Top up evaporated water with fresh water. Clean skimmer cup (more often if necessary). Do a small water change if that is your routine.

**Monthly.** Do a water change if you haven't been doing them weekly. Change activated carbon and any other chemical media that may need replacement. Vacuum gravel and power blast detritus from rock surfaces with a handheld powerhead pump, or siphon out any pockets of debris.

### Marine troubleshooting

A marine aquarist (novice or old hand) may run into a problem now and then that is perplexing and worrisome. Sometimes the problem is just unsightly, or in the worst case, it may involve the death of valued specimens. The novice, of course, is more prone to such problems, but even experienced marine aquarists are surprised once in a while. I have had the opportunity to talk with many marine aquarists over the years, and to run many a marine tank myself, since the first edition of this book; thus I have been exposed to many of the problems and difficulties that can be experienced. So as an aid to marine aquarists, I have listed the most common problems, and a few rather uncommon difficulties that might occur, along with the possible causes and solutions.

The chart on pages 158–161 does not include all the problems that can plague a marine aquarist (I don't know all of them yet), but if you have a problem, there's a good chance you may find an answer, or a least a clue, here. Note that many of the symptoms listed in this chart can have different or multiple causes. I have tried to mention the most likely causes for each symptom, but please be aware that a chart like this is inherently oversimplified. Captive marine ecosystems are complex, and it is easy to misdiagnose a problem, especially if one does not have broad experience with marine systems. Therefore, if you have a problem, don't just assume that the first thing you come across that sounds like it might apply is truly the cause of the problem. Check out all the potential problems and discard them one by one until you have only a few real possibilities left. General environmental problems within the system are listed first, and more specific, fish-related problems are listed later. Note, however, that disease and distress is often caused by a combination of events or conditions in both the environment and the organism. A good environment (light, water quality, habitat, and diet) is the best prevention and basic treatment for disease and distress!

The chart doesn't give complete information on each possible cause. It is intended only as a guide to steer you toward a solution to the problem. One should refer to the section of this book where that subject is discussed (see the Index), or to *The Marine Aquarium Reference*, or to other

The good aquarist spends some time every day observing his or her animals and system.

books, videos, or websites that deal with these subjects in great detail (see the Selected References at the end of this book).]

Note: Even after the passage of many years, the problems listed in the chart still plague many experienced aquarists. True, there are now many new problems created by techniques and technologies that have been developed to maintain and even breed fish and invertebrates that were considered impossible to keep in marine aquariums a few years ago. But these are the basics, and most marine aquarists, especially those who are somewhat new to the hobby (the most interesting and challenging hobby out there, in my opinion) will find some answers—or at least clues to some of the problems that they may encounter.

| Symptoms | Possible cause(s) | Possible solution(s) |
|---|---|---|
| Yellowish water | Lack of water change, exhausted activated carbon, and/or heavy algal growth | Water change and additional or renewed activated carbon filtration |
| Red slime algae on bottom and sides of tank | Improper lighting, high nutrient load (especially in a reef tank) | Remove nitrate and especially phosphate from system water, remove all detritus from system, consider treatment with erythromycin (this may destroy filter bacteria) |
| Brown dust-like algae on bottom and sides of tank | Diatom bloom, improper lighting, high levels of silicic acid (silica) in system water | Remove excess nutrients, use deionized and/or RO water for all freshwater additions |
| Persistent foam and/or shiny film on surface | High level of dissolved organic compounds; tank may be overcrowded or overfed | Water change, add protein skimmer, add surface skimmer |
| Reduced water flow from filter | Dirty filter media; caked filter bed and/or clogged airstones | Clean filter pads or bed, replace some filter media, replace airstones |
| Cloudy water, green or white | A bloom in the tank water of microscopic algae (green) and/or bacteria (white) | Reduce lighting (algae bloom), increase/add fine mechanical filtration, reduce nutrients |
| Cloudy white water, tiny bubbles in eyes and fins of fish | Teensy-weensy, itty-bitty, teeny-tiny air bubbles in the water | Relieve supersaturation of air in the water, look for an air leak in the intake side of the pump |
| Fish trying to jump from the tank | External toxin such as pesticides | Water change and/or add heavy; new activated carbon filtration |
| Fish gasping at the surface and/or showing rapid respiration | Low oxygen levels, possible toxins, possible *Amyloodinium* infestation | Increase aeration, water change, treat for *Amyloodinium* |
| Fish shimmying, rapid gilling (respiration), hanging in one place, apparent weight loss in small fish, fish death, "wipe out" or "toxic tank syndrome" | Bacterial toxins, usually *Vibrio* (vibriosis) | Move fish to different system or treat in treatment tank with antibiotics (neomycin at 250 mg/gal and streptomycin at 40 mg/gal) |

# chart for marine aquarium systems

| Symptoms | Possible cause(s) | Possible solution(s) |
|---|---|---|
| Fish display rapid respiration, rapid, irritable movement, little feeding activity | New tank syndrome, ammonia and/or nitrite poisoning | Check ammonia and nitrite levels, change water, move fish |
| Fish holding mouth open, abnormal swimming patterns, excess mucus production, slow respiration, listlessness | *Amyloodinium* infestation, *Ichthyophonus*, high $CO_2$ levels, piscine TB, fungus disease, copper poisoning | Look for *Amyloodinium*, increase aeration, look for other disease in fish, check copper level |
| Fish mildly irritable, invertebrates stressed, something not quite right, fish may be inactive or too active | Possible electric charge in system water, possible temperature problem (too high or too low), possible low pH, possible high nitrite level | Check/clean/replace electrical equipment, ground tank water, adjust temperature and pH, increase aeration, do a water change |
| A pool of water slowly enlarging on the floor around the tank | If water level in tank is dropping at about the same rate as pool is expanding, look for crack in bottom or side of tank. If tank level is not dropping, there may be a leak in filter sump (or perhaps the bathtub in the next room is overflowing) | Fix leak (Note: If you have this problem, and you had to run through this chart to figure it out, you may want to switch to collecting stamps.) |
| Tiny whitish specks, dust-like, on sides and fins of fish, fish respiring rapidly and brushing against rocks | *Amyloodinium* infestation | Freshwater dip, copper treatment of fish and tank |
| Small white pimples on sides of fish | *Cryptocaryon* ciliate infection | Freshwater and formalin dip (1 minute), 30 minute to 1 hour saltwater formalin bath, copper treatment, repeat as necessary |
| Rough white areas on sides of fish with excess mucus and skin loss | *Brookynella* or other ciliate infection | Freshwater and formalin dip (1 minute), 30 minute to 1 hour saltwater formalin bath, repeat as necessary |
| Tiny black spots on sides of fish, mostly on tangs | Turbellarian worm infestation (Black Ich) | Formalin bath, frequent cleaning of filter and tank bottom |

| Symptoms | Possible cause(s) | Possible solution(s) |
| --- | --- | --- |
| Extended eyeball (popeye or exophthalmos) | Fish TB, internal fungus infection, bacterial infection | Bacterial treatment, TB treatment, feed antibiotic-treated food |
| Rapid respiration, open mouth, raised scales, fins clamped | Fish TB | TB treatment, streptomycin (40 mg/gal) |
| Soft, distended abdomen (dropsy) | Fish TB, internal bacterial infection, parasites, tumor | TB treatment, feed antibiotic-treated food |
| Frayed and red-edged fins, open sores on sides, fins may be clamped to body of fish | Bacterial infection (*Pseudomonas*, *Vibrio*), possibly secondary to parasitic infection; high level of dissolved organics in system | Antibiotic treatment: neomycin, tetracycline, erythromycin, streptomycin; water change; reduction in tank population; improve lighting |
| Apparent blindness, fish may be unusually dark or pale in color | Fish TB, internal fungus, bacterial infection (*Vibrio*) | TB treatment, feed antibiotic-treated food |
| Fish swimming in circles and/or upside down, disoriented, shrunken stomach, ragged fins, poor color, cloudy eyes | Internal fungus infection (*Ichthyophonus*) | No proven cure, good diet and good environment best control and preventative |
| Cotton-like, wispy external growths | External tufts of fungus and/or bacterial growth (*Saprolegnia*, Columnaris) | Treatment with malachite green, acriflavine, Furanace, copper |
| Cauliflower-like, small white clumps on fins and/or mouth parts | Viral disease (*Lymphocystis*) | No cure, good diet and good environment speed recovery |
| Sunken abdomen | Starvation, possible cyanide poisoning | Supply proper diet |
| Slow decline, feeding without thriving, loss of appetite, loss of vigor | Possible cyanide poisoning including liver, kidney, and intestinal damage | No cure, good diet and good environment aid recovery if recovery is possible, attempt to eliminate cyanide |
| Stress intolerance, deep shock at netting and/or environmental disturbance | Liver damage, great fatty infiltration of liver tissue as a result of poor diet | Remove fat from diet, particularly animal fats designed for freshwater fish; reduce feeding |

# chart for marine aquarium systems

| Symptoms | Possible cause(s) | Possible solution(s) |
|---|---|---|
| Hard, swollen abdomen, good health otherwise | Eggbound, eggs in female developed fully but not spawned; possible encysted parasite | Treat normally, eggs will gradually be absorbed or will remain encysted |
| Frayed fins, marks on the body, not feeding, hiding | Harassment by other fish | Remove or isolate victim or harassing fish |
| Erosion of skin around eyes, and in and around pores of lateral line | Lateral line or "Hole in the Head" disease, probably caused by inadequate diet or light | Add vitamin C and B and perhaps E to the diet, find a food with "stabilized" vitamin C, feed green algae |
| Anemones turn white, shrink, and die | Inadequate intensity and/or spectrum of light, high nutrient level; starvation. | Improve lighting, water change, add protein skimmer, feed regularly |
| Hard corals do not grow and may even recede | Lack of calcium, high nutrient levels, high salinity | Add calcium, improve water quality, check salinity |
| Green hair algae invades hard corals | High nutrient levels (nitrate and phosphate) | Water change, remove nutrients in tank and in makeup water |
| Stony corals fading, soft corals stretching upwards ("trumpeting") | Inadequate lighting | Increase light intensity, increase blue peak in spectrum, move specimen toward light source |
| Algae (*Caulerpa*) turn white and die back | Loss of essential nutrients in the system, algal reproduction | Add iron supplement to system, harvest excessive algal growth |
| A chocolate chip cookie floating in the tank | This can be a baffling problem, but the most likely cause is an unauthorized fish feeder, probably below the minimum age recommended by the International Association of Professional and Amateur Fish Feeders, Marine Division (IAPAFFMD) | A net, a heavy cover, and a serious talk about what little fishies eat. *The Marine Aquarium Handbook: Beginner to Breeder* |

CHAPTER

*7*

# Fish Selection

*What to Look for: Condition and Compatibility*

Acquiring a new fish, whether for an old aquarium or a new one, can be both an adventure and an occasion fraught with anxiety and weighty considerations. Choose well and you may have a fish that will live for years, giving countless hours of viewing pleasure, perhaps even finding a mate and spawning in your system. Make a poor choice, and the specimen may last only a matter of days or weeks, or it may grow into the bad actor that bullies or even starts consuming your other prized fishes.

The very least that marine aquarists should do is to avoid purchasing specimens that cannot be properly fed and cared for, or specimens that were collected with destructive harvesting methods, such as cyanide or dynamite. They should also work to advance responsible collection and the cultivation of marine aquarium species.

In years past, collection, holding, shipping, and distribution techniques were designed with the convenience of humans in mind; many fish arrived at their final destinations poisoned, stressed, diseased, and starved. Many marine fishes did not survive more than a few weeks after being captured on the reefs.

Today, things are a bit better. We—meaning hobbyists, retailers, and wholesalers in North America and collectors, buyers, and exporters in the source countries that produce live tropical marine life—are becoming more and more aware that harvesting methods that destroy the environment and the resources also destroy the future of humanity. More and

Young Sailfin Tangs, *Zebrasoma veliferum:* a good choice for a larger community tank.

more local fisherfolk are learning net collection techniques and abandoning the use of paralyzing cyanide squirt bottles. But destructive collecting practices still exist, and the job of educating all concerned is never-ending. Organizations such as the Marine Aquarium Council (MAC), The Marine Aquarium Society of North America (MASNA), and other regional and local marine aquarium societies are working hard to educate people in the use and conservation of natural resources, and need the support of marine aquarists.

As time goes on, marine aquarists will increasingly be able to choose "certified," "sustainably harvested," "net caught," and "captive bred" livestock, which are superior from an environmental point of view and often less stressed and more likely to thrive as well.

## Condition

That healthy, alert, beautifully colored specimen in the tropical fish shop or a friend's tank may have had many a rough time before it became adjusted to aquarium living. Choosing the best prospect among the many temptations in a good aquarium shop involves asking a set of questions.

Is this fish in good shape? Is it eating greedily? Will it eat for me? Is that spot a scar or a parasite? Was the fish collected with cyanide? Will he get along with the other fish in my tank? Will his coloration clash with my wallpaper? Most of these questions, and others like them, you have to answer for yourself. Your dealer may know some of the answers, but chances are, he puts his faith in a wholesaler who has given him good fish in the past, and he doesn't know the history of each fish in his stock. One of the most important considerations, and one that I may be able to give you a little help with, is whether or not the fish is in good health. There are two basic areas for your evaluation: appearance and behavior.

Look closely at the eyes, mouth, skin and scales, abdomen, and fins when you judge the appearance of a prospective acquisition for your marine aquarium. The eyes should be bright and clear and normally set in the head. Internal bacterial infections are often first seen in the eyes as a cloudy grey mist, or in more advanced cases, as an outward protrusion of the eyeball (exophthalmos, or "popeye"). Sometimes only one eye is affected, so be sure you observe both eyes when you evaluate the fish. Cloudy eyes and/or popeye can be treated; Neomycin is usually effective, but you, and the retailer, should know about it if you decide to buy the

A good local aquarium shop offers the chance to observe many species side-by-side, to pick specimens that are in the best possible condition, and to ask questions of the staff.

fish. A fish with sunken eyes (eyes that seem too small for their sockets) is bad news, especially when the fish displays shallow respiration and little movement. This condition may be a result of exposure to a poison, and the fish's days are probably numbered.

The mouth should open and close normally in respiration and feeding. Most species seldom open their mouths more than just slightly during normal respiration. A fish that keeps its mouth wide open all the time has problems that are hard to cure and is usually on a downhill ride. Respiration rates vary with species, age, and size; but extremely rapid gilling, except when the fish is upset by being chased with a net or fighting with other fish, is also a sign of trouble. Disease or parasitic infection (*Amyloodinium*) is the usual cause of rapid respiration, and the fish merits very careful evaluation when this condition is observed. The tissues of the mouth should be firm and uninjured. Mouth parts are often torn in fights, and these tears are potential sites for fungus and bacterial infections.

Young Spotted Unicornfish, *Naso brevirostris*, is peaceful but requires a large aquarium.

The skin and scales should be smooth and well colored. Indistinct, discolored blotches on the upper sides are usually a sign of an internal disease, especially when linked with rapid respiration. Uplifted or raised scales are also bad—they could indicate piscine TB. Scales should be indistinct unless their edges are accentuated by the natural coloration of the fish. Missing scales are indications of fighting and are potential sites for infections. Fish are generally very hardy creatures, and given a good environment and good nutrition, they can usually repair minor damage quite rapidly if they are not deeply stressed, poisoned, or diseased.

A fish usually stops eating when it is taken from its oceanic home and subjected to crowded holding situations and unnatural foods. The period of starvation lasts until the fish encounters a wholesaler, retailer, or hobbyist that takes the pains to set him up in at least a semi-natural situation and offer food regularly until he begins to feed. During the period of starvation, the fish subsists on energy stored in its fat and liver, and no great harm is done unless the fish goes without food past the point where the liver can recover. In a healthy fish, the abdomen or stomach area should be well rounded and slightly convex in profile. As the fish loses condition, the abdominal profile becomes straight and then concave. In extreme cases, the stomach is pulled up almost to the spine and the dorsal muscles are wasted and shallow. Needless to say, such a fish seldom recovers. The condition of the abdomen offers clues to the recent history of the fish and some indication of how easy it will be to get him to eat. Beware the sunken stomach.

The fins should be clear, with smooth edges, and the fish should extend them to their full spread with some frequency. Tightly clamped dorsal, anal, or pelvic fins are a sign of problems. Frayed fins indicate fighting or bacterial infections. Fins with frayed and bleeding edges and red spots have bacterial infections. If not checked, these will turn into open sores and invade the body, usually where the pelvic or pectoral fins touch the sides, and ulcers on the body will result.

*Amyloodinium* is often first seen on the fins. The cysts on the body of a light-colored fish might be overlooked, but the white pinpoints are noticeable on thin fins. A few *Amyloodinium* cysts on a fish can be readily treated with a freshwater bath and a copper medication, but this parasite can quickly get out of hand and overrun a stressed fish in a few days. If one fish in a tank has *Amyloodinium*, it's a sure bet that the others either have or soon will have the infection. If you spot *Amyloodinium* in the tanks of a dealer, be sure to point it out to him, for it can cause a dealer heavy losses of money and good will if allowed to progress unchecked.

Behavior is an important clue to the general health of the fish. It helps to know something of the normal behavior of your prospective fish, for then you can properly evaluate his (or her) actions. If the fish is normally nocturnal or secretive, then there's nothing wrong with hiding under a rock or in a

> **WARNING SIGNS:**
>
> Be extremely wary of buying a fish with white spots, clamped or frayed fins, cloudy or sunken eyes, or a reluctance to feed.
>
> ❖

corner. A fish of this persuasion, however, swimming slowly in the middle of the tank with fins clamped tight to its sides, is in trouble. Conversely, a fish that normally swims about in the open waters above the reef should not hide continuously. Feeding is a very important sign of well-being. If a

Small Spiny Puffer, *Diodon holacanthus*, in normal swimming mode with spines flattened. Right: same fish, inflated with water, showing its erect spiny defenses.

fish feeds well on standard aquarium fare, the chances are that he is either in good condition or strong enough to shrug off any minor ailments. An active interest in his surroundings is also a good sign. The fish should respond quickly and actively to movements just outside and inside the tank. Although the term "bright-eyed and bushy-tailed" may not apply to fish, the basic concept does; so when you pick out your fish, look for the ones that are bright-eyed and full-finned. A large part of the skill of a good marine aquarist lies in the selection of compatible fish that have the promise of surviving well in a home aquarium.

## Compatibility

There are perfectly good reasons why some fish are compatible in community aquariums and others are not, why some fish communities are peaceful and others are like a frontier bar on a Saturday night. Unfortunately, there is no sure way of knowing what behavioral interactions are going to occur between specific fishes in a particular aquarium situation.

The relationships between species that make up natural communities—not just fish but invertebrates, plants, and bacteria as well—have developed over millions and millions of years of living together and surviving to reproduce in a harsh and changing environment. Predator and prey, parasite and host must coexist on the species level for each to survive. Each species must maintain its numbers within an optimum range—too many and the food supplies dwindle, too few and the reproductive effort is not adequate.

When we build a marine aquarium, the inhabitants we select bring along all their accumulated instinctive behavioral baggage—one of the things that makes a marine aquarium so fascinating and unpredictable. After all, a marine aquarium is like a multimillion-piece jigsaw puzzle. All but a few pieces are missing, however, and the few that we have may not fit together just right, or in exactly the same way that they did in nature. In the vastness of the reef and nearby environs, there are species that seldom encounter each other, species whose separate instinctive methods of fulfilling their drives for food, protection, and reproduction never bring them directly into competition with one another. Packed into an aquarium environment, however, they must interact with each other as they compete for available food and space.

The more active, mobile, and aggressive species usually get the lionfish's share of attention, food, and occasionally, a tankmate. Some fish can almost never coexist with other fish in a small aquarium for one of two reasons. Either they feed so aggressively and actively on other fish that tankmates can find little shelter from them, or they are so docile and restrictive in their food habits that most other fish easily outdo them in the competition for food and space. Fish in these categories should be kept in tanks by themselves or with tankmates chosen by trial and error, and in these cases, experience is the best teacher. Most of us do not choose to undertake a study of species compatibility and the intricacies of coral reef ecology. We are content with knowing how certain species of fish and invertebrates commonly behave in marine aquariums, and how to anticipate, and thus avoid, loss and damage of valuable fish. To this end, it is helpful to have an understanding of why some fish are aggressive toward others.

**SPECIES PROFILING:**

Before bringing a new fish home, be sure you know how large it will grow, what it eats, and what it will take to make it thrive.

❖

The most important considerations in assessing compatibility are species, individual size, state of sexual maturity and activity, feeding habits, size of the aquarium, numbers of fish in each species group, and type and amount of habitat built into the aquarium. All these factors help determine the nature and intensity of aggressive behavior between aquarium inhabitants.

Table 2 summarizes the kinds of aggressive interactions that can take place in marine aquariums. The most obvious type of aggression is the predator/prey interaction. There is little question as to why a large grouper is aggressive toward a small damselfish. The interaction is quickly settled by the disappearance of the damselfish, either into the grouper or into the protective network of the reef. The aquarist uses this aggressive behavior to good advantage when feeding silversides (minnow-like marine feeder fish) to a prize grouper or lionfish. Few aquarists are so naive

## Table 2  Types of aggressive behavior in the marine aquarium

| Type of aggressive interaction | Recipient of aggressive behavior | Example |
| --- | --- | --- |
| Predator/prey | Perceived food organism | Moray eel consuming a small clownfish |
| Territory protection | Others of the same or similar species | Juvenile angelfish and jewelfish attacking others |
| Mate and status protection | Other fish of the same species | Paired clownfish attacking others |
| Spawn protection | All other fish near the nest area | Triggerfish |
| Instinctive feeding patterns | Corals | Butterfly fish feeding on coral polyps |

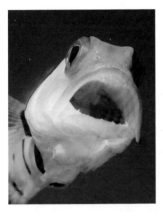

as to expect the lion to lie down with the damsel in the aquarium. Most of the fish we keep in aquariums feed on smaller fish or invertebrates in the wild.

### Predator/prey relationships

Fish-eating fishes, except for sharks and barracudas, usually take their prey in one gulp, so food organisms are seldom larger than a mouthful. Therefore, size differences are important considerations. A moray eel can coexist with a large angelfish, but a small clownfish may only be a tasty tidbit. The three factors that work to the aquarist's advantage when keeping predatory and prey species in the same aquarium are size, familiarity, and habitat. A small fish may coexist with a large predator on a peaceful, if tenuous, basis for a long time simply because they both have a recognized habitat in the aquarium. The small fish avoids the predator and the well-fed predator is not stimulated to attack the familiar tankmate. Another small fish added to the aquarium is seldom so lucky. The predator's attention is drawn to the unfamiliar fish, the fright and anxiety behavior patterns displayed by the new fish arouse the feeding instincts of the predator, and a strike is made.

Under these conditions, the long-time tankmate may also become a target. However, it has a better chance of survival since it is familiar with the protective cover and behavior patterns in the aquarium. Protective habitat, such as honeycombed rocks and coral growths that provide numerous safe havens, are necessary in tanks that hold groupers, lionfish, moray eels, and other predators as well as small reef fish. Even with the protection of extensive habitat and a good feeding program, however, small fish will occasionally disappear.

If one wishes to maintain fish with a predator/prey relationship in a large tank, it is often helpful to separate the species with a partition of glass or transparent plastic for a week or so to allow the prey species to become acclimated to the tank and established in the mind of the predator. The reasons for other types of piscine aggression are not so obvious. Proper habitat is the key to survival in nature. Although numbers of some species, such as High-hats and cardinalfish, can peacefully share a small habitat, others, such as angelfish and some damselfish, require some individual space. In nature, each species requires a particular type of habitat to survive. Jewelfish require fire coral; clownfish need anemones; Neon Gobies must have large coral heads; High-hats need dark, intricate reef formations; small angelfish need sponges and crevices; and so it is with all fish species—some with broad and some with restricted habitat requirements. The fish that occupies, and holds onto, the right crevice, the right section of the reef where the proper food organisms occur, is the fish that will survive.

### Territory defense

What would you do if you returned home one day and found a stranger fixing dinner in your kitchen and his suitcase in your bedroom? "Nice place you got here, buddy, I'm sure you won't mind if I move in for a while." With a little help from the police, I'm sure said stranger would soon find himself in different surroundings. In other words, you would aggressively remove the intruder from your private space. Individuals of many fish species protect their own living space (food, shelter, and potential spawning sites) from others of their species in basically the same manner.

A little Queen Angelfish may comfortably occupy the same crevice with a High-hat, a blenny, a pair of gobies, a few cardinalfish and a puffer, but will not tolerate another Queen Angel within three feet, or more.

Dragon Moray Eel, *Enchelycore pardalis*, will attack and swallow smaller tankmates.

Orchid Dottybacks, *Pseudochromis fridmani*,
are now captive bred and make great reef fish.

Other species do not compete for exactly the same resources as the Queen and therefore are not a threat to its existence. These other species occupy different apartments in the same building, but another Queen would be moving into the same apartment—not an acceptable living arrangement. The original owner has the power of occupancy—a power great enough to enable him to drive off even a slightly larger angelfish. When such an encounter takes place, a little nipping and posturing usually sends the intruder off to find an unoccupied apartment a few coral heads away. The angelfish may occupy this space for a few weeks or months until he outgrows the area and moves on to a new habitat more suitable to his size. Another small angelfish soon finds the deserted habitat and moves in, much to the delight of the tropical fish collector who has "staked out" that particular hole and collects a Queen Angel at the same spot every month or two.

In the aquarium, the same instincts prevail even though there is no shortage of food or shelter. A territory is a territory, and no other small angel is allowed within a certain distance. If this distance happens to be four feet and the aquarium is only three feet, then somebody has a problem, and it's usually the smaller of the two angels. In nature, the loser has a vast expanse of ocean bottom to escape into, but in an aquarium he is imprisoned with the owner of the territory. He can't fight back because he already lost the fight, and the winner can't stop fighting because the loser won't go away. The result is either a dead fish or one that is so intimidated that he seldom ventures from a secluded hiding place.

Size is important to the intensity of intraspecific aggression. Often a large angelfish will tolerate a small fish of the same or closely related species because the size difference puts them in slightly different ecological niches and territorial aggression is muted. Another way of diffusing territorial aggression in an artificial situation is to contain many fish of the same size and species together, perhaps 20 to 200, in a relatively small tank. Aggression is then so diffuse, because there are so many fish, that no one fish can become dominant, and no one fish can become the sole target for the aggression of all the others. All the fish give and take a little aggression and all survive. There is some indication that fish reared in such a situation are not as aggressive toward others of their own species as wild fish; however, this tendency probably disappears after the fish is kept alone for a while.

I use young angelfish to illustrate territorial aggression because it is often pronounced in these species, and aquarists often try to keep them together, which is usually a mistake. Two small angelfish of the same species can seldom be kept together unless there is a significant size difference, and even in this situation, the smaller fish is barely tolerated and shows little or no growth.

### Sexual territory (mate protection)

As a general rule, the more distantly related the species, the more tolerant they are of each other. In certain families of marine fish, notably some species of angelfish and wrasses, a harem type of relationship exists between the sexes. One physically large male, often distinguished by color and form as well as size, maintains a territory with several females and aggressively protects his females from intrusion by other males. Some groupers may also exhibit this pattern in natural populations, but this is difficult to observe. It is interesting to note that protogynous hermaphroditism (functional females changing to males) is found in each of these, as well as in other families of coral reef fishes.

The loss of the male in these harem groups apparently stimulates a large female to begin to change into a male, which can take place within a matter of weeks. Behavior patterns change along with form, color, and sexual organs. An opposite pattern, protanderous hermaphroditism, occurs in anemonefish. In this case, one large, dominant female, a smaller male, and a variable population of subadult fish inhabit a large anemone or area of anemones. The subadults are tolerated by the pair, but are kept in their place and do not develop into adults. Upon the loss of one of the pair, the largest subadult becomes an active male. If the female is lost, the active male changes to a female and pairs with the now-maturing subadult male.

**CHANGING SEXES:**

Hermaphroditism is common in coral reef fishes, and sex change in the aquarium can lead to unexpected aggressive behavior.

❖

We are discovering and investigating these fascinating physiological and behavioral changes, which are apparently common in coral reef fish. We have much yet to learn, much that will advance our understanding of how to care for these fish in aquariums. The development of aggressive behavior in a tank that has long been peaceful may be due to the onset of sexual maturity or even sexual change. Individuals of some species protect their status within a sexual hierarchy as well as, or perhaps without regard for, a specific territory. For example, one male pygmy angel, *Centropyge* sp., may tolerate, interact, and even spawn with several females in a single aquarium; yet the introduction of another male may cause intolerable aggression and loss of the new male. If the aquarium is large enough, however, a new female may fit into the harem and not cause undue problems. It is also possible for a small juvenile clownfish to occupy an anemone with a pair of the same species and suffer no more than an occasional nip; and if the relationship is well established, the juvenile will grow only very slowly. A mature intruder into a tank with an established clownfish pair stands little chance of survival, unless it is so big and powerful that it can displace one of the pair. A female will be violently attacked by the resident female and a new male will be harried and picked upon by both male and female.

It is possible to have two, or perhaps three, pairs each establish a territory in a large tank, but this usually happens only if the fish have grown up in the tank together. Once sexual maturity and subsequent pairing takes place in anemonefish, each mature fish protects its status by attacking all who might threaten this status.

### Reproductive territory (spawn protection)

Spawn protection is more intense and focused than status protection. This aggression is directed at all species of fish that venture near the nest. It only exists when a spawn is present or imminent. Damselfish and clownfish are most commonly observed protecting spawns since their nests are usually somewhat exposed. Royal Grammas and Neon Gobies, on the other hand, are secretive spawners, their nests well hidden under a rock or in a crevice. Even though the nests are well hidden, an observant aquarist will notice the increased aggressive activity exhibited by the male near the entrance to his carefully guarded treasure. Many species we keep in aquariums become adults at a relatively small size and form strong pair bonds between a male and female. Most commonly encountered in this category are some species of butterflyfish, gobies, clownfish, a few angelfish and, to a certain extent, Royal Grammas. These fish are often easier to keep as mated pairs than as singles, but when paired they seldom tolerate other fish of their own or similar species in the same aquarium.

### Random aggression

Territorial protection is present in many species to a greater or lesser degree and usually results in loss or intimidation of one or more tankmates. There are some fish, however, that are so aggressive that few, if any, fish can be kept with them, and some species of triggerfish are the prime example. They nip and bite the fins and bodies of all other fish kept in the same tank. This is not territory protection in the true sense; it is merely an aggressive, non-specific feeding behavior that targets any victim who cannot avoid the slow-swimming triggerfish in the confines of the aquarium. (Once the triggerfish gets near its prey, it is quick on the trigger.) Invertebrates are also subject to this never-ending torment. This is just an extension of triggerfish behavior on the reef. They investigate anything that might be remotely edible with nips from their sharp teeth and small, but powerful, jaws. One day as I was collecting angelfish, I thought I had lost half an ear to a curious Grey Triggerfish. (Incidently, Grey Triggerfish fillets are good eating.)

Triggerfish are among the most colorful and responsive of marine fish and are easy to keep, by themselves, in an aquarium. A few are appropriate community fish, even in a reef aquarium, but most are less than trustworthy, especially as they reach larger sizes and sexual maturity. However, even the known troublemakers are well worth a separate tank just to observe their behavior and beauty. Some triggerfish are said to recognize their owners and can even be taught to perform particular behavior patterns when food is offered. Behavior patterns, developed over millions of years, that adapt a species to life in a particular ecological niche do not fundamentally change when the fish is placed in the confines of an aquarium. The fish adapts to the aquarium only to the extent allowed by these innate behavioral patterns. Some species have behavioral characteristics that allow them to adapt to aquarium conditions quite well. The clownfish, for example, has a restricted range in nature, is active during the day, feeds on a wide variety of food organisms, and is of small adult size—all characteristics that allow it to survive with vigor in a typical marine aquarium.

### Shy, delicate, and dietarily restricted fishes
Incompatibility is not always a result of unconstrained aggression caused by predatory behavior and territorial or reproductive defense. Some species, such as the Jackknife Fish and other reef drums, are physiologically delicate, do not withstand capture and handling very well, and have a wide natural range in nature. Fish that remain associated with reef structures usually acclimate better to captivity in small tanks than fish that range widely over the reef and open ocean. It is difficult to keep these fish in good condition during capture and shipping, and they seldom withstand this stress well enough to survive in an aquarist's tank. Small specimens usually do much better than large fish.

Other species, such as mandarinfish and wild seahorses, may be physiologically hardy enough to survive capture and transport very well, but are so restrictive in diet and/or so shy in feeding behavior that they often starve before taking typical aquarium foods. Such fish are best kept in a tank devoted to that one species, and the aquarist must be sure to meet

Juvenile Chevron Tangs, *Ctenochaetus hawaiiensis*, will mature into dark-striped adults.

the dietary needs of the species with the proper foods and feeding regime. Mandarinfish, incidently, and some other difficult-to-keep small fish that require tiny invertebrate prey species, do quite well in reef tanks and other systems with much live rock and natural invertebrate fauna. So despite the docile nature and spectacular form and color of some fish, such as Jackknifes, mandarins, some puffer fish, and shrimpfish, they do not adapt well to life in a community tank, although a careful and attentive aquarist can create a good captive environment for these difficult species. Reef tanks now supply the kind of captive environment that many of these delicate species require.

## Survival

There are many pathways to survival on the reef. Some species have found that there is safety in numbers, and interspecific competition for food and shelter has been reduced to the point that they can exist in groups or schools to the benefit of all the individuals. Surgeonfish, some damsels, grunts, jawfish (providing there is enough bottom area), cardinalfish, and some wrasses and reef drums (High Hats) are examples of fish that form compatible living groups. Fish that live in groups or schools in nature usually get along well with their own, and most other species, in the

Green Mandarinfish, *Synchiropus splendidus*, demand special care and feeding.

aquarium environment. Survival in the aquarium, however, is much different than survival on the reef.

The greatest compatibility problems in the aquarium usually occur when the aquarist brings a valuable new prize acquisition home to an old, established tank with fish that are well adapted to the tank and each other. Occasionally the new fish will be met with indifference, especially if it is a large fish that does not establish a particular territory, or if the aquarium is relatively uncrowded. But more often, the old timers harass the newcomer unmercifully. There are several things the aquarist can do to ease the introduction process. New habitat, a rock or piece of coral added along with the new fish, may provide the new arrival with some cover unfamiliar to the established fish. Changing the position of all the tank habitat is a bit more drastic, but it causes confusion in the established territories and allows the new fish to find a spot in the subsequent reestablishment of space claims. However, if the new fish is a large specimen of a species that is known to be aggressive, it is probably better to add it without any establishment aid, since the old fish will be better able to maintain an already established position against a larger intruder.

One of the best methods of bringing a new and delicate fish into an active community tank is to separate the new fish and a bit of habitat from the rest of the tank with a transparent piece of glass or plastic for about 10 days. This allows the old timers to see and accept the new fish before they can attack. It also allows the new fish to develop the behavior patterns of an established fish and defend its status when it does move into the tank's social structure.

The development of coral reef tank systems has created many new challenges in the area of compatibility of marine organisms. The fish-to-fish interactions that we used to worry about seem relatively simple compared with those of the whole mix of fish, plants, hard and soft corals, and other invertebrates now packed together in one little tank. Advanced marine aquarists are still—and will be for quite some time—working out the compatibility problems that show up in these environmentally complex small marine systems.

In general, it is important to know the feeding habitats of any fish placed into coral reef tanks, especially whether or not corals are included in the diet of the fish. Some butterflyfish, for example, feed on coral polyps and can quickly destroy valued hard coral specimens. Various species of corals are also incompatible with each other. If placed too close together, they expand and touch each other and the polyps wage "war" with their stinging cells. One coral will usually prevail and may even kill the other if one of them is not moved. Anemones can move about the tank and may find a location where they damage other invertebrates. A good reef aquarist is aware of these interactions and keeps the reef tank under close observation to avoid any coral "wars."

A great many good books and articles are now available that add to the marine aquarist's understanding of fish and invertebrate condition and compatibility. It isn't possible to list them all in this space, but look for books by Scott Michael, Julian Sprung, Charles Delbeek, Bob Fenner, John Tullock, Alf Jacob Nilsen, Svein Fosså, Joyce Wilkerson, Anthony Calfo, Ron Shimek, Rudie Kuiter, Gerald Allen, Michael Paletta, and Matt Wittenrich, among others. The more you read, the more you learn, the more you know, the better the aquarist you will become.

**Coral Beauty**

**Yellow Assessor**

**Yellowtail Damselfish**

**Orchid Dottyback**

## Angelfish
Cherub, *Centropyge argi*
Coral Beauty, *Centropyge bispinosa*

## Assessor
Blue, *Assessor macneilli*
Yellow, *Assessor flavissimus*

## Blenny
Midas, *Ecsenius midas*
Redlip, *Ophioblennius atlanticus*
Tailspot, *Ecsenius stigmatura*

## Cardinalfish
Banggai, *Pterapogon kauderni*
Pajama, *Sphaeramia nematoptera*
Threadfin, *Apogon leptacanthus*
Yellowstriped, *Apogon cyanosoma*

## Clownfish
Ocellaris, *Amphiprion ocellaris*
Percula, *Amphiprion percula*

## Damselfish
Blue Devil, *Chrysiptera cyanea*
Goldbelly, *Pomacentrus auriventris*
Humbug, *Dascyllus aruanus*
Yellowtail, *Chrysiptera parasema*

## Dottyback
Neon, *Pseudochromis aldabraensis*
Orchid, *Pseudochromis fridmani*

## Firefish
Magnificent, *Nemateleotris magnifica*
Purple, *Nemateleotris decora*

## Goby
Clown, *Gobiodon citrinus*
Neon, *Elacatinus oceanops*
Shrimp, *Amblyeleotris* spp.,
    *Cryptocentrus*, *Stonogobiops* spp.

# (10–30 gallons)

References: *A PocketExpert Guide to Marine Fishes; Adventurous Aquarist Guide: The 101 Best Saltwater Fishes*, Scott W. Michael (Microcosm/TFH).

## Groupers, Basslets, Grammas
Chalk Bass, *Serranus tortugarum*
Royal Gramma, *Gramma loreto*
Peppermint Bass, *Lipropoma rubre*

## Hawkfish
Flame, *Neocirrhites armatus*
Longnose, *Oxycirrhites typus*
Pixie (Falco's), *Cirrhitichthys falco*

## Jawfish
Pearly (Yellowhead),
  *Opistognathus aurifrons*

## Lionfish
Dwarf (Zebra), *Dendrochirus zebra*

## Wrasse
Fairy (*Cirrhilabrus* spp.)
Flasher (*Paracheilinus* spp.)
Golden (Canary), *Halichoeres chrysurus*
Sixline, *Pseudocheilinus hexataenia*

Royal Gramma

Longnose Hawkfish

Chalk Bass

Dwarf Lionfish

Sixline Wrasse

Flasher Wrasse

Indian Yellowtail Angelfish

Lyretail Anthias

Comet (Marine Betta)

Snowflake Moray Eel

## Angelfish
Halfblack, *Centropyge vrolikii*
Indian Yellowtail,
   *Apolemichthys xanthurus*

## Anthias
Bartlett's, *Pseudanthias bartlettorum*
Lyretail, *Pseudanthias squamipinnis*

## Butterflyfish
Pacific Doublesaddle,
   *Chaetodon ulietensis*
Klein's, *Chaetodon kleinii*
Lemon, *Chaetodon miliaris*
Raccoon, *Chaetodon lunula*
Yellow Longnose, *Forcipiger flavissimus*

## Clownfish
Clark's, *Amphiprion clarkii*
Maroon, *Premnas biaculeatus*
Tomato, *Amphiprion frenatus*

## Comet
Marine Betta, *Calloplesiops altivelis*

## Damselfish
Bluegreen Chromis, *Chromis viridis*
Domino Damsel, *Dascyllus trimaculatus*

## Filefish
Fantail, *Pervagor spilosoma*

## Hawkfish
Arc-Eye, *Paracirrhites arcatus*

## Moray Eel
Goldentail, *Gymnothorax miliaris*
Snowflake, *Echidna nebulosa*
Zebra, *Gymnomuraena zebra*
Chainlink, *Echidna catenata*

## Puffer
Porcupinefish (Spiny Puffer),
   *Diodon holocanthus*

# (40–75 gallons)

References: *A PocketExpert Guide to Marine Fishes; Adventurous Aquarist Guide: The 101 Best Saltwater Fishes*, Scott W. Michael (Microcosm/TFH).

## Tang
Convict, *Acanthurus triostegus*
Yellow, *Zebrasoma flavescens*
Sohal, *Acanthurus sohal*

## Triggerfish
Bluechin, *Xanthichthys auromarginatus*
Picasso, *Rhinecanthus aculeatus*
Bursa, *Sufflamen bursa*

## Lionfish
Spotfin, *Pterois antennata*

## Wrasse
Checkerboard, *Halichoeres hortulanus*
Christmas, *Halichoeres ornatissimus*
Cuban Hogfish, *Bodianus pulchellus*
Harlequin Tuskfish, *Choerodon fasciatus*
Lunare, *Thalassoma lunare*

**Porcupinefish (Spiny Puffer)**

**Yellow Tang**

**Yellow Longnose Butterflyfish**

**Bluechin Triggerfish**

**Clark's Clownfish**

**Harlequin Tuskfish**

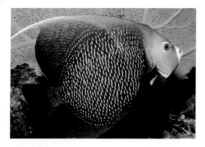

French Angelfish

Maculosus (Map) Angelfish

Volitans Lionfish

Foxface Rabbitfish

## Angelfish

Blue, *Holacanthus bermudensis*
Koran, *Pomacanthus semicirculatus*
French, *Pomacanthus paru*
Grey, *Pomacanthus arcuatus*
Maculosus (Map),
   *Pomacanthus maculosus*
Passer, *Holacanthus passer*
Queen, *Holacanthus ciliaris*

## Butterflyfish

Auriga (Threadfin), *Chaetodon auriga*
Heniochus (Longfin Bannerfish),
   *Heniochus acuminatus*
Golden, *Chaetodon semilarvatus*
Vagabond, *Chaetodon vagabundus*

## Grouper

Coney, *Cephalopholis fulva*
Miniata (Coral Hind),
   *Cephalopholis miniata*
Panther, *Cromoleptes altivelis*

## Lionfish

Volitans, *Pterois volitans*

## Puffer

Dogface (Blackspotted),
   *Arothron nigropunctatus*
Guinea Fowl (Golden),
   *Arothron meleagris*

## Rabbitfish

Foxface, *Siganus vulpinus*
Magnificent, *Siganus magnifica*

## Shark

Epaulette, *Hemiscyllium ocellatum*
Whitespotted Bamboo,
   *Chiloscyllium plagiosum*

## Tang

Naso, *Naso lituratus*
Sailfin, *Zebrasoma veliferum*
Spotted Unicornfish, *Naso brevirostris*
Purple, *Zebrasoma xanthurum*

## Triggerfish

Clown, *Balistoides conspicillum*
Crosshatch, *Xanthichthys mento*
Niger, *Odonus niger*
Pinktail, *Melichthys vidua*
Sargassum, *Xanthicthys ringens*

INDIAN TRIGGER

## Wrasse

Bird, *Gomphosus varius*
Banana (Sunset), *Thalassoma lutescens*
Yellowtail Coris, *Coris gaimard*
Diana's Hogfish, *Bodianus diana*
Formosan or Queen Coris, *Coris frerei*
Hardwick's, *Thalassoma hardwickii*
Rockmover (Dragon),
    *Novaculichthys taeniourus*
Spanish Hogfish, *Bodianus rufus*
Surge, *Thalassoma trilobatum*
Yellowtail Coris, *Coris gaimard*

Purple Tang

Sailfin Tang

Miniata Grouper (Coral Hind)

Niger Triggerfish

Magnificent Rabbitfish

Pinktail Triggerfish

# Introduction & Quarantine

*Purposes and Methods*

Wᴀʏ ʙᴀᴄᴋ ɪɴ 1864, Lᴏᴜɪs Pᴀsᴛᴇᴜʀ ᴘʀᴏᴠᴇᴅ ᴛʜᴀᴛ ᴛʜᴇʀᴇ ɪs ɴᴏ sᴜᴄʜ thing as spontaneous generation. Therefore, everything that shows up in your marine tank, except for airborne bacteria and algal spores, is there because someone, somehow, put it there. This goes for disease organisms, parasites, copepods, and macroalgae as well as fish, invertebrates, and coral rock decor. Consequently, it is wise to stop and consider how things that you don't want, such as disease organisms and chemical toxins, might find their way into your tank and what can be done to prevent their introduction. Remember that introduction of a nasty life form doesn't happen only during the initial setup; in fact, this is the period when you are most concerned and aware and work hardest to avoid contamination. Slip-ups usually occur after a year of trouble-free operation, when you've developed the "Oh, I can throw anything in there and it does fine" attitude.

## Introductions

We are most concerned with preventing the introduction of the marine protozoan parasites *Amyloodinium*, *Cryptocaryon*, and *Brooklynella*, and the bacteria *Pseudomonas*, *Vibrio*, and *Mycobacteria*, since these organisms cause most of the disease problems in marine tanks. Although it is true that a healthy fish in a good environment can fight off a few bacteria,

Disease problems frequently occur when fishes are transported and subjected to stress.

Most disease outbreaks in home aquariums occur when one or more new fish are acquired and introduced into a community tank without passing through quarantine.

protozoan parasites are another story—they can quickly destroy a tank of fishes if introduced and allowed to reproduce unchecked.

The second concern (only because it is relatively uncommon) is the introduction of "unnatural" toxins such as nicotine, pesticides, rodent poisons, heavy metals, perfume, paint fumes, and industrial chemicals. Anything that enters the tank has to be considered a possible source of contamination, especially if persistent problems are occurring, and the history of each routine introduction should be traced to make sure it is above suspicion. Keep in mind, however, that a marine tank is not an operating room, and you need not try to keep it "clean and sterile." Indeed, that attitude could almost give one an ulcer. Algae and detritus are part and parcel of most marine aquariums; we are only interested in avoiding the introduction of something from an already-contaminated marine

# Table 3  Sources of disease in a marine aquarium

| Mode of Contamination | Methods of Prevention |
| --- | --- |
| Introduction of new saltwater either as initial fill or as water changes | Natural seawater should be treated (dark storage for two weeks) to prevent introduction of protozoan parasites. Synthetic seawater is safer, but be sure containers and hoses are rinsed in freshwater if they have recently held saltwater from another source. |
| Introduction of active filter media when seeding a new tank | The only precaution here is to know and trust your source. |
| Introduction of new fish and invertebrates | Quarantine is the answer. See the following section. |
| Introduction of live rock | "Live rock" covered with attached invertebrates and algae can add much natural beauty and interest to a marine tank, but can also introduce protozoan parasites. Quarantine for a week or so in a fish-free tank is good insurance. Do not accept rock from another aquarium that has had any disease outbreaks. |
| Fish and invertebrate food | Every day food goes into your tank, and if you do a good job as an aquarist, the food is varied and from both plant and animal sources. Generally, any food that has been processed (frozen, cooked, dried, freeze-dried, canned, etc.) is free of parasites. The greatest danger comes from live foods (brine shrimp, plankton, live minnows, worms, etc.), and next in line are dead unprocessed foods (shrimp, fish flesh, and algae). The answer is to be careful, but not paranoid. Find sources you can trust. Don't introduce water that live foods are packed with, rinse natural foods, and thaw and drain frozen foods. |
| Introduction and transfer of coral, rocks, or other decorations | Be sure all coral or rock not intended to be alive is properly processed. Rinse and scrub well any transfers from possibly contaminated sources. |
| Introduction through nets, siphon hoses, and cleaning implements | It's easy to pick up a net, use it to remove a dead fish from a tank, put down the net, then pick it up a few minutes later and use it in another tank. Get in the habit of rinsing all nets and cleaning materials in fresh water after each use and storing them in a dry place. Not only will they last longer, but possible parasite transfer will be prevented. |
| Introduction from airborne spray or splash-over | Aquariums set up close to one another, or over and under each other, have the potential for spreading problems through drip and spray. Isolate the tanks as well as possible by space and covers, and in the unfortunate instance that a tank develops a parasite problem, prevent any spray, splash, or drip. |
| Introduction through casual or accidental means | "Oh look, Barbie, Uncle Mike's fishy is on the floor. Let's put him in that tank over there. I wonder why he isn't swimming?" Good covers on tanks are important for obvious reasons. They keep fish in and little fingers out. The better your control of the over-the-tank environment, the fewer accidents you'll have. |

source or the accidental introduction of external poisons.

Perhaps the most common disease (and probably the most dangerous to captive fish populations in a marine aquarium) is caused by the *Amyloodinium* parasite. This parasite exists as a free-swimming dynospore, a cyst on the external surfaces of a fish, and as a cyst on the bottom of the tank. Thus it can enter a tank (1) with water from a contaminated source, (2) with gravel, live rock, an infected net, or a decoration from a contaminated tank, or (3) attached to a new fish (the most likely way).

Be sure to see the section on *Amyloodinium* in Chapter 9 for more information on diagnosis and treatment. It is important to be aware of the various ways a parasite can gain entry to an aquarium system. Table 3 on page 191 lists the most common modes of contamination with *Amyloodinium* and other parasites and toxins and offers suggestions on prevention.

The best preventative for protozoan parasite introduction, besides careful selection and a good dealer, is a one- to two-minute freshwater bath before introducing a new fish to a tank. As long as the freshwater is the same temperature and close to the same pH as the tank water, the fish is only momentarily inconvenienced; but most external parasites not deeply embedded in flesh or mucus quickly take up water until they burst from the increased internal osmotic pressure or drop off as cysts. If you also avoid introducing any of the water the fish were packed in and dipped in, there is very little chance of contamination. (In the case of *Amyloodinium*, the parasite cyst only falls off the fish and remains alive on the bottom of the bath bucket. *Never add the freshwater from any freshwater bath to the marine aquarium!*)

**THE FRESHWATER BATH:**

A short dip in freshwater will help kill or at least dislodge any external parasites from a newly acquired fish.

❖

### Introducing a new fish

Following the simple procedures of selecting top quality fish, giving a one-minute freshwater bath before introduction to a tank, providing a two- or three-week stay in a quarantine tank, feeding a varied diet, and adhering to a good maintenance schedule will give you a marine tank relatively free of death and disease.

A good method of introduction, assuming the fish is not severely

A juvenile French Angelfish gets a quick dip in freshwater that is of the same temperature and pH as the water it arrived in. A fish may lie on its side, but it should be removed promptly if it shows signs of extreme distress and rapid breathing.

stressed, is in relatively good condition, and came in a bag that was packed with oxygen, is to float the packing bag, unopened, in the quarantine tank for about 15 minutes to allow the temperatures to equalize. (Turn off the lights to avoid stressing or overheating the fish.) Then open the bag and add water from the tank, equal to about one fourth the bag's original volume, to the bag. This allows the fish to gradually get used to the tank water and you to observe the fish's behavior as you introduce the water. If the fish becomes stressed when the tank water is added, something is wrong and the introduction process must be watched very carefully. Add the same volume of water about every 15 minutes three more times. Remove water from the bag and discard it before each addition of tank water to prevent the bag from filling. Now take a good look at the fish.

Same fish in the QT, or quarantine tank, a small aquarium where it can easily be treated with copper, formalin, or other medications if necessary. PVC pipe offers hiding places.

If he is respiring very rapidly, listing to one side, and in general looking very stressed, it's probably best to skip the freshwater bath and put him directly into the quarantine tank, unless there is obvious evidence of parasite infection.

If the fish is in good shape, however, a one-minute freshwater bath is good insurance. Make sure the freshwater is the same temperature and close to the same pH as the tank water (7.8 to 8.1 should be about right). Lift the fish with a clean net or hands and place him in the container of freshwater. Cover the container with something transparent to keep the fish in and allow observation. Time the bath and watch for signs of shock. If severe shock occurs remove him from the freshwater bath and place him in the tank immediately. Otherwise, after one minute, put the fish in the quarantine tank and give him a day or two to settle down before worrying about whether or not he is eating. Other cleansing methods include the use of copper compounds, medicinal dyes such as methylene blue, and antibiotics for periods of days or weeks before introduction to display tanks. Such treatments add to the stress on the fish and are best avoided unless a disease becomes evident during the quarantine period or fish from a particular source consistently display disease.

## Quarantine

The term "quarantine" can mean different things to different aquarists. To some it's a sterile-looking, medicated, bare tank that houses new fish for a day or two to see if any disease develops, and to others it's a second, fully set-up, smaller tank that maintains new fish and invertebrates for several weeks to be sure all is well before introduction to the main tank. Both methods have their advantages and disadvantages. The bare tank allows the effective use of medication, good observation of the fish, and the opportunity to keep the tank bottom clean. However, the fish cannot survive long or well in such a setup, and the water should be discarded after each use. In my opinion, the bare tank finds its best application as a treatment tank, for use when a disease has been detected and a course of medication determined.

A small tank, 10 to 15 gallons, set up with a biological filter and some tank decor for hiding, is more functional for quarantine than a bare tank. It allows a new fish to be maintained under good aquarium conditions for two to four weeks to get used to the water, the tank routine, and available foods away from the competition of the main tank. If a fish does bring a problem home with it, this should be evident within two or three weeks and, depending on the disease, treatment can be effected in the quarantine tank or in a bare treatment tank. A small quarantine tank is a lot easier to keep free of disease than a large display tank, and can be used to brighten up another corner of the room. Also, if necessary, a 0.2 ppm copper treatment level can be better maintained in a small tank that does not contain calcareous gravel or rock.

An important side benefit of using a quarantine tank is that a new specimen can be target fed without competitors present. An established community of fishes may make it difficult for a newcomer to get enough to eat at first, and if the fish has been underfed during shipping it may go into a downward spiral, hiding and losing strength. A few weeks in the

A large reef display at the Waikiki Aquarium: public aquariums exercise extreme caution when introducing new specimens to any display, for fear of allowing parasites or diseases to enter the system. Quarantine of new animals typically lasts a minimum of three weeks to a month.

peaceful isolation of quarantine allows it to become well nourished and get accustomed to the water and foods you provide.

There is generally much less concern for quarantine when dealing with corals and other invertebrates, and generally there is less of a problem with parasites in invertebrates than in fish. Also, many of the coral parasites are confined to specific host species or genera of hosts, whereas fish parasites, for the most part, reproduce quickly, spread to many different species of fish, and attain epizootic levels of infection in closed systems. But this doesn't mean that an aquarist can ignore the potential for parasite problems with corals and other invertebrates.

One example of a coral pest that multiplies to plague proportions in a reef tank is *Tegastes acroporanus*, the so-called Red Bug. It is a parasitic copepod, small and rather flea-like, and it targets *Acropora* stony corals, sucking nutrients out of their flesh. One treatment used at Oceans, Reefs & Aquariums (ORA) involves the use of dips in a dilute solution of iodine or in water containing a heartworm medication known as *Milbemycin oxime* (Interceptor) usually prescribed for dogs.

Quarantine procedures are not difficult to establish for corals and invertebrates; a second, smaller, well-lighted tank with high water quality will do the job, and it is wise to have this capability. Careful observation of any new acquisition is critical, especially if it comes from an unknown source. Be sure to observe the new coral at night a few hours after dark, since many parasitic organisms are only active during nighttime hours.

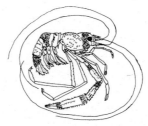

# Diseases & Distress

*Identification and Treatment*

THIS CHAPTER IS INTENDED TO BE AN EASY-TO-FOLLOW FIRST-AID, disease-prevention, and control guide. It covers The Dirty Dozen, the most common health problems you are likely to encounter in a home marine aquarium. The emphasis is on treatments that are basic, effective, and within the scope of most marine aquarists to obtain and use with modest cost and relatively little danger.

## Problems

Suppose, despite your best efforts to avoid contamination, a disease is introduced to your aquarium. This is not an uncommon occurrence in marine aquariums, and sooner or later every marine aquarist has to deal with a disease problem. This section is designed to help you identify the problem and suggest a method of treatment. Disease diagnosis is an involved and complex subject, however, and although this chapter will help you cope with the most common problems a marine aquarist encounters, I encourage you to seek out other references and learn all you can about marine fish diseases and treatments.

    Most fish and invertebrate health problems fall into one of three major categories:

    1. Problems caused by poor environmental conditions

    2. Problems caused by poor nutrition

    3. Problems caused by an organism that causes disease

Yellow Tang exhibiting classic signs of extreme emaciation with sunken muscle masses.

Newly imported Maroon Clownfish with multiple health warning signs.

Usually, poor environmental conditions and/or poor nutrition cause debilitation, create stress, and reduce the natural resistance of an animal to disease organisms. A disease can strike quickly, within a few hours or up to a few days or a week, but problems due to poor environment and/or poor nutrition develop slowly over weeks and months. Generally, if the problem comes on quickly, suspect a disease organism; if the problem develops slowly, try to improve conditions and nutrition. There are exceptions, of course; piscine TB and some parasites may be chronic and plague the fish for a few months or more, while a drop in oxygen levels in the tank may affect the fish very quickly. But with the application of a little common sense, the rapidity of onset is a good clue to the source of the problem.

Note that the very best disease control in an aquarium consists of prevention, and the very best disease prevention technique consists of providing good nutrition and a good environment and using a quarantine procedure. Good environmental conditions, good nutrition, and quarantine will not eliminate the possibility of disease, but will certainly reduce the incidence of it and greatly increase the ability of the fish to withstand the stress of disease and treatment. When disease and distress happen, and they will, a good marine aquarist must know what to do.

First of all, it is important for a marine aquarist to understand something about the relationship between fish and disease. Fish have a natural resistance to disease, and, in nature, disease-causing organisms seldom destroy their host; if they do, they also usually die. A natural balance, which has developed over eons of evolution, exists between host and parasite, and both have adapted to survive within the natural web of life in tropical seas. The aquarium, however, is an unnatural environment, and whatever the natural balance may be on a coral reef, it no longer exists in the captive environment. Parasites, bacteria, and host are contained in a restricted environment where nutrients that feed bacteria and algae can accumulate to very high levels, natural nutrition may not be available, and natural controls on bacteria and parasites are seldom present. It is the responsibility of the aquarist to provide what is lost from the natural environment. Does this mean that you have to keep a shark to eat any fish that might get sick? No, there are limits to your responsibility, but you should do all you can to keep the life that you removed from the sea as healthy as possible. When disease is detected, it is important to act quickly—intelligently, but quickly.

## Disease identification

There are three steps to solving a disease problem:

1. Determining that a problem exists
2. Identifying the cause of the disease or source of the distress
3. Successfully curing the fish and eliminating the disease or cause of distress

The first step—determining that a problem exists—may seem very simple: "Gee, when I got up and looked at my tank this morning, half the fish were dead and the rest were covered with little white spots." The real key to disease control, however, is to catch the problem as soon as it appears. The aquarist quoted above is actually saying that the first time in well over a week that he really looked at his fish, he discovered a problem that had existed for some time. Make it a point to observe your fish carefully every day, or at least every two or three days. Make sure they are all present, their behavior is normal, and there are no white spots, fuzzy skin, cloudy eyes, red fins, or open sores.

Atypical behavior is often the best first indicator of disease, so watch for fish that are not feeding or are rubbing against rocks, listlessness, color changes, and other unusual appearance and behavior patterns. These are the things that tell you to look more closely and keep the tank under careful daily observation. The more quickly a disease is identified, the better the chances for treatment and recovery. Once you have determined that a problem exists—that things are not right with one, several, or all of your fish—the first thing to do is to stay calm and analyze the problem.

Don't act until you are reasonably sure of the cause of the distress and have a carefully thought-out plan of treatment. Panicking and treating a tank with a dose of copper, for example, does nothing to cure a bacterial disease and may even make it much worse. Remember that the treatment can sometimes be worse than the disease, so never rush blindly into treatment. Frequently, and especially in a neglected or overlooked situation, treatment will be complicated by the presence of two or more problems. An unchecked *Amyloodinium* infestation, for example, often allows a secondary bacterial infection to get started because of damaged skin and mucus layers and general stress. A fish weakened by harassment from other fish or poor environmental conditions is also a likely victim of bacterial disease. Keep in mind that certain basic problems, such as bad environment and poor diet, can be the underlying cause of continuing disease problems. There are several important things to note and consider as you observe the fish. Think about the following questions and keep the answers in mind as you try to identify the cause of the problem.

1. How long has the tank been in operation?
2. Has biological filtration been fully established?
3. What are current ammonia and nitrite levels?
4. When was the last water change and filter cleaning?
5. How many fish and what species are affected?
6. What is the tank water temperature?
7. What is the pH of the tank water?
8. How long ago was the newest fish introduced?
9. When was the tank last treated with copper, if at all, and is there any free copper left in the tank water?
10. How long has the distressed fish been in the aquarium?

11. What and how often do the fish eat?
12. Any past disease problems? If so, how long ago and due to what cause?
13. Any recent unusual introductions, such as ornaments or chemicals?

Keeping a logbook to document your aquarium activities will easily provide answers to these questions and will greatly increase your skill as a marine aquarist.

After you are sure that a problem is present (and hopefully you catch it so early that you can't be sure without careful observation), it must be identified and a course of treatment determined. It is difficult to prepare a checklist or key to follow in order to arrive at a specific cause of distress, because many problems cause similar symptoms. The troubleshooting chart in Chapter 6 may be helpful in focusing on the possible causes of various problems.

Careful evaluation of the problem and attention to the following chart of ailments (Table 4), and the discussions of symptoms and treatments, should enable you to cope with the majority of disease problems that may develop. There are a great many diseases of marine fish that may appear in an aquarium, far too many to discuss them all in this book. Just a few of them, however, cause most of the problems. These few, the most frequently encountered ailments, are listed in Table 4 in the order of the frequency with which they are likely to occur. This is somewhat subjective, being based solely on my own experience. The only reason for listing them in this order is to suggest to you which ailments seem to be most common. Actually, the ones that most marine aquarists most commonly encounter are the first few on the list, and these are also the ones that respond best to treatment.

Another feature of the list in Table 4 is the checkmark that indicates whether the ailment is usually common to all fish in the tank, fish of one closely related species group, or just one or two individuals in an otherwise healthy tank. Two checks indicate the most common circumstance, even though it may also occur more broadly.

### Diseases, symptoms, and treatments

This part of the disease and distress section provides basic information about the most common ailments, a description of the most obvious

## Table 4  The Dirty Dozen Ailment Chart

| Descriptive names | Scientific name | all fish affected | one species affected | several fish affected |
|---|---|---|---|---|
| Amyloodinium, Oodinium, Coral fish disease, velvet disease, oodiniasis, saltwater ich | Amyloodinium cellatum | ✓✓ | ✓ | |
| Cryptocaryon, white spot disease, cryptocaryonosis, saltwater ich | Cryptocaryon irritans | ✓ | ✓✓ | ✓ |
| Brooklynella, clownfish disease, angelfish disease, skin spot disease | Brooklynella hostilis | | ✓✓ | ✓ |
| Poor diet | Nutritional deficiency | ✓ | ✓✓ | ✓ |
| Poor environment | | ✓✓ | ✓✓ | |
| Toxins present | | | | |
|   Generated within the tank | | ✓ | ✓✓ | |
|   Introduced into the tank | | ✓✓ | ✓ | |
| Harassment | Insufficient living space | | | ✓ |
| Fungus disease | | | | |
|   Internal fungus, Ichthyophonus | Ichthyosporidium hoferi | ✓ | ✓ | ✓✓ |
|   External fungus | Saprolengia | | ✓✓ | ✓ |
| Piscine TB (fish tuberculosis) | Mycobacterium marinum | | ✓ | ✓✓ |
| Black ich, tang turbellarian disease | Turbellarian worms | | ✓✓ | ✓ |
| Bacterial disease | | | | |
|   Vibrio disease, saltwater furunculosis, "wipe-out" | Vibrio anguillarium | ✓ | ✓ | ✓✓ |
|   Fin rot, red spot disease, ulcers, Pseudomonas | Pseudomonas sp. | ✓ | ✓ | ✓✓ |
| Viral disease, cauliflower disease, lymphocystis | Lymphocystivirus | | ✓ | ✓✓ |
| Fish flukes | Benedenia melleni | ✓✓ | | ✓ |
| Fish lice | Argulus sp. | ✓✓ | | ✓ |
| Old age | Passage of time | | | ✓ |

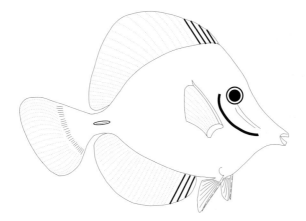

Yellow tang, *Zebrasoma flavescens*

symptoms, and details of one or two treatments that, in my experience, usually effect a cure or solve the problem. The recommended treatments have been developed from a number of sources, including my own experience, and many, if not most, of the suggested chemicals and antibiotics are available in the pharmaceutical section of your favorite aquarium store in a commercial preparation. Be sure to read the labels of commercially sold aquarium pharmaceuticals to know what the active ingredients are and how to use them. First, two very important points:

• Always read the ingredients and directions on aquarium pharmaceuticals and use as directed.
• Always keep aquarium pharmaceuticals out of the reach of small children.

Some medications can also be obtained from drugstores, animal supply (feed) stores, and scientific and chemical supply houses. There are usually a variety of effective treatments for each malady, and I have tried to include the ones that are most effective and most available.

### Amyloodinium

*Amyloodinium ocellatum* is also known as coral fish disease, white spot disease, velvet disease, or, most commonly, saltwater ich. The name "ich," incidently, is an abbreviation for the freshwater parasitic ciliate, *Ichthyophthirius multifiliis*, which is very similar to the saltwater parasitic ciliate, *Cryptocaryon irritans*. The name was originally used by freshwater aquarists and then started being applied to the marine parasite.

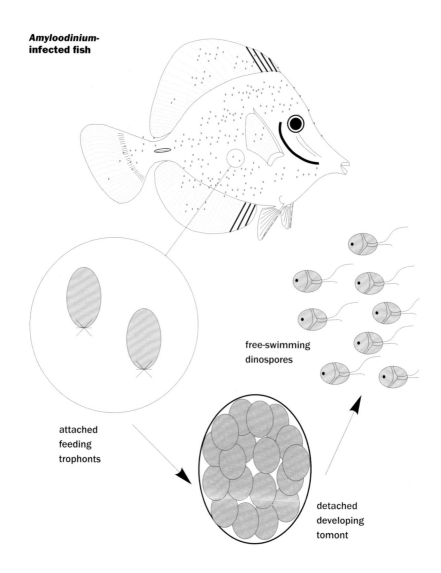

**Amyloodinium-infected fish**

free-swimming dinospores

attached feeding trophonts

detached developing tomont

The secondary names for *Amyloodinium* are, in common usage, sometimes also applied to the protozoan disease *Cryptocaryon*. There is a tendency for the novice aquarist to use the term "ich" for any condition that results in a white spot on a fish. Beware of this confusion, because mistreatment can be the result. *Amyloodinium ocellatum* is a marine one-celled alga, a dinoflagellate, a member of the same group of organisms that causes red tides in marine waters. *Amyloodinium* does not cause red tides, but it is parasitic on fish during one stage of its life cycle, and in a closed or open marine aquarium system, this can be as devastating as a red tide. The reason *Amyloodinium* can be such a scourge is that, unlike some other marine pests, it can readily complete its life cycle in the aquarium, and can quickly reach numbers that overwhelm the captive fishes. In nature, its numbers are kept in check by planktonic predators, dilution by ocean currents, the movement of fish, and the cleaning activity of parasite pickers. It is very rare to encounter a wild fish with a severe case of *Amyloodinium* parasitism, although fishes with a few *Amyloodinium* cysts (trophonts) tucked away here and there are not rare at all.

The life cycle of this parasite begins with the release from a mature cyst (tomont) of up to 250 very tiny, free-swimming algal cells called dinospores. The tomont cyst either is trapped in the mucus of the host fish or has fallen off to the bottom of the tank. Division of the daughter cells within the tomont occurs within three to six days, depending on temperature. The higher the temperature, the more rapidly the dinospores mature and drop off the fish. The free-swimming dinospores must then find a host fish to obtain the nutrients needed for further development; they cannot live long without a host. Some strains may not survive 48 hours, but others may last up to a month. High temperatures also reduce the time that the dinospore can survive in the free-swimming state.

When the dinospore comes in contact with the external tissues of the host, it attaches itself to the fish. Since fish are constantly pumping water through their gills, these soft respiratory tissues are the most frequent sites of infection. After attachment, the dinospore becomes a cyst (more properly termed a trophont) and sends filaments (rhizoids) into the tissues of the host to draw nutrients for its further development. After several days, the filaments are withdrawn and the parasite becomes a tomont (another type of cyst). Cell division occurs and mature dinospores eventually develop and are released, and the life cycle begins all over again.

The number of dinospores produced depends on the nutrition obtained in the trophont stage, temperature, and the genetic characteristics of the strain. The tomont cyst usually falls off the host fish at maturity (if it isn't caught in mucus and cell debris in the gills), and development is completed on the tank bottom or some other resting place. Depending on temperature, the life cycle of *Amyloodinium* is completed in 6 to 12 days. Often, an aquarist not familiar with the life cycle of *Amyloodinium* will notice that the cysts on the fish are gone and assume that the parasitic infection is miraculously cured and all is well. Then, 6 to 9 days later, the cysts reappear on the fish like traffic on the freeway at 8:00 A.M. on Monday morning, and the aquarist is scrambling to save the fish with freshwater baths and copper cures.

One or two, or even half a dozen, of these parasites would have little effect on a fish in the open ocean; however, it is easy to see that in a closed system aquarium this parasite can reach population levels that totally overwhelm any fish that may be present.

### Symptoms

*Amyloodinium* infestations typically begin in the gills. Damage to the delicate gill tissue stimulates the fish to produce excessive mucus, and this condition restricts the exchange of respiratory gases. The result is an increased respiratory pace (rapid gilling), which may be the first outward sign of *Amyloodinium* infection. As the infestation progresses, the cysts become visible on the fin membranes and body surfaces. These cysts are about the same size and color as grains of table salt and, especially on light-colored fish, are difficult to see. They can usually be first observed on the clear fin membranes, and show up best on the body when the fish is viewed lengthwise along its side and light reflects off the numerous tiny cysts.

Infected fish often scratch their sides on the bottom or on rocks, and sometimes shake or shudder while swimming. As the infestation progresses, colors fade, a powdery or dusty appearance becomes very noticeable as the cysts proliferate, and secondary bacterial infections often develop. Respiration is now very rapid, and the fish begins to lie on its side on the bottom of the tank. It is usually too late at this point to save that particular fish, but some of its less infected tankmates may pull through if treatment is quickly provided. The time period between the first observation of rapid respiration and terminal infestation may be as short as 3 to 4 days or may be two weeks or more, depending on temperature, tank population, type and efficiency of filtration, and the resistance of individual fish to this parasite.

### Treatment

A successful treatment for *Amyloodinium* consists of treating both the infected fish and the infected tank. If the parasite is not eradicated from the tank, reinfection will occur no matter how effectively the fish have been treated. *Amyloodinium* can be treated successfully with formalin, copper, hydrogen peroxide, quinacrine, malachite green, and a number of other compounds. The most common treatment used in large and small marine systems is copper in the form of cupric sulphate complexed with citric acid or chelated with EDTA. A solution of just copper sulphate quickly precipitates out of saltwater; copper sulphate complexed with citric acid stays in solution much longer (at least a few days); and copper sulphate chelated with EDTA remains in a saltwater solution for considerably longer, but is less toxic to the parasite, and most chelated copper medications require treatment at higher apparent copper levels.

The most effective, no-nonsense treatment for *Amyloodinium* is as follows.

**The freshwater bath:** Prepare a freshwater bath of 1 to 3 gallons, depending on the number of fish to be treated. Dechlorinate the tap water if necessary by aerating it for several hours, or add one small crystal of sodium thiosulfate or one drop of a weak solution of sodium thiosulfate per gallon. (*Note:* If the freshwater contains chloramine and not just chlorine, it may not be very easy to remove the chloramine. Chapter 2 has more information on removing chloramine from freshwater.) The pH of the freshwater should not be more than 0.5 points off that of the tank water. Add baking soda (start with 1 tsp. per gallon of freshwater) or a commercial buffer if the pH is too low. Remove all the fish from the infected tank and give them a one- to two-minute bath in the bucket of freshwater. The fish can easily withstand the abrupt change in external osmotic pressure, but the parasites have no protection (unless they are deeply embedded in mucus) and quickly swell and burst. Thus the freshwater bath efficiently frees the fish of most parasites, as well as their potential offspring.

However, I have learned that some of the cysts can still pose a threat. I always thought that the cysts on the fish burst after the fish was placed in a freshwater bath, because I had read that this was so in various reference books; and when affected fish were removed from a freshwater bath, it was obvious that the cysts were gone and the tissues around the cyst area were ragged, giving the appearance of a cyst that had burst.

Then one time we had some half-inch clownfish that were badly infected with *Amyloodinium* cysts. Since they were such small fish, I gave them a freshwater bath in a small fingerbowl and watched the process under the dissecting microscope. Sure enough, the cysts disappeared and there were little ragged spots on the tiny clowns where the cysts used to be. Then I noticed a lot of little white specks scattered over the bottom of the fingerbowl. I removed the clownfish and kept the specks in the fingerbowl under observation for several hours. No change was noted. Then I sucked up some of the specks in an eyedropper and placed them in a fingerbowl of saltwater. I left the fingerbowl of saltwater on the table and observed it once in a while over the next few days. After a day or two, most of the little white specks were gone and there were numerous tiny dinospores swimming about in the saltwater in the fingerbowl.

**DURABLE CYSTS:**

Unlike the mature dinospores, *Amyloodinium* cysts do not burst in freshwater. Always discard water used in baths.

❖

So a freshwater bath does not burst all the cysts, but only makes them fall off the fish. They are then able to complete development if they get back into saltwater, and continue the life cycle if they can find a host. Never put the freshwater from the bath into a marine tank!

After the freshwater bath, the fish are placed in a treatment tank with only an airstone for aeration and water circulation, and some rocks or flower pots for fish shelters. A 5- to 10-gallon tank is a good size unless a large number of fish need treatment. Avoid placing coral, limestone, and other calcareous materials in the treatment tank, since they tend to remove copper from the treatment water. Treatment for fish infected with *Amyloodinium* consists of a 3-week exposure to a copper level of 0.2 to 0.3 ppm (parts per million) to destroy all dinospores that have been liberated before they can encyst on a fish, and, if the fish are held in a separate treatment tank, exposure to an antibiotic (neomycin, erythromycin, tetracycline, or Furanace) may help to control secondary bacterial infections. Refer to the bacterial disease treatment section for dosage or follow the instructions that come with a commercial antibiotic treatment for marine fish. If a copper level of 0.15 to 0.2 ppm can be maintained for three weeks, this is adequate to destroy *Amyloodinium* dinospores. (Some scientific studies show that dinospores are destroyed by copper and tomonts are not, and other studies demonstrate the opposite result.) However, 0.15 ppm is the minimum effective dose, and it may not be adequate under normal aquarium conditions where proper levels of copper are difficult to maintain. Most fish are not harmed by levels up to 0.3 ppm, thus concentrations slightly higher than 0.15 (0.2–0.25 ppm) provide a more sure cure. That way, even if a slight drop in concentration occurs, the treatment will still be effective.

Treatment of the fish is only half the cure. The *Amyloodinium* cysts resting on the bottom of the tank or in the filters must also be eliminated. There are two ways to do this, both effective, and the best way for you depends on your own attitudes and methods. Time and temperature can be used together very effectively. The *Amyloodinium* life cycle, like that of all organisms with no internal temperature control, progresses faster at high temperatures because the chemical reactions of life take place more quickly. As mentioned above, *Amyloodinium* requires a host fish to survive and generally, the free-living dinospore stage survives for only a few days without one. (Some strains, however, can survive 15 to 30 days before finding a host.) Therefore, the life cycle of the parasite can be broken if the fish hosts are removed from the system and not returned until after all the dinospores have hatched and died for want of a host. The process can be speeded up by increasing the temperature to 85°F, perhaps even to 90°F. All *Amyloodinium* cysts and dinospores can be eliminated from an aquarium in two weeks (three is almost a sure thing) if the fish hosts are removed and temperature is elevated—and if the fish do not carry the parasite back with them when they are returned to the tank. The bottom substrate should be thoroughly cleaned and all detritus removed at the start of the treatment to remove any *Amyloodinium* cysts that may remain in the bottom debris. The bare bottom of any tank with an external filter should be siphoned clean.

**Treatment in reef systems:** *Amyloodinium* is usually not as big a problem in reef tanks as it is in fish tanks. This is not to say that this parasite does not occur in reef tanks. On the contrary, it can be a major problem in some coral/fish reef tanks when fish sensitive to the parasite are in the tank and can't be removed without pulling out every piece of rock and coral, which is seldom a worthwhile endeavor. The special characteristics of a reef tank—super filtration, strong water movement, and the presence of lots of filter feeders—tend to keep parasite populations in check and even occasionally seem to eliminate them. Most often, however, the parasite remains in the system at a low level of infection, and may someday become a serious problem if other fish are added to the tank. The only way to clear a reef tank of *Amyloodinium*, aside from removing all corals and other invertebrates and treating with copper, is to keep the tank completely fish-free for at least a month, preferably two. The fish must be captured and removed or the parasite will probably find a host and survive at low levels. Even a resistant fish may harbor a few cysts and keep the parasite viable. If the fish cannot be captured and removed, the aquarist must either wait for the fish to succumb to the parasite, keep only fish that are resistant, or live with an occasional outbreak of *Amyloodinium*. Note that copper treatments are absolutely deadly to most invertebrates kept in a reef aquarium.

**Copper treatment:** If you do choose to treat the tank with copper, the most effective method is to remove any invertebrates and all calcareous objects. Sometimes it is not possible to remove all calcareous material, especially when the sand bed or coral gravel substrate is composed of a calcareous media. If an undergravel filter is in use, it should be cleaned very well before treatment, to remove detritus and some, hopefully most, of the free *Amyloodinium* cysts (tomonts). The tank can be treated with or without removing the fish to a treatment tank. If no other tank is available, give the fish a freshwater bath to remove the cysts (trophonts) that are currently on the fish, and replace the fish in the tank. Treat the tank with a 0.3 ppm dose. (If all fish and invertebrates have been removed from the tank, the initial treatment can be as high as 0.6.) Test the copper level the next day (if the tank has never been treated with copper and if calcareous material is present, the copper level may have dropped to almost zero) and elevate the dose back to 0.25. Wait two days, test the copper level again, and bring it up to 0.20 if necessary.

Thereafter, test copper levels every other day and maintain the dose at about 0.2 for two to three weeks. The fish may be replaced in the tank after two to three days if necessary, since the copper levels that are maintained in the tank water will prevent reinfection. Be sure to test the copper level before replacing the fish in the tank, especially if an elevated copper dose was added to the fish-free tank. Adjust the copper level to 0.2, or close to this, when the fish are replaced in the tank. If copper levels are too high, lower the concentration with water change or activated carbon filtration.

The copper concentrations must not be allowed to fall below 0.15 during the treatment period. After treatment, free copper in the tank water can be removed with activated carbon filtration, and the invertebrates replaced after copper levels fall to zero.

Once a tank is treated with copper there will always be some precipitated copper in the tank, and the water should always be tested before retreatment with copper, especially if species sensitive to copper are kept. Symptoms of copper poisoning in marine fish are slow respiration and listlessness.

For the more casual aquarist, there are shortcuts for this treatment method that can be effective, although less precise and far more dangerous to the fish. The simplest method is to just dose the tank with a double dose of copper treatment at the first sign of *Amyloodinium* (hopefully winding up with a 0.3 ppm level). Add a second single dose two days later and another single dose three days later, and keep your fingers crossed in hopes that this will take care of the problem. It may, and then again it may not. The tank can be retreated whenever *Amyloodinium* is observed, for the presence of *Amyloodinium* is a good sign that copper levels are below 0.05 ppm. A freshwater bath for those fish most heavily infested will also be helpful. They can be returned to the tank immediately if the tank has been treated with copper. Such a shortcut is not good treatment technique, but it's better than none as long as copper levels do not rise above 0.4 ppm—and even this may be too high for some sensitive fish species.

**Now a word or two about copper:** Copper is not a cure-all. In fact, the primary, almost only use of copper in the marine aquarium is to medicate for *Amyloodinium* infestations. This parasite is so common that without judicious use of copper treatments, collecting, shipping, stocking, and keeping marine fish would be extremely difficult. There are, however, several problems inherent in the use of copper. First of all, it is a poison to fish as well as to *Amyloodinium*. The only reason we can use it is because it is slightly less toxic to fish than to dinoflagellates, and by carefully regulating the dose, we can wipe out the *Amyloodinium* and not injure the fish. The second problem is that it is difficult to maintain the proper level of free copper in an established marine aquarium. Many organisms, including bacteria and algae, and also detritus and calcareous material, remove copper from the water and can rapidly reduce its concentration below the effective level. However, repeated applications may quickly push the concentration into the toxic zone (0.5 ppm and up) for fish.

The third difficulty is that even low levels of copper are quite toxic

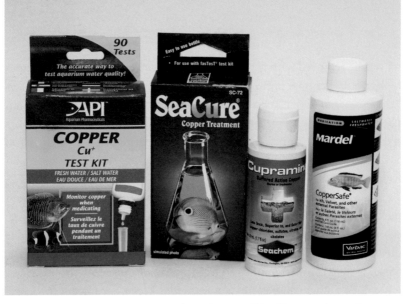

Copper-based medications are commonly used to treat fish with external parasites.

to many invertebrates, such as anemones and corals, and should never be used when these animals are in the tank. There is also evidence that copper treatment inhibits biological filtration to some extent, putting the biological filter at risk if high copper treatment levels are used. Note, too, that the presence of heavy metals, especially copper, contributes to the growth and development of *Vibrio* bacteria. Thus, treatment with copper may cause or contribute to vibriosis, a virulent bacterial infection! So try to avoid the use of copper in the main tank by using an effective quarantine system (Chapter 8), and before you use copper, be sure that you have an *Amyloodinium* or ciliate problem and not a bacterial infection.

**Copper treatment preparation:** Proper copper levels are relatively easy to maintain in a bare treatment tank if the copper solution is correctly prepared. There are many copper preparations available on the market today and most are compounded to deliver a 0.15 ppm concentration at a dose of one drop per gallon, but some deliver 0.25 ppm at the same dosage. It's important to know what concentration of copper is programmed to end up in the tank with a commercial preparation. The best way to find this out is to put a drop into a gallon of saltwater or 10 drops into 10 gallons and test the resulting concentration with a copper test kit. The copper in most commercial preparations is complexed, usually with an acid, to keep the copper in solution as long as possible. Other medications such as formalin are frequently added.

Unfortunately, treating a marine aquarium with copper is not a simple, straightforward operation. Even if you know precisely what concentration of copper the medication is designed to deliver, the tank may not be at all cooperative. Each aquarium setup has a certain capacity to pull free copper from the water. Old tanks with a lot of detritus and calcareous material and infrequent past copper treatments can pull out much more copper than clean tanks with silica sand filters. It's possible to treat a tank with a full dose of copper, only to have copper levels fall to almost zero in the space of a few hours. This is why it's important to test copper levels in the tank to make sure that the proper treatment level is maintained.

If you've a mind to, you can make up your own copper treatment solution. I'll give two formulas below, the first for those with access to a laboratory type gram scale and metric volume measurements and the second for those with only kitchen equipment and no other alternatives.

1. Dissolve 2.23 grams of copper sulphate (pentahydrate) and 1.5 grams of citric acid in 1 liter of freshwater to prepare the stock solution. Treatment with this stock solution at 1 milliliter per gallon of tank water results in a maximum concentration of 0.15 ppm. If the amounts of copper sulphate and citric acid are doubled, the resulting solution will produce a concentration of 0.3 ppm at a dose of 1 ml per gallon.

2. If you are really stuck and can't get a commercial preparation or find someone to weigh out the chemicals for you on a gram scale, and don't understand all this metric stuff anyway, you can still prepare a stock solution. Copper sulphate and citric acid can usually be purchased at a drugstore or a plant nursery. The copper sulphate should be in the form of small blue crystals (it's sometimes called bluestone) about 1/16–1/8 inch (1–3 mm) long. Dissolve 1 level teaspoon of copper sulphate and 1 rounded half teaspoon of citric acid in 3 liters of freshwater. If you can't measure out 3 liters (100 ounces), use 3 quarts plus 4 ounces. A 1-gallon jug makes a good mixing and storage container for this stock solution. One milliliter (ml) of this stock solution per gallon of tank water should deliver about 0.3 ppm copper. There are about 5 ml per teaspoon (20–25 drops per ml), so 1 teaspoon of this solution for every 10 gallons of tank water will produce about a 0.15 ppm concentration. Note that this method of preparation is quite inaccurate, and there is a substantial risk of over- or under-treatment, especially if you do not test the aquarium water for copper concentration.

When adding any medication to your tank that calls for a certain dose per gallon, remember that there is more than just water in your tank. Any rock, sand, coral skeletons, or other decorations, as well as the fish, take up space, reducing the total volume of water. To determine how many gallons of water there are in the tank, multiply the length times the width times the height of water, all in inches, and divide the product by 231. This will give you the number of gallons that space will hold. Then deduct 10% or more, depending on the individual tank, to allow for the volume of the fish, the filter, and the decorations.

### Cryptocaryon (White Spot Disease)

Cryptocaryosis is also known as cryptocaryonosis, saltwater ich, and, most commonly, White Spot Disease. It is caused by the ciliate *Cryptocaryon irritans*. Inexperienced aquarists frequently confuse *Cryptocaryon* and *Amyloodinium*. Although the two diseases are quite different, they do have some similarities. The ciliate *Ichthyophthirius multifiliis* causes the fearsome "ich" that is the freshwater counterpart of *Cryptocaryon irritans*. Like *Amyloodinium*, *Cryptocaryon* can complete its life cycle in a closed system aquarium and also has the capacity to overwhelm and destroy captive fish.

The tomite is the motile, infective stage of the life cycle. They are small, ciliated protozoans about 50 microns long, and their function is to find a host fish within a day or two or die in the attempt. Once they attach to the gill or body of a host, they develop into the second stage, the parasitic trophont. This stage burrows into the host and feeds on the host's tissues, often causing extensive damage. The well-fed trophont eventually stops feeding and encysts, becoming the outwardly inactive tomont stage. This final stage may stay trapped in the mucus of the fish or may fall off and drift to the bottom. Within 6 to 10 days, about 200 new tomites may emerge from the tomont and seek another host fish to begin the cycle all over again.

Despite similarities in their life cycles, it has been my experience that *Cryptocaryon* does not overwhelm aquariums as rapidly as *Amyloodinium* does. Perhaps fish have a greater natural resistance to *Cryptocaryon*, although the individual trophonts of *Cryptocaryon* seem to inflict greater damage than single *Amyloodinium* dinospores do. However, whenever any of your fishes displays white spots of any kind, it is essential that you promptly investigate and diagnose the condition.

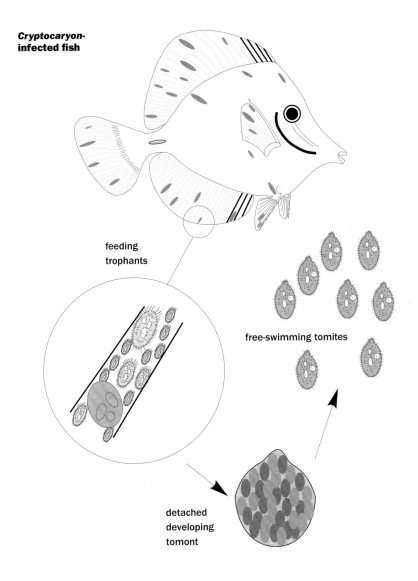

**Cryptocaryon-infected fish**

feeding trophants

free-swimming tomites

detached developing tomont

### Symptoms

Although *Cryptocaryon* frequently infects the gills and causes respiratory distress, the first sign of the disease is usually several to a dozen white spots on the body and fins of the host fish. These spots are about the size of a pinhead and look very much like a small single pimple. The fish do not have the "dusted" or "salted" appearance that characterizes a severe case of

*Amyloodinium*, unless, of course, both parasites are present. These discrete white pustules become more numerous as the disease progresses. The gills become clogged with tomonts, mucus, and tissue debris. Bacterial infections invade the lesions caused by the trophonts, and the fish declines rapidly. Scratching on the bottom or on rocks is a common symptom. Loss of color also occurs in patches or blotches as the erosion of the trophonts destroys pigment cells.

### Treatment

As with *Amyloodinium*, the fish and the tank must be successfully treated to eliminate *Cryptocaryon* infestation. There are several methods of treatment that generally give good results. Unfortunately, copper is not as effective against *Cryptocaryon* and other ciliates as it is for *Amyloodinium*, although it does attack the free-swimming tomite stage and is therefore useful, but other medications are necessary. The first step in treatment is a freshwater bath, which will explode all trophonts and tomonts on the surface of the fish. This is not as effective as it is with *Amyloodinium* because *Cryptocaryon* burrows deeply and is protected by mucus and tissue.

**Formalin treatment:** The traditional treatment for *Cryptocaryon* consists of a 1-hour formalin bath (½ hour for sensitive species) every other day for a total of three baths, and a copper treatment for the aquarium (as described in the *Amyloodinium* section). In this case, the fish can be returned to the aquarium after each bath, as it is also under treatment. If you do not wish to treat the tank with copper and plan to maintain the fish in a separate treatment tank with a light (0.15 to 0.2 ppm) copper treatment, the tank can be cleansed of *Cryptocaryon* with a time-temperature treatment of 10 days at 85°F. This period allows four to six days for all tomonts to release their tomites, and at least three days for all tomites to die for want of a fish host. Another way to break the life cycle of *Cryptocaryon* is to keep the fish under treatment in a small, treated tank and then remove the fish and clean and sterilize the tank, and totally change water every three days. This completely breaks the life cycle of the parasite and prevents reinfection.

**The formalin bath:** Prepare the formalin bath by adding 1 ml of formalin for each gallon of saltwater in the bath (1 teaspoon to 5 gallons). Aerate this preparation very actively, because formalin tends to reduce oxygen saturation, and carefully time the hour of treatment. If signs of shock appear, terminate the bath immediately. Formalin is a commercial preparation of a 37% solution of formaldehyde gas. It is commonly available at drugstores and janitorial supply houses. Full-strength formalin is potent stuff, so don't inhale it or get it in your eyes or on your skin. Formalin works as a preservative (and poison) by denaturing protein. Proteins, as you know, are the basic building blocks of life, and formalin, figuratively speaking, rushes in and changes the arrangements of the blocks and binds them permanently together so that the chemical reactions of life cannot take place. At very low exposure levels, formalin destroys the parasites without affecting the fish. It also does the same thing to most bacteria, thus a good dose

> **FORMALIN USE:**
> Although effective in treating parasites and infections, formalin will kill a biological filter and must only be used in a dip or hospital tank.
>
> ❖

can wreak havoc with a biological filter. Formalin breaks down over a period of weeks in solution, so it stays active for some time. It is a useful treatment tool for *Cryptocaryon, Amyloodinium,* external fungus, external bacteria, fish flukes, and fish lice, but keep effective doses in a separate treatment tank or you may pickle organisms you don't want pickled.

I think the best treatment for cryptocaryosis, in terms of effectiveness and ease of use for most marine aquarists, consists of first removing the fish to a treatment tank. The main tank can then be treated with copper or left without fish for 10 to 15 days. If the fish are set up in a treatment tank, then the treatment tank should carry a 0.15 to 0.2 copper level. The fish should be given a 1-minute freshwater bath with 1 ml of formalin per gallon added to the bath water. Transfer the fish to a standard 30-minute to 1-hour saltwater formalin bath and then return them to the treatment tank. The bath process can be repeated after three days, especially if any recurrence of *Cryptocaryon* is noticed on the fish. After two weeks under copper treatment, the *Cryptocaryon* infestation should be cured.

**Quinacrine treatment:** A treatment developed by Dr. Edward Kingsford works well on *Cryptocaryon.* This treatment uses the antimalarial drug, quinacrine hydrochloride (atabrine hydrochloride), at a dosage of 4 to 6 milligrams per gallon applied directly to the infected tank. Note: this drug is no longer available and aquarists will probably not be able to find it on any market. I have retained this section, however, since some

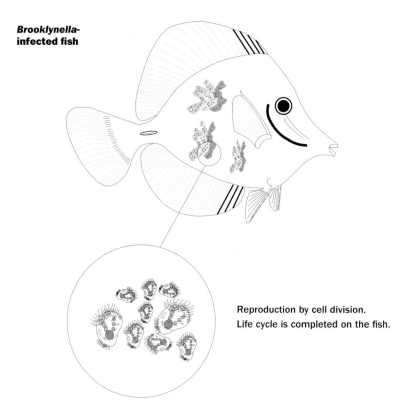

**Brooklynella-infected fish**

Reproduction by cell division.
Life cycle is completed on the fish.

aquarists may wish to use it if it becomes available once again. Other antimalarial drugs, i.e., quinine hydrochloridide and quinine sulfate, may also be effective against *Cryptocaryon* at dosages of 1 gm per 100 liters of water. Antimalarial drugs do not affect the biological filter, but are active against protozoans. They may also affect anemones and corals, so remove these animals from the tank before treatment. Carbon filtration removes quinacrine, so these filters should be taken off and flushed with fresh water to remove any stray cysts before reuse.

The treatment requires two doses of 4 to 6 milligrams of quinacrine hydrochloride, spaced 24 hours apart, applied to the infected tank. Light levels should be reduced during treatment, so the tank lights should not be turned on. After 10 days, residual quinacrine can be removed by activated carbon filtration. A water change after treatment is also a good idea. This medication leaves a yellow stain in the tissues of fish and invertebrates, which gradually disappears.

**Malachite green treatment:** Another effective treatment for *Cryptocaryon* and other ciliates is a 5-day exposure to malachite green. One or two drops per gallon of a 1% solution makes up the treatment bath. After four to five days in a treatment tank, the White Spot Disease should be gone.

### *Brooklynella* (Clownfish Disease)

*Cryptocaryon irritans* is not the only ciliate parasite that plagues marine fish. It is the most common, but there are others just as nasty. *Brooklynella hostilis* is known for its occurrence on clownfish and is often called Clownfish Disease.

Other species of ciliates parasitic on marine fish are *Uronema marinum*, *Miamiensis avidus*, and *Caliperia* sp. The diseases caused by these and possibly other species of ciliates differ in expression and virulence depending on the species under attack, the condition of the host, and environmental conditions.

Small French and Grey Angelfish from Florida are often infected during the warm summer months, and other species, such as the Cuban Hogfish may also develop ciliate infections. The stress of capture, handling, and closed systems, as well as exposing them to high concentrations of these parasites in poorly kept systems, may reduce the resistance of the fish to the ciliate attack, and cause a small occurrence that might well be shrugged off in the wild but could bloom and kill the fish in captivity.

#### Symptoms

At first the fish has small, whitish spots with indistinct borders on its sides and sometimes on the fins. These small whitish areas begin to enlarge, and soon mucus and skin begin to slough off and the affected areas become red and raw with loose scales. In some host species, the ciliates may also invade the internal organs and blood system of the host. The disease advances rapidly and the fish usually dies within a few days. Small fish suffer the most from the effects of this parasite.

#### Treatment

As with *Cryptocaryon*, copper treatment is ineffective without co-treatment with formalin, quinacrine, or malachite green. The formalin treatment recommended above for *Cryptocaryon* is probably the best that a marine hobbyist can do to cure other ciliate infections as well.

**Nutritional deficiency**
(starvation)

## Poor diet/starvation

A diet that provides all the essential nutrients is necessary to keep marine fish in good health over a long period of time. Fish suffering from malnutrition become susceptible to many other maladies, and although death may be caused by a specific disease, the underlying problem is a fish weakened by malnutrition. Except for total starvation, nutritional deficiencies do not occur quickly. They are the result of habitual poor feeding practices and, unfortunately, some fishkeepers do not expend the little bit of extra effort that would keep their fish well fed. Underfeeding is a common problem. Most fish need to be fed at least once a day; twice is better. Reef tanks offer constant grazing to smaller fishes, but these, too, need daily feedings.

In nature, many fish, particularly plankton pickers and sponge- and algae-browsers, feed almost constantly during their active hours. In an aquarium, they can do very well on two or three feedings per day, if the food provides their basic nutritional needs. Underfeeding becomes a problem when no one feeds the fish for days at a time and then, after a big argument about who's supposed to feed the fish, someone sprinkles a little dry flake food in the tank and then lets it go for another few days. Fish don't have to eat a lot to be healthy, but they do need the right foods on a consistent schedule.

Overfeeding is bad for the fish and bad for the tank, especially consistently overfeeding dry or frozen foods. Some aquarists cannot walk past a fish tank without feeding the fish a little sprinkle of food. This may make the fish-feeder feel good, but it quickly overloads the fish and the tank. Small fish that consume too much flake food too often have a tendency to bloat after feeding and become so buoyant that they have difficulty staying near the bottom. Feeding the same food week after week without change promotes underfeeding for those fish that don't or can't eat well on the offered fare, and nutritional deficiencies for fish that require a wide range of nutrients. Many species require vegetable matter, preferably algae, in the diet to provide roughage and the proper balance of nutrients. One condition that often plagues marine fish is the fatty degeneration of the liver. Feeding most marine fish a diet high in animal fats gradually causes fat to infiltrate the liver, and that organ then declines and eventually stops working. Do not feed freshwater feeder fish or goldfish to marine predators, and ignore any old aquarium tomes advocating the feeding of beef heart and other terrestrial proteins. By the same token, rich marine foods like squid should not be fed too frequently.

When fatty liver degeneration occurs, the fish is very susceptible to stress, often going into complete shock when disturbed or netted from the aquarium. Sometimes a fish in deep shock will not recover and will die from the shock, but often it gradually recovers consciousness. Fatty liver degeneration may be reversible, but I have not successfully restored a fish that suffered from the obvious symptoms of this condition. See the section on foods and feeding in Chapter 10 for a positive approach to marine fish feeding practices.

### Symptoms

The symptoms of malnutrition are very much like, and often the same as, the symptoms of a variety of diseases. However, some of the things to watch for that may be attributable to dietary deficiencies are a tendency to bloat after feeding, a sunken stomach, overall thinness (especially behind the head under the dorsal fin), fading colors, loss of color in blotchy areas, erosion of the skin behind the head (especially angelfish), and general listlessness. A large fish can live a long time without feeding. If the proper food is not available, or if another condition prevents the fish from feeding, it will slowly starve. When this happens, the abdomen of the fish slowly shrinks upward toward the spine, giving the lower profile of the fish a decidedly concave appearance. The musculature on the sides behind the head also wastes away and the fish becomes quite thin. A fish in this condition is not feeding, or is feeding very little, and most probably will not survive.

### Treatment

Provide a good, varied diet that includes something for all the various types of fish in the tank. One would not feed a cow and a tiger the same diet and expect both to survive, so don't feed a tang and a grouper the same food either. Refer to the foods and feeding section (Chapter 10). Several brands and formulas of frozen, complete diets for marine fish are now available, and some even include stabilized vitamin C in the preparations.

### Head and lateral line erosion (HLLE)

This is a condition that often plagues fish, particularly tangs and angelfish, in marine systems. It also occurs on butterflyfish, groupers, damsels, and other species. The fish appear to be in good health in terms of body shape, feeding behavior, and general tank deportment, but color is often faded or washed out, and the tiny pores that make up the lateral line sensory system and extend along the side of the body and wind around the face and eyes of the fish are enlarged, and external layers of the skin in the vicinity of these pores seem to erode. Large areas of the face and head, particularly about the eyes, are often affected and lose pigment. Eventually, if the condition is not reversed, the fish waste away and become susceptible to various diseases. (This condition is sometimes confused with Hole in the Head Disease, which is also disfiguring but is suspected to be caused by *Hexamita* or *Spironucleus* flagellates. This disease is characterized by pitting of the forehead area and around the eyes. It is usually treated with metronidazole.)

One simple, single specific cause for this condition has never been demonstrated; however, some evidence implicates poor diet—a deficiency of vitamin C (ascorbic acid). Anecdotally, a number of aquarists report that feeding foods rich in stabilized vitamin C seems to cure, or at least improve the condition of, affected fish. George Blasiola found that the addition of vitamin C in the diet improved this condition in a study done with one species of surgeonfish, the Palette Tang. Access to natural algae is also reported to be beneficial. Improvement in lighting or exposure to natural sunlight is also reported to improve this condition, and

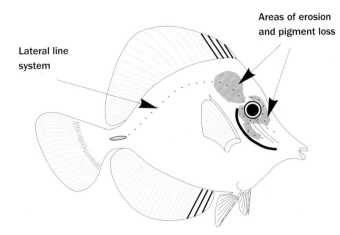

**Head and lateral line erosion (HLLE)**

even elimination of stray electrical charges in the system by grounding the saltwater with a stainless steel probe attached to a good ground is said to have a beneficial effect. Finally, some aquarists have come to suspect the fine dust particles from activated carbon as a possible cause. Jay Hemdal reported that afflicted fish sometimes improved when moved to clean water in systems without activated carbon. One theory is that the dust particles may lodge in tiny pores in the victims' skin. Systems with very efficient protein skimming, which can remove carbon particles, seemed to lower the incidence of HLLE. At this time the best treatment seems to be to improve water quality or move the fish to a very clean system, be sure not to use dusty activated carbon, keep a good skimmer running, and feed a varied diet with plenty of vegetable matter (especially marine algae and *Spirulina*) or that contains stabilized vitamin C.

### Poor environment

The aquarium environment has been thoroughly discussed in other areas of the book, and obviously, a bad environment can have detrimental effects on the fish. Some of the most common problems are a lack of the proper kind and intensity of light, inadequate circulation through the biological filter, high organic load (yellow water) and/or high $CO_2$ levels and subsequent drop in pH, and high or low temperatures. Some of these maladjustments of the aquarium environment can cause ammonia and/

or nitrite toxicity (discussed under toxins), but more often they lead to general debility and reduce the lifespan of the fish.

### Symptoms

Fish subjected to a poor environment show a fading of color, often due to a whitish film over the body (which may be a touch of external fungus or excess mucus production or both); are very susceptible to bacterial infections; lack a strong interest in feeding; and may stay in one small area of the aquarium with little ranging movement.

### Treatment

Check water chemistry, the filtration system, and physical factors (light, temperature, water flow, etc.) to make sure that all is well. If you still can't identify the cause of the problem, and if no disease is evident, make a 50% water change, clean detritus from the bottom substrate and filters, change or add fresh activated carbon, and watch the fish carefully for either improvement or the indications of a disease.

## Toxins

Fish toxins get into aquariums in one of two ways: they develop within a tank through natural biological processes, or they are introduced from an external source. Since these are very different in cause and effect, they will be discussed separately.

### Internally generated toxins

A poor environment can cause toxins such as ammonia, nitrite, phenol, cresol, hydrogen sulfide, indole, and skatol to develop in the tank. The latter three are the result of anaerobic (oxygen-lacking) bacterial processes and are very odorous. They develop only when a dirty outside filter has been turned off for several days and then turned on without cleaning or flushing, or when an undergravel biological filter is so clogged that aerated water does not circulate through all or part of it. Both conditions show severe neglect by the aquarist. A good aquarist usually discovers the problem when toxin levels are still very low and contribute only to a generalized poor aquarium environment, as discussed previously. However, sometimes things degrade quickly and toxins reach a level where they cause severe distress, and even death, before the aquarist is aware of their presence.

The average marine aquarist may encounter two problems caused by internally generated toxins. These are ammonia and/or nitrite poisoning ("new tank syndrome") and a sudden, inexplicable loss of almost all the fish in a healthy looking tank within 12 to 24 hours ("wipe out" or "whole tank wipe out"). "Wipe out" or "toxic tank syndrome" is not a particularly uncommon occurrence, but it is very misunderstood, and the effects are usually attributed to a disease. The syndrome most often occurs in tanks heavily populated with young fish of a single species, although it can occur in any type of closed marine system. The water is often very clear and uncolored, with no trace of ammonia or nitrite, and it usually has an acceptable pH when the syndrome occurs. Many aquarists believe that efficient protein skimming is an effective way to prevent wipe-out syndrome.

My experimentation has shown that a virulent toxin is released from the biological filter and is often species-specific, or may be more toxic to certain species than to others, especially when numerous young fish of one species are present. Possibly a substance released from the fish stimulates the filter bacteria (not necessarily nitrifying bacteria) to produce a toxic substance; or perhaps a new type of toxin-producing bacteria is stimulated into a population bloom. Fish showing early symptoms of toxic tank syndrome that are removed and placed in a totally different system almost invariably recover, and those left in the affected system almost inevitably die. Laboratory investigations show that no ammonia/nitrite levels or *Amyloodinium* are present. Total water changes slow, but do not stop, the syndrome.

**VIBRIO SUSPICIONS:**
Mysterious whole-tank fish wipeouts or "toxic tank syndrome" may be traced to toxins released by *Vibrio* bacteria.

❖

Although I knew that tanks of fish were mysteriously "wiped out" from time to time, it was always easy to put the blame on many possibilities such as tobacco, insecticide, *Amyloodinium*, bacterial disease, or anything else that could cause such mortality. The specific nature and apparent source of the toxic tank syndrome was not apparent to me until I began to work with large numbers of young, tank-reared fish in closed systems. Extensive work with very large numbers of small fish in small, closed systems enabled me to identify the symptoms of this syndrome and subsequently trace the cause to a toxin released from the biological filter. It is possible that this toxin can be removed by chemical filtration; however, very little is known about it, and much additional research needs to be done. I do have some strong suspicions.

Bacteria in the genus *Vibrio*, possibly the species *V. anguillarum*, have many characteristics that make them a prime candidate as the cause of this syndrome. They proliferate rapidly, displace other species of bacteria, attack fish externally and internally, and produce a toxin that is quickly lethal to fish whether or not the live bacteria are actually present. My best guess is that toxic tank syndrome is caused by a toxin released by large populations (a bloom) of *Vibrio* bacteria residing in the biological filter, and quite possibly on the external surfaces of the fish themselves.

**RAPID RESPONSE:**
Be ready to act immediately if toxic-tank syndrome or ammonia poisoning is suspected. Fish deaths can come in just six hours.

♣

Reducing the amount of toxin currently present and in production by moving the fish to a new system, changing water, cleaning the biofilter, and treating the fish with an antibiotic should reduce the toxic effect on the fish and relieve the symptoms. Leaving a large population of *Vibrio* bacteria in the system, however, probably just prolongs the bloom and postpones the development of lethal levels of toxin. The best treatment, especially in the case of large numbers of small fish of the same species, remains a transfer to a new, unaffected system. Modern, well-maintained systems filtered with protein skimmers, ozone reactors, trickle filters, and activated carbon and resins limit the accumulation of detritus and dissolved organics, and apparently control bacterial blooms. Thus, a marine fish breeder with a modern closed system may not have as great a problem with toxic tank syndrome as we did in the past.

### Symptoms

Ammonia/nitrite poisoning leads rapidly into bacterial disease because of the impaired functioning of the kidneys and liver. Excessive mucus is also produced in the gills and rapid respiration is one of the first signs of ammonia/nitrite toxicity. (If a water test shows no ammonia or nitrite, suspect *Amyloodinium*.) The fish may also keep their mouths open and move restlessly about the tank. In extreme cases, movement is rapid and the fish may try to jump from the tank; eventually colors fade, eyes get dull, and the fish goes into shock and dies.

The "toxic tank syndrome" progresses very rapidly. As little as six hours may pass between onset and death, but usually 24 to 30 hours pass before it's all over. Only the most virulent of bacterial diseases or severe poisoning destroys fish this rapidly. Only a few fish out of several hundred survive this syndrome.

The early symptoms are very rapid, shallow respiration and shimmy-like swimming movements that keep the fish active, but do not move them about the tank. There also seems to be tremendous weight loss, especially in small fish, which gives them an emaciated appearance over-night. Possibly the biological mechanisms that maintain osmotic barriers break down and the fish lose body fluids to the surrounding saltwater. Young fish also tend to group in schools facing the water flow and shim-my and shake almost in formation. Unless removed from the system, the fish soon lie on the bottom and die.

### Treatment

Note that a high pH, 8.3 to 8.5, increases the toxicity of ammonia. If your fish show signs of ammonia poisoning and the pH is high for some reason, lowering the pH will bring the fish some relief. This would be a rather unusual occurrence, however, for pH in a marine aquarium rarely rises above 8.0 to 8.2 unless there is a great deal of algal growth, and if there is, the algae keep ammonia levels low. Ammonia/nitrite poisoning usually occurs during the early life of the aquarium before the nitrifying bacteria are established or when the activity of the bacteria are repressed by medication, especially antibiotics, or after filter removal or cleaning. The best treatment is removal of the fish to a balanced, ammonia/nitrite free environment. If this is not possible, remove the most severely affected fish (or the most valuable) to an aerated bucket or unfiltered tank for sev-eral days until the ammonia/nitrite levels in the display tank drop. Add 1 ml per gallon of a 1% by weight methylene blue solution to the holding water to aid respiration and provide a mild medication against fungus problems. A Furanace (nifurpirinol) preparation is also very effective in this situation. Leaving ammonia/nitrite-sensitive fish in an unbalanced tank, even with a water change, is usually a death sentence. The only real cure is to allow the tank to build the nitrifying bacteria population levels necessary to balance the animal load in the tank.

Persistent toxicity problems with newly made synthetic seawater may be the result of a new water treatment process for municipal water supplies. This process binds ammonia and chlorine in a stable compound that remains in the water despite typical treatments to remove chlorine from tap water. See Chapter 2 for a description of the problem and its remedy.

Fish suffering from the initial symptoms of toxic tank syndrome present a slightly different situation. Usually the only way to save the fish is immediate transfer to another, totally separate system. Water changes slow the progress of the syndrome, but do not prevent its reoccurrence 24 to 48 hours later, especially if only biological filtration is in use. There are two methods of treating the tank for this syndrome. The first is a good filter cleaning and water change and 5 to 10 days of "rest" from fish occupation. The tank should be watched carefully for the next several weeks to catch any reoccurrence. It is wise to change the species composition of the tank after a bout with a wipe out, for the tank may become "sensitized" to a particular species group.

The second method is sterilization of the entire affected system—tank, filter, and decorations—and re-establishment of the biological filter. Entirely new bacterial populations develop, and any sensitivity to a species group that may have developed in the tank is destroyed. Tank sterilization is probably the best thing to do if two or three wipe outs occur within a 6- to 9-month period. See the end of this chapter for details on tank sterilization.

### Externally introduced toxins

Outside poisons seldom find their way into a tank, but when they do, they create many difficult problems. There are three ways such poisons can get into a tank:

1. On or in something the aquarist introduces into the tank
2. Accidental introduction
3. Sabotage!

A poison strong enough to cause death and distress was probably introduced within a few days, or more likely, within a few hours of the onset of the symptoms. If you suspect a poison from an external source, review everything done to the tank within the last three days. Suspect new ornaments, new food, new water, and any unusual introductions. Remove these, if possible, and investigate carefully. Medications, perhaps? A double dose, or more, of copper? Glass cleaners carelessly used on or around an aquarium? More than one person treating or cleaning the tank?

Think about who had access to the tank (did your three-year-old nephew put moth balls from the closet into the tank?) Could the culprit be paint or chemical fumes, cigar butts, perfume spills, or martinis after a party? How about the most obvious—a zealous insecticide or pesticide sprayer working behind and under the tank in the vicinity of the air pump intake? Sabotage is another problem altogether, and if you worry about it, you're either paranoid or you've got problems way beyond the scope of this book.

### Symptoms

Severe poisoning is very evident from the behavior of the fish. In most instances, there is violent swimming around the tank mixed with moments of rapid, heavy respiration. Fish will frequently jump from the tank, shudder and shake, and finally convulse and die. When this happens to all the fish in the tank, you know something is terribly wrong. Perhaps worse than this, though, is the mild case of poisoning that gradually kills the fish off one by one and is difficult to distinguish from the effects of a disease. The only way to separate the symptoms of poisoning from those of disease is to note that the fish do not respond to treatment, that a disease can not be demonstrated, and that new fish always come down with the same symptoms. If this is the case, it's time to look for a possible cause of subtle poisoning.

### Treatment

Obviously, the first step is to find and remove the source of the poisoning. Once again, the value of keeping a notebook on aquarium activities is very evident. This will help you track down the time of new introductions, food changes, and other things that may reveal the source of the problem. A good filter cleaning and a water change should put the tank back in shape once the problem has been corrected. Activated carbon and adsorbent/absorbent fiber pads, such as the Poly-Filter, can remove many contaminants. Sterilization of the tank is a drastic step and should be a last resort.

## Harassment

Harassment can consist of the outright destruction of one or two fish in a tank or subtle repression of a fish. Most reef-dwelling fish require a certain amount of space between themselves and other fish of the same or closely related species. The territory that an individual or a pair establish and protect ensures noncompetitive feeding, shelter, and reproductive areas, and prevents pair-bond confusion. This is a most complex and variable aspect of the study of reef fish ecology, and new findings and concepts are frequently published. The study of fish in aquariums can provide insight into fish behavior patterns, as long as the artificiality of the environment is understood.

Harassment of one fish by others to the point of severe repression or death most commonly occurs when a new fish is introduced into an aquarium where a fish of the same or a closely related species has already established a territory. If that territory includes the entire tank, the new fish is harassed until it is destroyed. In nature, the loser in such an encounter would quickly move on to an unoccupied area to find "lebensraum," or living space. However, in the aquarium there is no place to go, and harassment continues until the intruder is dead. If the tank is large enough for more than one territory for that species, then the new fish may find a scrap of bottom or a hole to call his own. Although the fish can exist in this situation, he takes his life in his own fins when he ventures forth, and is always quickly chased back to his own area. Slow starvation is often the end result.

Territorial defense is usually not as keen in young fish, or the territories protected are smaller, and seems to break down altogether if large numbers of one species are confined in a small space. Intraspecific aggression can develop into harassment in a static tank if a number of young fish are kept until they grow larger and pair-bond formation begins. This can happen abruptly or gradually as two fish, usually clownfish or damselfish, begin to repel others of their own or closely related species.

### Symptoms

Harassment is usually obvious. In severe instances, the harassed fish is physically damaged, with fins frayed and scales lost, and is often seen cowering in an upper corner of the tank, respiring rapidly. The aggressor also respires rapidly and moves restlessly about the tank with quick, aggressive attacks on the hapless intruder. The behavior of the fish and the initial absence of bacterial infection in the wounds easily distinguish aggressive interactions from disease.

### Treatment

Removal of the harassed or harassing fish, or partitioning of the tank to separate the fishes, is the only treatment for incompatible tankmates. A lecture on how to "play nice" seldom works. After separation, the injured fish should recover on his own unless he is badly chewed up, but watch and make sure that bacterial infection does not set in. It may be necessary to isolate the injured fish in a treatment tank with an antibiotic treatment.

## Fungus diseases

Fungal diseases in fish, especially internal infections, are not uncommon and are very difficult, if not impossible, to cure. Fortunately, fish have a natural resistance to funguses. If good nutrition and a healthy environment low in dissolved organics are provided, fungus infections are rarely a problem. Internal fungus infections, commonly called *Ichthyophonus*, are usually caused by *Ichthyosporidium hoferi*, a parasitic fungus in the class Phycomycetes. This fungus is not detectable until the advanced stage of the disease causes degenerative changes in behavior and appearance. This organism has caused massive death of herring in nature. Feeding the raw flesh of fish infected with *Ichthyosporidium* is the surest way to infect a fish held in a marine aquarium. Unfortunately, there is no positive cure. Many fish seem to be able to contain and control this organism and evidently live many years with this tiny, parasitic time bomb ticking away inside their vital organs. Stress and poor nutrition may weaken the defenses of the fish and release the fungus to destroy the spleen, liver, brain, and other organs.

External fungus infections are usually caused by organisms in the genus *Saprolegnia*. These are visible as cotton-like tufts about the mouth or as a thin, whitish coating on the sides of the fish. The appearance of external fungus usually indicates that there is an underlying problem, either nutritional or environmental, that should be corrected.

### Symptoms

Symptoms of internal fungus infections do not appear until the disease is well advanced. Loss of appetite and listlessness are the first symptoms as the fungus proliferates in the liver and kidneys. Dark nodules under the skin may appear along with areas of upraised scales. The infection soon passes to the nervous system and causes exophthalmos (popeye) and loss of equilibrium. The fish swims in random circles, often swimming upside down. This gives this disease the common names of **Staggers Disease** and **Whirling Disease**. The abdomen may also fill with fluid and be distended (dropsy). There is nothing that can be done for a fish in the later stages of this disease.

External fungus infections do not destroy the life function of the fish and are easier to deal with. *Saprolegnia* appears as cottony tufts near the mouth or on the fins; occasionally, growth about the mouth is great enough to obstruct feeding and can cause starvation. External fungus also occurs as a thin, white coating on the sides of the fish. It can easily be distinguished from *Amyloodinium* because *Amyloodinium* occurs as discrete specks and fungus infections appear as a variable white film with thick and thin areas. Severe cases can erode the skin, introducing secondary bacterial infection that eventually enters the abdomen and destroys the fish.

### Treatment

When it becomes obvious that a fish is infected with either internal or external fungus, there are two important concerns besides the infected fish: the health of the other fish in the tank, and the tank environment. Fungus infections are very hard to treat, and care must be taken to prevent them from spreading. A water change and, if necessary, a filter cleaning and increased dietary variety are the best preventative steps to take. Also, an effective UV water treatment unit is helpful in preventing the spread to other fishes. Usually only one or two fish show the symptoms of internal fungus disease, and these should be isolated and given good water quality and good food. I know of no really effective medication, and if the fish show no signs of improvement after a few days to a week, it is best to destroy them. Fungus is most often transmitted by healthy fish feeding on an infected dead fish or contaminated fish flesh. Remove dead or dying fish from aquariums immediately and be careful about feeding raw fish flesh. Raw fish flesh and some raw shellfish can introduce internal fungus disease to a marine aquarium.

A persistent case of external fungus may be treated by removing an afflicted fish from the tank, holding it carefully, and swabbing the fungus area with a cotton ball or a cotton-tipped swab soaked in an iodine medication. Copper sulphate solution, malachite green solution, or 2-phenoxyethanol can be applied in the same way, but these are all experimental procedures and could be worse for the fish than the external fungus. Given a good environment and good food, a fish can usually lick a mild case of external fungus by itself.

## Sporozoa

Sporozoans cause a great many fish diseases, including Whirling Disease of salmonids, boil disease in several species of farmed fish, and what is usually called **Seahorse Disease**. There are probably many sporozoan diseases that affect marine tropical fish, but few studies have been done on tropical sporozoans. Sporozoan infections may commonly be misdiagonised as internal and/or external fungus disease or piscine TB and, like bacteria, may also often be present in and on fish without causing a life threatening disease. Myxosporidians and microsporidians are sporozoans and the identification of species requires sophisicated laboratory techniques and is usually confused and difficult. The microsporidian *Glugea* sp. is most well known and the disease it causes is commonly termed Seahorse Disease. It causes the formation of well-defined, dense white patches over the bodies of seahorses, pipefish, boxfish, and other fish—usually fish with hard, plate-like scutes covering the body.

It is also possible that a microsporidian may infect the eggs of clownfish. We had a problem during the very early period of clownfish culture with a white spot disease that developed in clownfish eggs at about day five after spawning. The white infection was located in the yolk of the egg, and the stunted embryo did not develop to hatching. The organisms present in the yolk were tentatively identified as microsporidia. Treatment with sulfathiasole and quinine seemed helpful, but many eggs were lost, despite treatment. The female eventually stopped spawning infected eggs and produced good eggs for several years thereafter. Formalin baths and/or quinacrine hydrochloride may be helpful treatments for microsporidian infections, but information on treating marine tropical fish is scarce.

## Fish tuberculosis

Fish tuberculosis, **Piscine TB** or **Fish TB**, is a widespread marine fish disease caused by the bacterium *Mycobacteria marinum*. There are a number of species in this genus, including the one that causes TB in man. Although *M. marinum* does not commonly infect people, there are reports of serious skin infections caused by *M. marinum*. In these instances, the aquarists were cleaning tanks that had held TB-infected fish and either had an open lesion or suffered a cut while working in the tank. The open lesions developed into abscesses that did not heal, and after several weeks, additional abscesses developed on the hand and arm. These infections did not respond to penicillin, and treatment was not effective until the anti-tubercular drugs isoniazid and streptomycin were given. This is a very rare human infection, but it can happen. Penicillin doesn't work on *M. marinum*, so if this does happen to you, tell your doctor that those nodules on your arm may be fish tuberculosis. If you have an open cut or sore on your hands or arms, keep them out of the aquarium or wear protective gloves. Disinfect the lesion very thoroughly after working in the aquarium.

Fortunately, fish TB usually hits only one or two fish in a tank, and the course of the disease is slow enough to allow time for treatment. Fish showing symptoms of TB should be isolated immediately, for although it is not highly contagious, it can lead to tank-wide mortality. Contagion is especially likely if fish that die of TB are left in the tank and healthy fish pick at and consume the soft parts of the dead fish. Feeding the raw flesh of saltwater food-fish species is another possible way of introducing this disease to a marine system.

### Symptoms

Piscine TB and internal fungus, *Ichthyosporidium*, have similar symptoms and can be confused. However, loss of equilibrium, and swimming in circles, sideways, and upside down, are not usually symptoms of piscine TB. The first symptoms are loss of appetite and general listlessness. The fish stays hidden and soon has little or no interest in feeding. Rapid respiration is usually noticed about this time also. The fish may remain in this stage of the disease for several weeks. The eyes may become clouded and exophthalmos (Popeye) usually develops. Another typical symptom is the development of whitish blotches and areas of raised scales. Finally, the fins become ragged, and the abdomen sunken, and the fish lies on its side on the bottom.

The fish may linger in this state for many days before it dies. The internal organs of affected fish degenerate and small grayish granulomas (tubercles) are found on and in the liver, intestines, spleen, and eyes. One type of piscine TB forms granulomas along the spines of young fish. These can sometimes be seen through the semi-transparent flesh as a whitish discoloration along the spines of small fish. Fish can live a long time with piscine TB. Often the fish may appear to be in good health, with no outward sign of the disease for months or years. Only on dissection are the tubercles typical of this disease found in the mesenteries, heart, spleen, liver, and other internal organs.

### Treatment

Piscine TB is a difficult disease to treat because it is internal and often chronic, and the effective drugs are not easily obtained—and often not very effective. Since there is a strong possibility that the average aquarist will not be able to obtain the proper drugs for treatment, the affected fish should be immediately isolated in a treatment tank to reduce the chances of infecting other fish. At the risk of sounding like a broken record, I must stress that piscine TB is most common in poorly maintained aquariums. A good environment and good nutrition keep the natural immune system of the fish in top condition and practically eliminate the occurrence, or at least the physical expression, of piscine TB.

If the disease is caught in the early stages, treatment with streptomycin and isoniazid may effect a cure. Kingsford, in his book (now out of print; see Selected References) also recommends rifampin and cycloserine, although these two may be difficult to obtain. Streptomycin may be found in some commercial aquarium medications or obtained at drugstores, veterinary supply stores, and animal feed stores. Isoniazid can be obtained through chemical supply houses and, since it does not seem to affect nitrifying bacteria, it can be used in a tank with an active biological filter. Be sure to turn off all carbon and UV filtration before adding any medication.

Add 40 milligrams per gallon of isoniazid and 40 milligrams per gallon of streptomycin to the treatment tank when the fish are transferred. Change water every three days, more often for small tanks and/or large fish, and re-medicate. Add 40 mg per gallon of isoniazid to the display tank to reduce the chance of infection. Soaking the food in streptomycin solution or adding 6 mg of rifampin per 100 grams of food increases the effectiveness of the treatment. If medicated food is prepared, it should be fed to all fish that have been exposed to the disease. Return fish to the

**Bacterial disease**

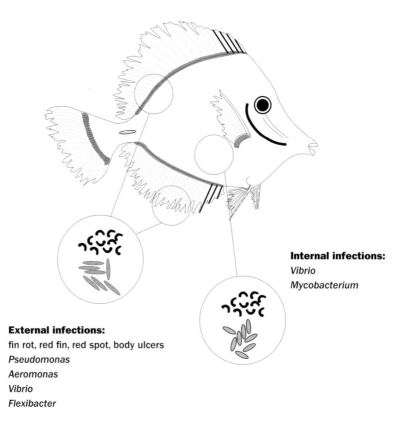

**Internal infections:**
*Vibrio*
*Mycobacterium*

**External infections:**
fin rot, red fin, red spot, body ulcers
*Pseudomonas*
*Aeromonas*
*Vibrio*
*Flexibacter*

display tank when they have apparently recovered. Do not return a fish if there is any question of recovery, for it is best to lose one or two rather than risk exposing all other fish in the tank. If most of the fish in a tank come down with TB, or if the disease persistently occurs in a particular tank, it is best to sterilize the tank and start again. Remember that any fish that was in a tank with TB-infected fish is capable of transferring this disease into any tank where it may be placed.

## Bacterial disease

The world is full of bacteria. Indeed, life as we know it could not exist without the activities of bacteria. Bacteriology has become a very complex discipline involving the most advanced techniques of taxonomy, biochemistry, and microscopy. One of the basic taxonomic tools of bacteriology was developed by the Danish physician Christian Gram in 1884. He discovered that bacteria could be separated into two groups depending on whether they retained (Gram-positive) or lost (Gram-negative) a violet color during a particular staining process. He didn't know it at the time, but this differential staining was caused by fundamental differences in the structure of the cell wall, which also affect the way antibiotics work on bacteria. Most bacteria that cause disease in marine fish are Gram-negative and some antibiotics, including penicillin, streptomycin, and sulfa drugs are not effective against them. *Pseudomonas* and *Vibrio* are the genera of the principle disease-producing bacteria in marine fish. The antibiotics neomycin and chloramphenicol, and secondly erythromycin and tetracycline, are usually effective against these bacteria. Other antibiotics may be even more effective, but they are also more difficult to obtain. Some of the above antibiotics are frequently found in aquarium pharmaceuticals or in farm-animal medications obtainable at feed stores. (Always follow the manufacturer's instructions to the letter; some of these drugs, such as chloramphenicol, can seriously harm humans if mishandled.)

Fish have a strong natural resistance to bacteria, so infections caused by *Pseudomonas* and *Vibrio* seldom overrun a fish unless there is stress and/or weakness already present. Old age, poor nutrition, poor environment, injury, harassment, fungus infection, etc. can all contribute to the debility that opens the door to bacterial disease. Occasionally, the environment is so poor that bacterial growth can bloom and overrun otherwise healthy fish. Cloudy water of a white, rather than clear or green, hue and persistent sores on the fish are symptoms of this condition.

### Symptoms

The most obvious symptoms of bacterial disease are reddened, frayed fins and open sores on the sides, usually near the fins. External ulcers are generally caused by *Pseudomonas* sp. and internal bacterial infections seem to be caused more often by *Vibrio* sp. *Aeromonas* is another genus of Gram-negative bacteria that attacks captive marine fish.

Usually, only one or two fish in a tank at any one time show symptoms of advanced bacterial infection. If all fish are severely affected, then the aquarium is in bad shape and a major overhaul is required. Common symptoms of bacterial disease include rapid respiration, a grey film over the eyes, bloody scales at the base of the fins, disintegration of the fins, and open sores on the body. Bacterial disease may also cause blindness in fish. Blindness in fish is usually evidenced by cloudy eyes, inability to see food or movements outside the tank, and lack of response to a net being moved slowly nearby. Excessive light alone, if there is such a thing in a marine aquarium, does not cause blindness, although it could increase stress levels in nocturnal fish or species from deep water. The lateral line system, that row of tiny pores extending along the side from head to tail, is the most frequent site of initial external infection. Bacteria can gain entry into a stressed fish through these tiny pores and the soft tissues of the gills. Internal organs are affected as the disease progresses; the fish stops eating, respiration rate increases, and eventually the fish lies on the bottom and dies. Some bacterial diseases may kill the fish in two to four days, but usually, especially in larger fish, the progression of the disease takes one or two weeks.

### Treatment

Only the affected fish need be treated if the infection is restricted to one or two fish and the other fish and the environment appear healthy. However, if most of the fish show signs of bacterial infection, it may be best to treat all the fish and sterilize the tank. This will prevent frequent re-occurrence of the same problems during the months to come. The tank cannot be treated with a strong dose of antibiotics without killing the nitrifying bacteria (they are also Gram-negative), so tank sterilization may be best in the long run for a severe or persistent bacterial disease problem.

The infected fish should be isolated in a treatment tank. A freshwater bath on the way to the treatment tank is a good idea in case there is a parasite problem, but it won't do much for a bacterial disease. Reduce light levels on the treatment tank to preserve the activity of the antibiotics and reduce stress on the fish. Add the antibiotic you choose to the treatment tank at the manufacturer's recommended dose. If there is no listed dose for aquarium fish, use neomycin at 250 mg per gallon, chloramphenicol sodium succinate (Chloromycetin) at 50 mg per gallon, tetracycline at 50 mg per gallon, or erythromycin at 40 to 50 mg per gallon. Positive results should be noted within three to four days if the antibiotic is effective.

If the treatment is not effective, try another antibiotic. Once the fish gets the upper hand over the infection, with the help of the antibiotic, recovery is rapid. Keep the fish in isolation until recovery is assured. Wait a day or two after ulcers are healed and eyes are no longer filmed over before replacing them in the display tank. An effective UV sterilizer on the display tank will be helpful in preventing a buildup of dangerous bacteria in the tank water.

If the bacterial disease seems mostly internal, and the fish is eating, it is a good idea to feed the fish an antibiotic food. One can then attack the bacteria directly inside the fish and not just on its external surface. Some internal antibiotic treatments are commercially available, and one can also put a few drops of an antibiotic solution on a porous food and feed it to the fish. The fish has to take the food quickly, however, to prevent loss of the antibiotic to the surrounding water.

**ANTIBIOTICS BY MOUTH:**
If sick fish are still eating, providing medication via their food can be an effective approach to treatment. Prepared fish foods with antibiotics are available at good aquarium shops, or the aquarist can add liquid antibiotics to dry and freeze-dried rations, which will rapidly absorb them. Powdered medications can be mixed with moist fresh or previously frozen foods.

❖

## Lymphocystis

This is the only viral disease that commonly affects marine tropical fish. It also goes by the name **Cauliflower Disease** because it causes a growth that looks something like a miniature cauliflower. The virus invades cells just under the skin of the fish (usually fins or lips are affected), and causes these cells to swell greatly (hypertrophy) and form a thickened cell membrane. These enlarged cells proliferate into a small growth with a characteristic form and color. The stress of capture, handling, and closed systems may reduce the resistance of the fish to the virus, thus outbreaks of *Lymphocystis* are not uncommon in newly captured fish. The virus does not kill the fish directly, although the growths may interfere with feeding or create a pathway for secondary bacterial infection. In many respects, *Lymphocystis* is similar to a wart on humans. Although the condition is unsightly and can alarm the beginning aquarist, given time and no secondary complications, fish will usually recover from a *Lymphocystis* infection on their own.

## Symptoms

The fish displays small, discrete, gray or whitish growths on lips and/or fins. These growths may appear all over the body in a severe case. The size of the growths is variable, but most are less than ⅛ inch (3 mm) in diameter. The surface of the growths is smooth and slightly irregular.

## Treatment

There is no treatment for *Lymphocystis*, and since the growths disappear in time, no treatment is recommended. However, if the growths interfere greatly with feeding or swimming, they can be removed (at the risk of spreading the virus and causing secondary bacterial infection). Use a sterilized curved fingernail scissors or a convex curved or straight toenail clipper to remove the growth at the base. Do this work while holding the fish

**Lymphocystis,
Cauliflower Disease**

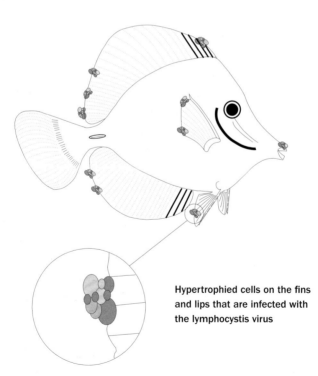

Hypertrophied cells on the fins
and lips that are infected with
the lymphocystis virus

above a treatment tank to prevent liberating viral material into the display tank. Antibiotic treatment is recommended to control bacterial infection. (Acyclovir, an antiviral treatment, has recently been reported to be effective against lymphocystis. Ointments containing acyclovir, smeared on the cauliflower-like growths, reportedly cause the growths to quickly recede. (I cannot vouch for the effectiveness of this treatment.)

## Metazoan parasites
There are numerous parasitic diseases of fish, internal and external, caused by relatively large multicellular animals (metazoans), mostly in the categories of worms and crustaceans. Some of these have complicated life cycles involving intermediate hosts and cannot reproduce in the aquarium, in which case they are only a threat to the infected fish. Others have simple life cycles and can, if given the chance, become a major problem. Fortunately, reproduction and growth is much slower than that of single-celled parasites (protozoans), and infestations can be caught fairly early. Two of these larger parasites that occasionally show up in marine aquariums are discussed below, and the recommended treatment for these can generally be applied to other metazoan parasites as well.

## Turbellarian worms (Black Ich)
The Yellow Tang, *Zebrasoma flavescens*, is particularly vulnerable to this parasite, but other tangs and sometimes angelfishes, butterflyfishes, and a number of other groups are occasionally infested with parasitic turbellarian flatworms in the genus *Paravortex*. Like *Amyloodinium* and *Cryptocaryon*, these parasitic flatworms can complete their life cycle in closed systems, and, left untreated, can destroy fish in small marine aquariums. A tiny free-swimming worm first finds and attaches to the skin or gills of a fish host. The tiny flatworm then feeds on the tissues of the host for five or six days, often moving freely about the fish, before dropping off to complete development on the tank bottom. After a few days on the tank bottom, the mature worm splits along its side and releases up to 160 young, free-swimming worms that then seek their own host fish.

### Symptoms
An infected fish displays numerous tiny dark spots, about the size of a period on a printed page or slightly larger, usually on the side of the body

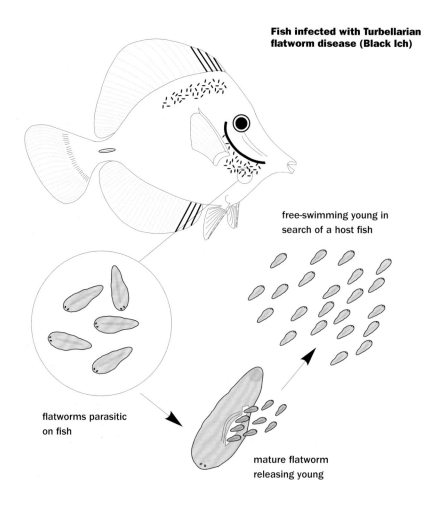

**Fish infected with Turbellarian flatworm disease (Black Ich)**

free-swimming young in search of a host fish

flatworms parasitic on fish

mature flatworm releasing young

just behind the gill opening, and sometimes on the fins. The worms are much easier to see on light-colored fish. Infected fish display scratching behavior, are listless, and are not inclined to feed.

### Treatment

The best way to eliminate this parasite is to use the formalin treatment described for *Cryptocaryon*. The bottom of the tank should also be kept very clean during treatment. This removes worms that have fallen off the host fish before they can reproduce.

## Fish flukes

*Benedenia melleni* are flattened, almost transparent parasites that attach to the gills and external surfaces of fish. They are usually only about ⅛ inch long, but may reach a length of ½ inch. Their transparency makes them difficult to see, and they are first noticed as numerous small bumps on the side of the fish. They may also infest the gills, but are usually evident on the body at the same time.

### Symptoms

Fish that are infested actively scrape and swim against the bottom, attempting to dislodge the parasites. Flukes can readily move from one fish to another, although they tend to remain with the same fish. Severe infestations invite bacterial infection by stressing and weakening the fish as well as by breaking through the skin and mucus layers.

### Treatment

*Benedenia* can reproduce in the aquarium, and although each generation takes several weeks instead of days, they can become epidemic. The best immediate treatment is a freshwater bath. Catch the fish as gently as possible to prevent dislodging the parasites, and transfer the fish to a freshwater bath as described under the *Amyloodinium* section. The flukes will turn opaque and drop off the fish very quickly. The fish can be left in the bath, under careful observation, up to eight minutes if all the flukes do not drop off in two minutes. The freshwater bath can be repeated every day or so, whenever the flukes are observed on fish, and the flukes will soon be exterminated—which is fine if you can get the fish out of the tank with very little effort. The traditional formalin bath, as described in the *Cryptocaryon* treatment section, is also effective against flukes and fish lice and can be used in conjunction with the freshwater bath. Be sure that all flukes are eliminated from the net used to catch the infected fish before placing the net into the same or another tank.

Another rather recently developed treatment for external worm and crustacean parasites is the addition of the chemical O,O-dimethyl 2,2,2-trichloro-1-hydroxyethyl phosphonate directly to the tank water. For some strange reason, this chemical is usually referred to only as DTHP. DTHP goes under the trade names of Dylox, Dipterex, and Proxol 80, as well as several others. It was developed as an insecticide and was found to be effective against many aquatic fish parasites. This compound is easily removed with activated carbon, does not disturb the activity of a biological filter, and breaks down into harmless compounds within a few weeks. Unfortunately, there is no way the average aquarist can test for the amount of DTHP present in tank water. A concentration of 0.75 to 1.0 mg per liter is an effective dose. This compound is very toxic to crustaceans, and so all shrimp, crabs, lobsters, and, to be on the safe side, all valuable invertebrates, should be removed from the tank before treatment. It is compatible with copper medications. Although DTHP is quite effective against flukes and fish lice and can be added directly to the tank, I recommend the traditional formalin treatment unless you have the laboratory expertise and equipment to calculate and prepare the proper dose of DTHP for your tank.

Parasite pickers, such as small French Angelfish, Neon Gobies, and Pacific cleaner wrasses, are helpful in controlling these large parasites. The slow reproduction rate of the parasite allows an active cleaner to defuse the population bomb.

### Fish lice (crustacean parasites)

*Argulus* is one of a number of genera of marine crustaceans that are parasitic on fishes and go by the general name of fish lice. Their appearance is variable. *Argulus* have flat, shield-like bodies that help them grip the surface of the fish, and the mouth parts are modified into a suction grip and sting. Most *Argulus*, however, are freshwater parasites.

Some parasitic copepods partially embed themselves in the host fish with only the paired, elongated egg sacs noticeably protruding. Others are not permanently attached to the host fish and can move from fish to fish, feeding on skin tissues.

It is important to recognize the difference between a parasitic copepod problem and an occasional bloom of free-living copepods. Parasitic copepods, especially epidemics of them, are rather rare in marine aquariums. On the other hand, a balanced aquarium with a solid functioning biological filter and good algal growth may frequently experience a bloom of tiny, free-living copepods. These tiny "bugs" are much smaller than parasitic "bugs" and swarm over the algae-covered sides of the aquarium. Occasionally they move over the sides of fish and give rise to fears of parasites. Actually, these tiny white copepods, less than a millimeter long, fit

**Metazoan parasites**

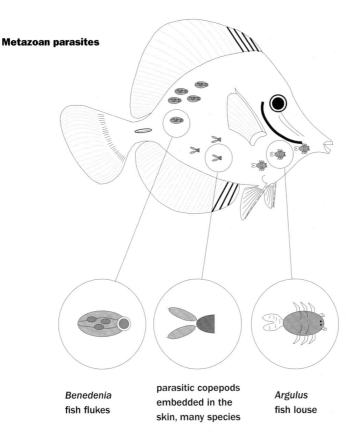

*Benedenia*
fish flukes

parasitic copepods
embedded in the
skin, many species

*Argulus*
fish louse

very well into the natural food chain of the aquarium. They feed on detritus and algal cells and are, in turn, fed upon by invertebrates and small fish. Their numbers can be controlled by more frequent filter cleanings, keeping algal growth under control, and strong filtering action through a UV unit or a small-pored mechanical filter. Control measures should be considered only if they are causing the fish obvious discomfort.

### Symptoms

Scratching and scraping behavior in fish indicates irritation from external parasites, and careful observation will reveal the presence of fish lice or other parasite problems. Sometimes these external parasites are almost completely transparent and can barely, if at all, be seen on the fish. They become opaque during a freshwater bath, however, and can be seen to drop off the fish. Do not add the freshwater to any marine tank.

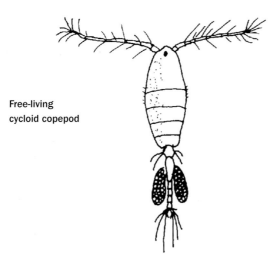

Free-living
cycloid copepod

## Treatment

Apply the same treatment as described for fish flukes. Embedded parasites may not respond to this treatment and if these are present, it is best to remove them individually with tweezers. Dab the point of removal with an antiseptic solution.

## Old age

Old age is not really one of the "dirty dozen." Fish, like all other animals, must die sometime, and if they bow out from old age in your aquarium, then you've done the best you can for them. A marine fish dying of old age in an aquarium used to be very unusual, so much so that it was seldom considered as a possible cause of death. Marine aquarium–keeping has now advanced to the point where keeping a fish one to five years, or even up to 15 years, is commonplace, so old age must now be considered when analyzing fish death. Many fish, for example Neon Gobies and jawfish, have only a one- or two-year life expectancy in the wild, and others rarely exceed a five-year life span. These fish often exceed their natural life spans when kept under good conditions, away from natural predators and disease. Marine fish, like all other animals, have immune systems that protect them from disease. The efficiency of this immune system declines with age, as do internal organs and musculature, and the fish become more susceptible to the onslaught of disease. So even if the death of an old fish can be blamed on a specific disease, old age may be the basic cause.

**Symptoms**

Old age often causes changes in the appearance of fish just as it does in other animals. Fins often get longer, teeth may become more prominent, colors may change, and even the shape of the head and slope of the back may alter. Unlike mammals, fish never stop growing. The rate of growth slows considerably when fish reach maturity, but it never stops, and fish continue to slowly increase in size under normal environmental and nutritional conditions. Large fish usually grow even more slowly in an aquarium, so it often appears that a fish reaches a terminal size in an aquarium, and given the limitations of the artificial environment, this may be the case. Older fish tend to be the larger and heavier individuals; however, considerable variation in growth rate prevents use of size or weight as an accurate index of age.

**Treatment**

There is no treatment, of course, for old age. Just keep in mind that fish do grow old, sometimes small fish do so quite rapidly, and this may make them more susceptible to common problems.

Please note: If you have to destroy and dispose of sick or dead fish, NEVER, NEVER release them in local waters. Although the chance that they will recover and establish a population of non-native fish, or that a new disease will be introduced to plague native fish, is rather remote, the possibility cannot be risked. The best way to dispose of a dead fish is to seal it in a plastic bag and send it out with the garbage, or maybe recycle it as fertilizer in the flower garden.

**Tank sterilization**

Sometimes, despite everything, it becomes necessary to "kill" a tank and begin all over again. This could happen because of severe neglect or an extremely persistent parasite or bacterial problem. Sterilization is almost like setting up a tank for the first time, and as far as the life forms in the aquarium are concerned, there is no difference. When the tank is sterilized, everything in the tank will be killed, so be sure to remove all animals and live rock. Animals removed from the tank may be carrying the bug that caused the problem, so they must be treated and quarantined for several weeks before putting them into other tanks, if one dares to risk this. Live rock that has been exposed to disease and parasites may need to be isolated even longer. (See below for a discussion of treating reef aquariums.)

The agent for sterilization is chlorine (sodium or calcium hypochlorite), the active ingredient in liquid bleach and in the granular bactericidal chlorine used in swimming pools. You don't have to worry about using too much chlorine (within reasonable limits) to sterilize your tank, but there must be a high enough concentration to do the job. The tank does not have to be dismantled to achieve sterilization. In fact, tearing the tank apart is a waste of time and effort unless there is an undergravel filter or plenum that has been disrupted and must be repaired. The first thing to do is to remove all colored plastic ornaments, if there are any, as these may become discolored by the chlorine. Leave rocks and decorative coral in place, as these must be sterilized also. Especially in old aquariums, it is a good idea to remove as much of the accumulated organic matter (detritus) as possible before sterilization. The chlorine must oxidize all organics present, and the less there is, the more thoroughly it can do its job. Also, there is a tendency for foam to form when the chlorine breaks down the organics, and in extreme cases, it is possible for the foam to overflow the tank and cover half the living room. (Someone—wife, husband, mother, or roommate—might never forgive you.)

The easiest way to remove the organics is to scrape the sides and stir the bottom well, then siphon out all the accumulated debris and dirty water. Refill the tank with freshwater—this is cheaper than saltwater and works just as well for this purpose. Put everything else that needs sterilization into the tank including hoses, tank covers (not lights), and cleaning tools. Chlorine is very hard on nets, so it is best just to dip and rinse them well for a few minutes in the chlorine solution, rinse with freshwater, and let them dry completely. Outside filters should be left operating, but their contents must be discarded. Keep the air pump or power filter running and water circulating just as if the tank were in normal operation. Circulating the chlorinated water will sterilize the inside of the tubes, pipes, and containers.

Now add about 1 tablespoon of dry granular chlorine for each 20 gallons, or a cup of unscented liquid bleach for each 20 gallons. This dose should be enough to sterilize the entire tank. Stir the bottom filter again to eliminate any static areas and let the whole mess cook in its own juices for 12 to 24 hours. After this period, check to make sure that all algae has turned white, if not disintegrated, and that there are no brown or black areas left on the sides or in the filters. If everything is not absolutely white and clean, then add another dose of chlorine and wait another 12 to 24 hours. It would be unusual, though, if the first application did not do the job.

The thing to do next, under some circumstances, is to neutralize the chlorine. It isn't good to put any chlorine into a septic tank, and it won't do the lawn any good either (Big, brown dead spots. No, I'm not going to tell you how I know this is so). Add hypo (sodium thiosulfate) or a commercial dechlorinator until the chlorine is gone. You can test for this with an OTO swimming pool test kit, or you can take a sample of the water, a cupful will do, and put in a few drops of food color. When the color of the food coloring doesn't change or bleach out, then there is very little, if any, chlorine left in the water. When the chlorine has been neutralized, the tank should be siphoned again and everything, including the gravel filter, rinsed with one or two changes of freshwater. After the tank has been cleaned and rinsed to your satisfaction, it can be refilled with saltwater and the process of conditioning the filter with nitrifying bacteria can begin again.

**AFTERMATH TACTICS:**

An aquarium that has been the scene of a devastating disease or that has persistent bacterial or parasite problems may need to be sterilized and restarted, including new biological filtration. Live rock can harbor fish parasites and may have to go through a quarantine procedure before being reused with a new population of fishes.

❖

In this modern age of reef tanks, sterilization is still an option, but it is a much more extreme option in tanks based on live rock and live sand. Chlorine, of course, makes live rock into dead rock. Perhaps a better option when a live rock tank must be broken down and cleaned is to carefully remove the rock and scrub each rock, carefully removing detritus and excessive algae, and then placing the rock in a quarantine system without corals or fish for three or four weeks. Some aquarists who have been through a tank wipeout with an infectious parasite have given live rock a freshwater dip and a brisk rinse before placing it in quarantine. This will remove excess organic material and also eliminate any dormant fish parasites that may be in the cracks and crevices of the rock.

A well-stocked fish shop can offer most aquarium medications and advice on their use.

## Summary

As a brief summary, here is a list of treatment Dos and Don'ts.

### Treatment DOs

- Do immediately remove dead and dying fish from aquariums.
- Do isolate fish for treatment.
- Do identify the problem before treatment.
- Do change water in the treatment tank every two or three days.
- Do keep the bottom of the treatment tank clean.
- Do provide shelter for the fish in treatment.
- Do keep light levels low in the treatment tank.
- Do keep track of ammonia and nitrite levels if the treatment tank has a biological filter.
- Do keep fish isolated until the cure is complete.
- Do keep aquarium medications out of the reach of children!
- Do use medications as directed.
- Do monitor copper levels in treatment water every one or two days.
- Do rinse any external filters with freshwater and change the media to prevent reinfection of a tank after treatment is complete.

**Treatment DON'Ts**

- Don't medicate unless necessary.
- Don't continue to add copper without testing the current copper level.
- Don't exceed 0.3 ppm copper. No more than 0.25 ppm copper for three weeks is all that should ever be necessary.
- Don't use antibiotics in a tank with a biological filter.
- Don't use copper in a reef aquarium. Remove and treat reef inhabitants in a separate hospital tank.
- Don't use an activated carbon filter with any type of medication unless the object is to quickly remove the medication from the water.
- Don't use a UV filter with any type of medication.
- Don't release live or dead fish in non-native waters. In fact, don't release live or dead fish in any natural waters; they may be carrying non-native parasites or bacteria that could cause a problem with native organisms.

*Further References:* I think you will find this chapter's information on marine fish distress and disease helpful for most of the problems that might arise. However, there are three very good books on aquarium fish health that I want to bring to your attention. *Fish Medicine*, by Michael Stoskopf (1993), is a big book, a compendium by many authors that is an excellent general reference, and *Fish Disease: Diagnosis and Treatment*, by Edward Noga (1996), is also a comprehensive scientific treatise on fish disease. The most aquarist-friendly is *The Marine Fish Health and Feeding Handbook*, by Bob Goemans and Lance Ichinotsubo (2008). When it comes to disease and distress in marine fish, this is the most detailed and up-to-date reference for the marine aquarium hobby.

CHAPTER

10

# Foods & Feeding

*What, When, and How*

FEEDING MARINE FISH PROPERLY IS JUST AS ESSENTIAL TO THEIR HEALTH and well-being as providing a good physical and chemical environment. In nature, fish are adapted physiologically and ecologically to certain types of food organisms. These specific foods provide the nutritional requirements of the fish within the specialized lifestyle of that species. The same variations in feeding habits found in land animals also exist among fish. Some species, such as the grizzly bear, feed on a wide variety of organisms, and others—like the Everglades Kite, which feeds only on the *Pomacea* (apple) snail—are very restricted in their diet. Whether broad or restricted, the natural diet provides the amount and balance of proteins, fats, carbohydrates, vitamins, and minerals that each species needs to maintain good health and reproductive capability.

Most marine aquarists do not structure the diet for their fish according to the exact composition, percentage, and origin of the proteins, fats, carbohydrates, and other dietary elements that their fish require. Actually, this would be very difficult and very expensive, since most marine aquarists are polyculturists—that is, they culture or keep a variety of fish that have a variety of dietary requirements. To a monoculturist, on the other hand, this is a very important consideration. He may have 500,763 individuals, more or less, of a single species—catfish, pompano, angel-

Feeding time for the Smithsonian Institution reef exhibit designed by Jeff Turner and heavily populated with planktivores, such as anthias, chromis, cardinalfishes, and fairy wrasses, that capture meaty foods in the water column.

Lemonpeel Angelfish, *Centropyge flavissima*, must have a variety of plant foods, including macroalgae and *Spirulina*, as well as carnivore fare such as *Mysis* shrimp and sponge.

fish, redfish, clownfish, or trout—in his tanks or ponds, and his children's inheritance on the line as well. In this case, it is very important to know exactly what dietary elements will produce a healthy fish with the characteristics required by the market, and the fish farmer has access to a specially formulated diet for each species based on extensive laboratory work and many rearing trials. Most marine aquarists, however, feed their fish commercially prepared diets or a fish food mix they prepare from what is available at the supermarket or seafood shop, and in almost every situation, these sources provide quite adequate nutrition for most marine aquarium fish. The aquarist does not have to know the scientific analysis of the foods fed to his or her fish to keep them healthy, but one should be familiar with the basics of marine fish nutrition.

This chapter will not go deeply into that science, but will acquaint the aquarist with the essential information. There is a vast scientific literature on the dietary requirements of freshwater and some marine fish, but this literature is almost entirely concerned with food-fish species. The advanced or professional aquarist can get a good overview of the science of marine fish nutrition in Steve Spotte's 1992 book, *Captive Seawater Fishes*, which has a comprehensive chapter on marine fish nutrition.

Fish with broad, unspecialized dietary requirements usually adjust easily to the foods and conditions of captivity, while fish with highly specialized diets may have difficulty. However, just because a fish feeds on only one type of organism in nature doesn't necessarily mean that that particular food organism must be available in the aquarium. A fish may be limited by its adaptive behavior patterns to certain food organisms, but still be capable of digesting and utilizing other foods. For instance, a wrasse specially adapted to feeding on certain crustaceans found deep within branching corals can meet its nutritional needs by eating other crustaceans, such as shrimp, or prepared fish foods when these are made available in an artificial environment.

There are two challenges that must be met when feeding captive marine fish. The first is to get the fish to accept a substitute for its natural diet, and the second is to provide all the nutritional requirements in the substitute food. Fish that consume a wide variety of foods in nature are usually most adaptable to aquarium fare. This doesn't mean that it is impossible to keep fish with very limited natural diets, such as some of the butterflyfishes, but giving these fish an adequate diet requires more care and effort.

## Natural foods

For maximum success with your fish, it is best to select species that are generalized feeders (columns 7 and 10 in Table 5 on page 258), and feed a good variety of foods. Table 5 is intended as a general guide to the natural food preferences of each major group of fishes. There are many exceptions to these groupings (for example, a few species of snapper are plankton pickers rather than generalized bottom feeders). However, the table will give you an idea of the content and structure of the natural diet of most fishes. Each of the 11 natural food groups from Table 5 is discussed in the following pages to provide basic information on natural diets. A possible substitute for each category of natural food is also discussed.

## Table 5  Principal food groups of the major types of fishes

(Two checks indicate the strongest preference.)

| Fish Type | Algae and seagrasses (1) | Algae (2) | Algae and detritus (3) | Sponges (4) | Plankton pickers (5) | Generalized bottom feeders (6) | Fish feeders (7) | Coral feeders (8) | Crustacean feeders (9) | Generalized invertebrates (10) | Parasite pickers (11) |
|---|---|---|---|---|---|---|---|---|---|---|---|
| Sharks | | | | | | ✓ | | | | | |
| Moray eels | | | | | | ✓✓ | ✓ | | | | |
| Squirrelfishes | | | | | | | | | ✓ | | |
| Groupers | | | | | | ✓ | | | | | |
| Hamlets | | | | | | ✓ | | | | | |
| Grammas | | | | | ✓ | | | | | | |
| Hawkfishes | | | | | ✓ | ✓✓ | | | | | |
| Cardinalfishes | | | | | ✓ | ✓ | | | | | |
| Sweepers | | | | | ✓ | | | | | | |
| Snappers | | | | | | ✓ | | | | | |
| Grunts | | | | | | ✓ | | | | | |
| Porgies | | | | | | | | | | ✓ | |
| Sea Chubs | ✓ | | | | | | | | | | |
| Mojarras | | | | | | | | | | ✓ | |
| Reef drums | | | | | | | | | ✓✓ | ✓ | |
| Goatfishes | | | | | | | | | | ✓ | |
| Damselfishes | | ✓ | ✓✓ | | ✓✓ | | | | | ✓ | |
| Clownfishes | | ✓ | | | ✓✓ | | | | | ✓ | |
| Wrasses | | | | | | ✓ | | | | ✓✓ | ✓ |
| Parrotfishes | ✓✓ | | | | | | | ✓ | | | |
| Flounders | | | | | | ✓ | | | | | |
| Gobies | | | ✓✓ | | | | | | | ✓ | ✓ |
| Blennies | | | ✓✓ | | | | | | | ✓ | |
| Jawfishes | | | | | ✓ | | | | | | |
| Scorpionfishes | | | | | | ✓ | ✓✓ | | | | |
| Spadefishes | ✓ | ✓ | ✓ | | | ✓✓ | | | | | |
| Batfishes | | ✓ | | | | ✓✓ | | | | | |
| Butterflyfishes | | ✓ | | | | | | ✓✓ | | ✓ | |
| Angelfishes | | ✓ | | ✓✓ | | | | | | | ✓ |
| Pompanos | | | | | | | | | ✓ | | |
| Tangs | ✓ | | ✓ | | | | | | | | |
| Triggerfishes | ✓ | | | | | ✓ | | | | ✓✓ | |
| Filefishes | ✓ | | | | | | | ✓ | | ✓ | |
| Sea robins | | | | | | | | | | ✓ | |
| Trunkfishes | | ✓ | | ✓ | | | | | | ✓✓ | |
| Boxfishes | | ✓ | | ✓ | | | | | | ✓ | |
| Puffers | | ✓ | | ✓ | | | | | | ✓✓ | |
| Frogfishes | | | | | | | ✓ | | | | |
| Seahorses | | | | | ✓ | | | | | | |
| Pipefishes | | | | | ✓ | | | | | | |
| Dragonets | | | ✓ | | | | | | | ✓ | |

## Column 1—Algae and seagrasses

The marine algae are generally broken up into two artificial groups, microalgae and macroalgae. The microalgae comprise all the small species that must be studied under a microscope. They include the one-celled, free-floating phytoplankton and the tiny filamentous and colonial growths that attach to solid substrate. The macroalgae, however, are large enough to be seen and examined without magnification, and range from small, thumbnail-sized growths to kelp plants 40 feet or more in height. The seagrasses—turtle grass, eel grass, and a few others—are not algae but are true aquatic flowering plants. They often cover vast areas of shallow bottom around coral reefs. Some fishes, such as parrotfishes and surgeonfishes, which feed primarily on algae, are true herbivores, the browsers and grazers of the sea bottom. These fish can get along for a while on standard aquarium fare, but nutritional deficiencies (sunken stomach, loss of color, inactivity) eventually develop. Marine algae—either dried or live—are the best vegetable matter to add to the diet, but leafy vegetables such as spinach, lettuce, romaine lettuce, and even freshwater aquarium plants such as *Riccia fluitans* or *Spirulina*, a freshwater alga, can be substituted.

## Column 2—Algae

There are many, many species of macroalgae that make up part of the diet of omnivorous fishes. Some of these are ingested incidentally as the fish feed on small crabs, shrimps, and mollusks, and others are deliberately eaten. These algae may make up 10–50% of the diet of many species, so vegetable matter should be a basic part of their diet in captivity. Clownfish and batfish, and of course tangs and angelfish, are good examples of fish that normally include a high percentage of algae in their diet.

## Column 3—Algae and detritus

Detritus is composed of a great variety of organic matter. Bits of algae, organic flocculents, solid wastes from fish and invertebrates, coral slime, bacterial debris, and small worms and crustaceans accumulate in sheltered nooks about the reef. This detritus and the tiny algae and invertebrates associated with it are a food source for many small fish. Some gobies, blennies, and damselfish are among those that utilize this resource. Detritus accumulates in all aquariums, especially in well-lighted tanks, and serves, among other things, to supplement the diet of species that normally feed on it. These species do well on normal aquarium foods, but may require old, well-established marine aquariums.

## Column 4—Sponges

Sponges are about the simplest of the metazoans (many-celled animals), and they exhibit many forms and colors. The typical bath sponge and vase sponge are only two of thousands of types of sponges. A number of species grow in the reef environment and provide homes for many species of small fish and invertebrates. Sponges are incidentally ingested in small volume by most herbivorous fishes as they graze algae, but only adult angelfish consume sponges as their major dietary component. In fact, sponges compose 70–97% of the diet of adult Atlantic angelfishes. Juvenile angelfish feed on small crustaceans and filamentous algae. Frozen rations containing edible marine sponges are now available, while most sponge-eating species do well on a varied diet of meaty foods laced with vegetable matter.

## Column 5—Plankton pickers (planktivores)

Many small fish make all or part of their living by hovering in the water over the reef or burrowing and feeding selectively on the planktonic organisms that continually wash over these areas with the currents. Zooplankters—primarily copepods, small shrimps, mysids, and many types of fish and invertebrate larvae—are the usual food items. The proteins in the larval forms of fish, shrimps, crabs, etc. are essentially the same as those found in adults, so these items make good food sources for plankton picking fish. Plankton may form only a part of the diet of some fish, so it's important to also supply some plant food, such as algae growths or leafy greens. Almost all larval fish feed on zooplankton, even if the adults are herbivores; so the planktonic pastures are really the foundation for all life in the sea. Plankton pickers in the aquarium do well on bits of shaved shrimp and fish, processed flake food, and other foods that drift about in the water before settling. Many plankton pickers will not take food items once they have landed on the bottom.

## Column 6—Generalized bottom feeders

This category is composed mostly of large, non-specific carnivores such as sharks, snappers, and groupers, and includes many groups with juveniles important to the marine aquarist. These fish are opportunistic feeders, although they may have a general preference for a specific group of food organisms. In nature, they feed on whatever foods are most abundant and available—vast schools of small fish, shrimp, juvenile lobster, swarms of polychaete worms, almost anything and everything during the season of its abundance. The flexibility of their food requirements make these fish easy to feed in captivity, although some species may have other physiological requirements that make them difficult to keep. Again, a varied diet with an emphasis on bits of fresh frozen shrimp, clams, fish, and other seafood will keep these fish healthy and happy until they outgrow the aquarium.

### Column 7—Fish feeders (piscivores)

Very few marine fish suitable for small home aquariums are totally piscivorous, a fancy name for fish eaters. Some of the scorpionfishes—notably the lionfishes, as well as the anglerfishes, frogfishes, and sargassum fish—come fairly close to being exclusively piscivorous. These fish can usually be trained to take other foods, but this requires time and patience. Slow-moving piscivorous fish are usually so well camouflaged that they appear to be part of the reef. Small fish blunder near them, often attracted by fin modifications that look like small worms or algae growths, and are suddenly engulfed by the monstrous (to them) vacuum cleaner action of the scorpionfish's mouth. These fish have a tendency to eat every other fish in the tank. They are best kept by themselves or with larger fish, and hand fed. To feed newly imported specimens, it may be necessary to offer live foods, such as feeder fish or grass shrimp, at first. It is possible to train frogfish and lionfish to take dead marine minnows (silversides), and even pieces of fish or crustacean flesh, by loosely attaching the food to a string, stick, or wire to give it motion. The feeding of goldfish and freshwater feeder fish should be avoided, as prolonged consumption of such foods can lead to fatty liver degeneration and death in marine predators.

### Column 8—Coral feeders

To feed on coral polyps (the soft animal hidden in the stony coral skeleton), a fish must be able to either crush the hard coral, reach a tiny mouth into small protected areas to remove the animals therein, or suck the polyps out of the stony skeleton. All of these specialized modes of feeding can cause problems for the marine aquarist. Unless you take care and pay attention when developing a diet for these fish, they will not be able to obtain proper nourishment. The tiny-mouthed butterflyfishes and filefishes are some of the most difficult of this category to feed. Bits of shrimp, scallop, frozen plankton, or live *Tubifex* and White Worms (*Enchytraeus albidus*), pressed into pieces of coral rubble or irregular rock surfaces, often stimulate these fish to begin feeding. This will also help the corallivores find food in a competitive aquarium situation; however, be sure to remove any uneaten food presented in this manner so it doesn't foul the aquarium.

### Column 9—Crustacean feeders

These species feed primarily on small crustaceans, but are not above picking up worms or clams from time to time. Small shrimps and crabs represent the major part of their diet, so some crustacean flesh should be a staple part of their diet in captivity. If fish in nature feed almost exclusively on one type of organism, it is important to include that general type of food in their diet. Then you can be reasonably sure that all their required nutritional elements are available to them. Offering frozen *Mysis*, enriched brine shrimp, or krill is perhaps the easiest way to get crustacean material into your fish's diet.

### Column 10—Generalized invertebrates

Many, if not most, small tropical marine fish feed on a wide variety of small invertebrates with a little bit of algae included upon occasion. Although one group of organisms—shrimp, snails, clams, worms, or crabs—may be most common in the diet of certain species, a broad variety of small invertebrates are represented. The organism of choice often changes as the fish gains in size and changes its habitat. Since the specific natural diets of most fish at different stages of development are relatively unknown, a variety of foods that includes some items from each basic group of invertebrates is most likely to provide all the basic nutritional needs.

### Column 11—Parasite pickers

A few popular marine aquarium fishes make part of their living, either as adults or during the juvenile stage, by removing external parasites from large fish. It is not unusual for a diver to watch a huge Green Moray

The Cuban Hogfish, *Bodianus pulchellus*, one of a large number of wrasses that greedily feed on a wide variety of meaty prey, including many small crustaceans.

Eel waiting patiently with open mouth while a Neon Goby flits about its head and mouth picking up food debris and small parasites. A large grouper will often lean to one side against a coral head and allow small angelfish and gobies to move over its body and gills, picking off external parasites, and jacks will turn dark and hang over coral heads with open mouths while gobies and wrasses move over them, picking off parasites. This cleaning behavior is quite fascinating and can readily be observed in a home aquarium if Neon Gobies are kept with larger fish. Cleaner wrasses, and even small French Angelfish, also often display cleaning behavior in aquariums. Obviously, one would not want to provide parasites as a food source in the tank; fortunately, some parasite pickers can do very well on a varied basic diet when parasites are not available.

## Available aquarium foods

There is a wide variety of foods available to marine aquarists, most at little cost, that will provide a good diet for almost all marine fish. Many of these foods are listed below, with comments, to help you develop the proper feeding program for your particular needs. There are three main categories listed: prepared diets, plant foods, and animal foods. Ideally, the fish in a traditional community tank should receive two small feedings of a prepared diet each day and one feeding from each of the other two categories once a day, or at least every other day, to keep them in top condition. Most aquarists, however, cannot put this much effort into a feeding regimen for their tanks. Even though three or four relatively small feedings of varied foods per day is best, most marine fish can get by nicely on two feedings per day. A good dry flake–food feeding in the morning and a feeding of natural animal and plant foods in the evening will keep most fish in good condition. The following information may be more than you need or want to know about foods and feeding; and although you should be able to keep your marine fish healthy and happy with only a few of these options, it's good to know about a broad range of available foods and feeding techniques.

### Prepared diets

The prepared diet specially compounded for marine aquarium fish can be a great aid to the marine aquarist; however, total dependence on a prepared diet can cause nutritional problems. Convenience is the most obvious advantage of the prepared diet, but equally important are inclusion of a variety of proteins plus a broad spectrum of trace nutrients including vitamins and minerals. Be careful of using diets compounded for freshwater fish, because these do not provide the proper nutritional balance for coral reef fishes. They can easily cause problems, such as fatty degeneration of the liver, if fed to excess. Prepared diets can be purchased already compounded—frozen cubes and dry flake foods are the most popular forms—or they can be made at home in a wide variety of mixtures. Four basic types of prepared diets are discussed below.

**Dry flake foods:** This is the most widely used, and abused, form of prepared diet. These are relatively inexpensive, considering the small amounts consumed by each fish and the convenience of feeding, and contain a wide variety of nutrients. The flake food you choose should be of high quality,

For optimum health, offer fishes a variety of foods, including several prepared rations.

35–45% protein, and should contain some plant material, ideally including marine algae, *Spirulina*, and carotene. The flakes should be large and crisp and not smell musty or moldy. Store the well-sealed container in a dry, cool place, not next to a hot light fixture or near the spray of an air lift. Don't buy more than you can use in a month or two, and make sure that the dealer's stock is fresh. Be sure to choose dry flake and pellet foods that are compounded just for marine fishes. Even though flake food for freshwater fish may be less expensive, marine fish are better off when fed a dry food compounded especially for them, particularly if a dry processed food is the major portion of their diet.

Remember that flake food is very dry and compressed, so it contains a lot of food energy in a small package. It's easy to habitually overfeed the stuff. Just think what it would be like to eat all your meals as a dry, highly compressed flake with only a glass of water to wash it down (and saltwater at that!). Coral reef fish do not normally feed on the surface, and when they do take floating food, they may also ingest air bubbles, which can cause excessive buoyancy and disturb the digestive process. If this is a problem, soaking the food in a small volume of water before feeding eliminates floating food and surface feeding. Small fish, such as young clownfish, may gorge on dry food and develop a case of the "bloats" as the food expands in their stomachs. When this happens, the abdomen of the fish is greatly distended and the fish must continually fight to keep from floating at the surface. The cure for this condition is to stop feeding for a day and then feed mostly a wet food mix with only an occasional light feeding of dry food. Don't depend entirely on a dry flake food—fish also need fresh plant and animal foods on a regular basis.

**The seafood paste mix:** There are many variations of a wet blended diet that you can mix up yourself, and if you have the time and interest, this is a good way to give your fish the best possible diet with the least amount of daily fuss. It will, however, take an hour or two to make up the food for one or two months of feeding—a relatively minor investment of time, considering the aesthetic and monetary value of your marine display. Building your own diet for your fish also has the advantage of being ad-

Table or Green Shrimp form the basis of a homemade marine fish food, which can include scallops, clams, and sushi nori or other seaweed in a nutritious frozen ration.

justable to suit the type of fish you favor. Go heavy on the greens, for example, if you favor tangs and angelfish.

The basic ingredient for this mix is fresh frozen shrimp, scallops, clams, fish, lobster (if price is no object), or other crustaceans. Ingredients that break down to a paste-like consistency when blended, such as shrimp, are preferred over those that become watery, like oysters. Clean the meat of all shells, scales, or skin and blend it with a little water to make a paste. A blender or a food processor works well for this task. If possible, use two or three types of seafood (shrimp, clams, squid, and/or a non-oily fish) to provide a variety of nutrients. Other types of meat can also be added sparingly for additional variety. While this mixture is still in the blender (the average aquarist shouldn't need more than two or three cups of prepared diet at any one time), add about 20% by volume of vegetable material. Ideally, add dried or fresh marine algae (*Caulerpa, Ulva, Hypnea,* etc.) or *Spirulina,* available in flakes or powder. Chopped spinach or leaf lettuce can also be used. A spoonful or two of dry kelp powder can take the place of some of the vegetable matter.

Blend the mixture and either add a crushed tablet of a multivitamin mineral complex, or better yet, make up your own dry powder from vitamins A and E (dry powder from capsules), vitamin C crystals, defatted liver powder (for B vitamins), and, for minerals, kelp powder, bonemeal, and dolomite. The egg quality of spawning clownfish is often enhanced by the addition of chitin. Make enough of the mixture to fill an ice-cube tray, several cups, or as much as you will need for a month or two. The consistency can be controlled by adding water if it's too dense and dry flake food if it's too wet. The mixture is then frozen, either in ice-cube trays or in spoonfuls flattened out on a waxed-paper tray. After the mixture is well frozen, the individual cubes or sheets can be stored in a plastic bag.

At feeding time, remove one of the cubes and snip off small pieces of the right size for your fish and drop them into the aquarium. A fine-gauge stainless steel grater can also be used to provide the tiny pieces that are just right for juvenile fish and plankton pickers. If the mix is the right consistency, it will hold together until it is consumed by the fish. It isn't good to just toss a chunk into the aquarium and forget it, for it can dissolve into the water if uneaten and add too much too quickly to the organic load of the aquarium. Those with many tanks may wish to use the gelatin mix.

There are, of course, many frozen marine-food formulas commercially available to the saltwater aquarist. Purchasing these is considerably more expensive than mixing and freezing your own, but they do offer certain advantages. Not the least of these is the convenience of not having to mix up your own formula. There is also the advantage of the inclusion of marine animals (krill, sponges) and marine algae that the average aquarist can't collect on an afternoon's excursion, and having these varied ingredients in the proper balance. Some of these mixes also provide color enhancers and vitamin C in a stabilized form that keeps it available to the fish despite months of frozen storage. Thus, commercially available frozen food mixes offer a lot to marine aquarists, but as with all products, read the label. Also look at the condition of the package. Has it been sitting in the store's freezer for five years? Has it been thawed and refrozen a time or two? If it is not a fresh product in good condition, then you're better off making it up yourself or finding it fresh and good from a local aquarium store with a constant turnover of frozen food selections.

**The gelatin mix:** This diet is similar to the seafood paste mix, but is a little more versatile and a little more fuss to make. The ingredients can be quite varied because the whole thing is held together with gelatin instead of the protein paste of the fish or shrimp. The basic ingredients for the seafood mix can be used as the base for the gelatin mix. Many other ingredients, such as trout pellets, kelp bits or powder, and algae, can be included either ground or whole. Use up to 10–15% by weight of unflavored animal gelatin and about 50% water to make the basic mix. Add a little less water if the basic ingredients are wet. It will probably take a few attempts before you settle on the best formula for your fish, so don't be afraid to experiment if you decide to use the gelatin mix. Dissolve the gelatin in the water at a temperature of 150–200°F. Add the melted gelatin to the other ingredients when the temperature falls below 150°F and stir until the mixture is smooth. Now add the vitamin and mineral supplements and, if you wish, a little green or red food coloring. The coloring helps the fish see the food and helps the aquarist find uneaten food so it can be removed before it decomposes. Pour the completed mix into a tray and chill until it sets. The mix can then be cut up into cubes and stored in a closed container in the refrigerator or freezer. Bite-sized pieces should be cut or grated from the cube at feeding time.

**The plaster mix:** This mix has certain advantages, but may not be worth the bother of preparation to the average aquarist. "Plaster mix?" you may be thinking. "Has this guy developed a crack in his think tank?" But no, there is a good reason for a plaster mix. Most of the herbivorous fishes, and some coral and sponge eaters, spend a great deal of time biting and scraping at the reef to consume the proper amount of coral polyps and algae. Life is much easier in the aquarium, and even if the fish get along on the change of diet, they miss the extensive feeding activity. In fact, in the absence of browsing activity, the dentition of some fish, such as puffers, may grow long enough to cause feeding difficulties.

The plaster mix allows these fish to feed under simulated natural conditions and gives them the exercise they need. The basis of the plaster mix is simple; just prepare a small amount of a pure plaster of Paris (calcium sulphate) according to directions. Trace nutrients, and food coloring if desired, can be added while the mixture is still fluid. Wet ingredients added too soon to the plaster mix often interfere with hardening, so you should fold them in just before the plaster hardens. Adding these ingredients too late results in a rough, unblended mass. Chopped shrimp and fish, dry high-protein marine pellets, dry flake food with algae flakes, *Spirulina*, and kelp or algae are good inclusions. Make sure all excess water is removed from the ingredients before folding them into the hardening plaster. The food ingredients should only make up 10–15% of the total volume.

Store any unused mix in the refrigerator or freezer. Even though the food items are encased in plaster, they will still spoil readily, so any uneaten food mix should be removed from the aquarium after four or five hours. This diet is most often used by public aquariums that keep large fish, but may be useful to the advanced aquarist who keeps surgeonfishes and parrotfishes. The average aquarist looking for a simulated natural feeding approach may also wish to experiment with the plaster mix diet.

### Animal foods: live

Since most coral reef fish consume animal food as a major portion of their diet, animal foods are most important to the marine aquarist. Fish, like most other wild animals, consume the entire live prey organism when feeding. This gives them access to the minerals found in the hard parts and shells of their prey, plus vitamins from the internal organs and proteins and food energy from the flesh and fat. Obviously, a variety of live food organisms is the best possible diet for most fish, but only a most unusual marine aquarist can supply his or her fish with an exclusive diet of varied live foods. However, there are a number of live foods that can be provided fairly easily.

**Brine shrimp:** Brine shrimp are the most common live food that marine aquarists offer their fish. They are generally available in small portions as live adults or as dry eggs (cysts) that the aquarist hatches as necessary. Opinions on the value of live adult brine shrimp differ greatly among marine aquarists. Although live, clean, and well-fed adult brine shrimp are generally conceded to be an attractive and nutritious food (but not as an only food) for most marine tropicals, some aquarists fear the introduction of bacteria and parasites from unclean cultures of brine shrimp. A highly recommended procedure to enrich live adult brine shrimp prior to feeding calls for adding lipid concentrate to their water about 12 hours before they are to be fed to your fish. The most-used concentrate is called SELCO, a liquid rich in highly unsaturated fatty acids (HUFAs) that contains high levels of essential Omega-3 fatty acids. Powdered *Spirulina* can also be used to enrich live *Artemia*.

Brine shrimp can also be obtained in frozen and freeze-dried forms, although freezing can rob them of much of their nutritive value (58% protein) if they are not handled properly. Thawing and refreezing, or slow initial freezing, causes ice crystals to form in the tissues. Ice crystals rupture cells and internal organs and cause most of the fluids to leave the shrimp as they are thawed before feeding. Not only does this limit the shrimps' nutritional value to the protein in the exoskeleton, but ingestion of a large amount of dry food can cause difficulties for marine fish.

Newly hatched baby brine shrimp (nauplii) can be very valuable to the marine aquarist. They can be used to feed small plankton-feeding fish such as damselfish and jawfish, many filter-feeding invertebrates, and young fish of many species. Brine shrimp are very small when they hatch, not much bigger than a comma on a printed page, but even so, you may be amazed at the large size of many of the fish that eagerly eat them. Hatching them from eggs is quite simple. All that you need is a gallon jar of full-salinity seawater or artificial salt mix (even a straight rock salt mix

Nauplius, 48 hours old

Nauplius, 24 hours old

Nauplius, 3 days old

Nauplius, 6 hours old

Adult Brine Shrimp

Hydrated eggs

Brine shrimp life cycle: easily cultured to provide live food in various sizes for finicky fish.

will do) and an airstone for aeration. Vigorously bubble the saltwater with the brine shrimp eggs so that they do not accumulate at the surface. The jar should be filled about half full to reduce spray. A cap with a hole for the air tubing or a plug of cotton also reduces spray from the hatching jar. A jug with a narrow neck works too, but it can't be cleaned as easily as a wide-mouth jar. One or two teaspoons of eggs should provide plenty of hatchlings for most aquarists. The eggs hatch within 24 hours at temperatures of about 80°F. At temperatures in the low 70s, hatching may take up to 48 hours. Hatching time and yield depends greatly on egg quality and the setup. Keep temperatures above 75°F and allow light, preferably sunlight, to reach the hatching jar.

For about 8 hours after hatching, baby brine shrimp sink to the bottom and empty eggshells float at the surface when aeration is removed.

If you use good quality eggs, it should be possible to easily separate the nauplii from the eggs at this time by inserting a small siphon into the jar and drawing off the hatchlings from the bottom of the jar. Be sure to wait 15 or 20 minutes after the hatch to let the shells and the hatchlings separate, and break the siphon before the floating eggshells reach the bottom of the jar. Newly hatched brine shrimp are strongly attracted to light and can be concentrated in one spot by shining a narrow beam of light.

Separation of the nauplii from their eggshells is difficult if you wait too long after the hatch (two or three days) to siphon them off, since the hatchlings become mixed with the eggshells at the surface. If this occurs, the best thing to do is to use light to concentrate the hatchlings away from the empty shells. An elaborate separation box can be constructed that allows the new hatch to swim from a dark compartment to a lighted compartment under a partial partition that prevents the floating eggs from leaving the darkened compartment. A simpler, but less effective, procedure is to place a piece of black paper with a hole in it (about an inch in diameter) against the side of the hatching jar. Position the hole a few inches above the bottom of the jar and shine a light on the hole. The baby brine shrimp will be drawn down from the surface and cluster about the light. They can be easily siphoned out once they have gathered in the lighted area.

A fine-mesh net can be used to separate the hatchlings from the culture water and concentrate them in a small area for feeding to the fish or invertebrates. Baby brine shrimp have dense, oily yolk sacs that give them an orange or yellow color. It is possible to overfeed young fish on new hatched brine shrimp, which causes fatty degeneration of the liver. Thus, feed baby shrimp carefully to young fish and be sure that they do not over-feed on this very attractive food. Post-larval clownfish about 12 to 20 days old, incidentally, can overfeed on baby brine shrimp to the point that their abdomens are so distended they look like they are about to burst. When so overfed, the young clownfish may drift to the bottom and die.

Brine shrimp eggs are properly termed cysts, and they have gone through the early stages of development while still attached to the mother.

These cysts (eggs) then drop off the female and drift to the shore of the brine shrimp ponds where, in most species, they must undergo a dry period before complete development and hatching can occur. It is after they are deposited in windrows along the shore that they are collected, processed, and packaged. The dry eggs are separated from the debris and bad eggs by straining the shoreside debris to concentrate and recover all the eggs, and then air-blowing the eggs in a chimney to blow out all the lighter, unhatchable eggs. The heavier, good eggs can be kept viable for many years when sealed in a vacuum pack.

Brine shrimp eggs can also be put through a process that "decapsulates" them. This process removes the hard, indigestible coating on the eggs and leaves only a soft membrane around the yellow-orange yolk. The eggs go from dark brown, to white, and then to orange during this process. The decapsulated eggs are stored in brine under refrigeration, and are able to complete development and hatch just as untreated eggs do. Larval fish are able to eat and digest even the unhatched, decapsulated eggs and do not suffer intestinal blockage and death from eating unhatched eggs. Decapsulation is a dangerous process and should not be attempted unless one has some experience in working with hazardous chemicals. The decapsulation process is described in *The Marine Aquarium Reference.*

**Live fish:** A number of popular marine aquarium fish—lionfish, some eels, groupers and small snappers, sargassumfish, and frogfish—either require or enjoy small live fish in their diets. Unfortunately, a steady diet of freshwater fish is not recommended, although freshwater feeder fish, guppies, and mollies can be used initially, and stay alive long enough in the marine tank to entice the predator to strike. Some aquarists who keep piscivorous fishes maintain breeding colonies of saltwater mollies as fodder fish for their marine predators. If you do feed small fish from a marine or brackish water source, be sure to give them a two-minute freshwater bath before feeding to remove external parasites. Fortunately, most marine predators can be taught to take substitute meaty foods offered enticingly on a feeding stick.

**Small shrimp and other crustaceans:** Occasionally feeding live food is one of the best things you can do for the diet of your marine fish. Some retail shops offer live *Mysis* shrimp and grass shrimp of many types. Small, live crustaceans are not too difficult to find for yourself in coastal waters, if you are willing to spend a little time and effort. A fine-mesh dip net or

**Grass or peppermint shrimp can help trigger a feeding response from reluctant eaters.**

seine worked in grass beds in fresh or marine areas will often provide a surprising number of small shrimp, amphipods, crabs, worms, etc., and most of these are excellent live food organisms for your marines. Give the marine organisms a quick dip in freshwater to reduce the possibility of parasite introduction. The freshwater dip (saltwater dip for freshwater organisms) is a good way to either kill or incapacitate the organisms so that the fish can snap them up before they find shelter in the bottom of the tank. You may be surprised at how much small crustacean life already exists in your marine tank. Fish usually feed only in the daytime, and many small crustaceans are active only at night. Old, well-established tanks and refugiums often develop a population of amphipods and copepods that can only be observed crawling about algae-covered rocks and tank walls several hours after dark. Examination of the tank by flashlight at some time well into the night may reveal aspects of your aquarium that you never knew existed.

**Live coral & substitutes:** In the early days of marine aquarium–keeping, we often used Rose Coral for feeding corallivorous fishes. Rose Coral is a solitary coral found near coral reefs in tropical seas, and the common species in Florida waters is *Manicina areolata*. Because it is a solitary coral, Rose Coral was easily collected, handled, and shipped, and most coral polyp–eating fish enjoyed an occasional treat of fresh coral. Live Rose Coral can no longer be collected in the Florida Keys, so it is no longer readily available as a specialty food organism for keepers of butterflyfish and other fish.

Owing to the swelling interest in fragmenting and propagating stony corals, we now have an abundance of captive-grown live "feeder" corals to offer to species that are dedicated corallivores. Fast-growing branch

Aquarists near a seacoast can harvest their own live foods, such as *Mysis* shrimp.

*Acropora* spp. corals are ideal for this and are readily accepted by most corallivores. After the fish are acclimated to captivity, it is possible to offer a coral substitute by pressing a shrimp paste, high-protein frozen reef-fish ration, or *Tubifex* worms into the matrices of dead coral branches or heads. As mentioned below, this may be the best presentation for finicky butterflyfish and other coral pickers.

**Tubifex worms:** *Tubifex* worms have always been popular with freshwater aquarists, but they have an application in marine aquariums as well. One very useful method of feeding *Tubifex* worms is to press a small ball of worms deeply into a coral skeleton and then place it in the tank. Hard-to-feed fish, such as butterflyfish, are often attracted by the movement of the worms and begin to feed actively. Use caution when feeding *Tubifex* worms. They can quickly foul a tank if overfed to marine fish. Be sure to wash the ball of worms very well before feeding and remove all dead worms and decaying organic matter. *Tubifex* worms, like the organisms mentioned below, should not be a major portion of the diet.

**Other possibilities:** Some marine aquarists with a background in freshwater fish–keeping may wish to experiment with other typical live freshwater fish foods such as White Worms (*Enchytraeus albidus*), blood worms (bright red larvae of *Chironomus* sp. midges), earthworms, and fruit fly larvae. These are good occasional foods and may have some special uses for certain fish, including conditioning broodstock, but remember that the proteins and fats are not those that marine fish digestive systems have evolved to handle. A diet rich in these foods will probably cause liver problems for marine fish. Make sure that these foods are cleaned before introducing them to the tank.

Live clams and mussels can be collected in (unpolluted) shallow coastal areas or easily obtained at any seafood counter. Large angelfish, butterflyfishes, and even some hard-to-feed fish, such as Moorish Idols, will often greedily attack live mollusks served on the half shell. Be sure to remove shells and any uneaten scraps from the aquarium to prevent fouling the water.

### Animal foods: dead (preserved)

Most marine aquarists cannot feed live foods to their fish on a regular basis; fortunately, most fish do well on foods that can be stored in the freezer or on the shelf.

Harlequin Filefish, *Oxymonacanthus longirostris*, feeding on a piece of *Acropora* coral skeleton that has been coated with a high-protein reef-fish food paste. Using this method, aquarist Matt Pedersen has succeeded in weaning this obligate corallivore species from live coral polyps to prepared foods, on which they have thrived and spawned (see photos on pages 330 and 331).

**Frozen krill, *Mysis*, brine shrimp:** An extensive menu of single-species frozen animal foods high in protein is now available to marine aquarists. The most popular are frozen enriched adult brine shrimp, *Mysis* shrimp in different sizes, ocean plankton, and krill, also sold in a variety of sizes. For

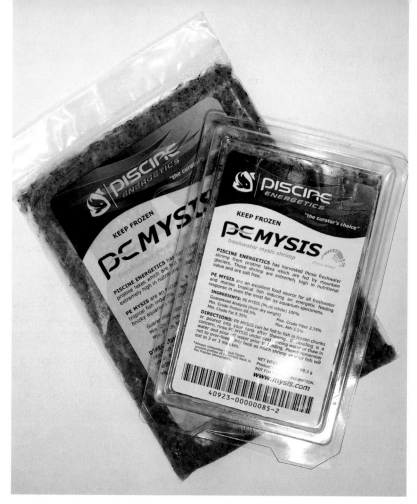

Good quality frozen *Mysis* shrimp has become a staple for serious marine aquarists. Although grown in cold northern lakes, it has an excellent nutritional profile, superior to that of most adult brine shrimp. Look for a brand with mostly intact, not broken, shrimp.

planktivores that need small-size prey items, frozen CYCLOP-EEZE® is a very rich ration provided by a bioengineered decapod crustacean cultured in cold northern lakes. Other frozen foods packaged for marine aquarium use include minced squid, clams, silversides (*Menidia menidia*, a marine minnowlike fish), sponge mixtures, and others.

Adding frozen fish foods, such as brine shrimp, directly to the tank as a small block and allowing the fish to snap them up as they drift off the block provides the most complete frozen protein possible for the fish. However, it also allows all juices and materials frozen in the food cube or block to escape into the tank. Thawing the block in water and straining the solid food from the accompanying liquid eliminates adding unnecessary organics to the tank, but it may also eliminate much of the nutritional value of the frozen food.

Brine shrimp are a good example. If the brine shrimp were quick-frozen live in clean water, it's best to just drop a small block in the tank and let the fish go to it. However, if the shrimp were frozen after they had been dead for a while, were frozen too slowly, or were thawed and refrozen one or more times, it's probably best not to feed them to the fish at all. Thaw a small part of the block in a clear glass and observe the result. If the water turns brown and the shrimp are nothing more than empty shells, it's a good bet the fish will gain little from eating them.

Freeze-dried brine shrimp, krill, and other foods have a strong tendency to float because they have no water at all in their tissues. It is best to soak these items in freshwater so that they sink and drift in the current when introduced into the aquarium.

**Table shrimp:** Green or table shrimp is one of the best basic foods for marine fish. Crustaceans of one type or another are a major part of the diet of many marine fish, and shrimp, being a common marine crustacean, is a good substitute for the natural diet. Shrimp can be obtained in frozen packages designated as tropical fish food, or as shrimp from the market in either fresh or frozen form, which is also excellent for marine fish.

There are numerous methods for feeding shrimp to marine fish. In almost all instances, the shrimp should be peeled and washed to remove the hard exoskeleton and excess fluids. Perhaps the easiest method of handling this basic food is to freeze the peeled, washed shrimp into a fist-sized ball and keep it in a plastic bag in the freezer. Select a metal grater that shaves particles of the proper size for the fish to consume in one bite. More than one size of grater can be used if small and large fish are kept together. The proper portion can be grated from the ball at each feeding time. Thus, one preparation of shrimp can last for several weeks and feeding is quick and simple. It is also possible to grate the entire portion of frozen, peeled shrimp at one time, either with the grater wheel of a food processor or with a bit of

**FOOD POLLUTION:**

Thaw a test portion of your frozen brine shrimp or other food. If it turns into a brown, watery mess, its food value may be suspect.

❖

elbow grease on a manual model. The shrimp bits can then be frozen in one-feeding portions, and feeding for the next few weeks consists only of dropping the premeasured frozen cubes of shrimp bits into the tank.

**Mollusks:** After crustaceans, mollusks are one of the most common food items in marine fish diets. Scallops, squid, clams, oysters, and conch are the most commonly encountered mollusks in food, bait, and fish-food products. All of the above can be utilized by marine aquarists in the same manner as shrimp. Most mollusks are not as "gelatinous" as shrimp, and although they are readily grated into small pieces when frozen, the pasty, binding quality of shrimp is absent. Alternate one or more of the mollusks with shrimp or blend them together to provide a good mix of marine animal protein.

**Processed plankton:** Marine plankton is now available as frozen, dried, and freeze-dried products. This plankton comes from the nutrient-rich cold waters of the Arctic and sub-Arctic regions of the Atlantic and Pacific oceans. It is composed primarily of small euphasid shrimp and/or calanoid copepods and is rich in protein (60–70%), wax esters, and lipids. Cold-water northern plankton is not a natural food of marine tropicals. However, it is a good, but rich, fish food, and one should be careful not to overfeed, especially with the dry form of the product. This cold-water plankton is rich in pigments and lipids, and feeding it should enhance the condition and color of your marine fish.

**Fish:** Ocean fish is another good source of animal protein for your marines. Most small reef fish do not commonly eat fish, as they are not equipped to chase and capture them. However, when an injured or dead fish presents the opportunity, most are quick to partake of their hapless comrade. Boneless fish flesh can be prepared and fed like peeled shrimp. Be careful not to overfeed, because fish flesh seems to have a greater tendency to foul the aquarium water than shrimp or scallop. All fish products, like all marine animal foods, should be frozen hard before feeding to reduce the possibility of parasite introduction. Fish roe and fish liver are also excellent foods for marines. These foods are best fed by snipping small pieces off a frozen block and feeding them slowly. Fish roe contains a lot of oil and shouldn't be fed to excess, but a little bit now and then will provide many of the nutrients and important pigments that may be missing or altered in other foods. Watch the color of your fish improve after feeding fish roe once or twice a week.

*Ulva lactuca* (Sea Lettuce) is easily cultivated and an ideal live food for herbivores.

**Other meats:** Lean beef, beef liver, and beef heart are often recommended for feeding to freshwater fish. An occasional feeding of these products is helpful if seafoods just aren't available and the only alternative is a constant dry food diet. If you must feed the meat of land animals, rabbit and chicken may be better because there is less fat in their flesh. Defatted beef liver powder is a good source of B-vitamins and can be added to the paste mix—and it doesn't add much fat to the diet. Remember that fish are cold-blooded (poikilothermic), and all digestion reactions take place at 70 to 80°F, the temperature of the aquarium water. Thus, they may not be able to efficiently digest or use the types of fats present in the flesh of warm-blooded animals. They are much better off with the flesh of animals that are similar to their normal prey.

### Plant foods

As mentioned previously, vegetable matter is an important part of the diet of most marine fish. Tropical marine algae, since they are the natural plant foods, should be included in the diet. Broad, thin, green algae such

Bay Anchovies, *Anchoa mitchilli*, and Silversides, *Menidia menidia*, are marine minnow-like fish that can be fed to many predators, such as lionfish, eels, and sea anemones.

as *Caulerpa* and *Ulva*, and meaty reds and browns such as *Gracilaria*, *Hypnea*, *Gelidium*, and *Dictyota*, are commonly found in stomach content analyses, and are the best ones to feed. These algae can be added to prepared diets or washed with freshwater and placed in the aquarium as browse for the fish.

Both live and dried marine macroalgae can be easily obtained by most marine aquarists. Live algae can also be cultivated in a refugium or in a spare aquarium placed in a sunny window or under lights. *Ulva latuca* (Sea Lettuce) and red *Gracilaria* are particularly well suited to cultivation. The nutrient-rich water removed from your display aquarium during water changes can be used to grow macroalgae.

Other substitutes for tropical marine algae are available. *Spirulina* flakes, wafers, and pellets can be purchased wherever freshwater fish foods are sold. Although cultivated in freshwater, *Spirulina* is an excellent food for marine herbivores. Pacific kelp and other algae are used as human food supplements and are available in health food markets, oriental food stores, and grocery stores, usually in dried form. Most marine fish will eat *nori*, the dried green seaweed sheets sold for sushi-making. Terrestrial greens can be supplied by including chopped spinach and/or turnip greens and an occasional leaf of bright green or red lettuce. Save the iceberg to be served with Thousand Island dressing; this lettuce does not have as much nutritional value as darker-leafed lettuce. Be sure to remove uneaten fresh greens after a day or two to prevent them from rotting in the tank. Dried macroalgae is often fed in plastic clips that attach to the inside wall of the aquarium.

## Feeding invertebrates

Most active invertebrates, such as shrimp, octopus, lobsters, and crabs, prefer a chunk of solid food that they can hold and tear apart with their mouth parts. These animals often feed at night and are adept at finding small food particles that the fish may have missed during the day. A few small pieces of frozen shrimp or fish dropped into the tank after lights out will usually keep these animals well fed, since they don't have to compete with the fish after dark.

Good algal growth in the tank keeps most of the slow-moving grazers like sea hares, nudibranchs, and sea urchins quite happy. If you live near the sea, a rock heavy with marine growth provides much food for invertebrates and some fish. However, beware of parasite introduction. Unless the live rock is put through quarantine, it may be best to restrict it to an invertebrate-only tank. Many of the invertebrates now kept are basically plankton feeders such as tube worms, some anemones, corals, and bivalve mollusks. They all have some sort of feeding mechanism that catches or filters out the tiny planktonic organisms that normally surround them. There are two ways to feed these animals with live organisms: introducing the food organisms to the tank or removing the invertebrates from the display tank and placing them in a feeding tank. Newly hatched baby brine shrimp are a very good food because they are nutritious, do not foul the aquarium, are easy to produce, and are readily taken by filter feeders. Wild-caught live ocean plankton is also very good, but in addition to being difficult to get, it may also introduce disease organisms.

A baster is a handy tool at feeding time. Concentrate baby brine shrimp in a cupful or two of saltwater and use the baster to direct a stream of brine shrimp nauplii into the vicinity of your filter-feeding

Tomato Clownfish nestles in a Bubbletip Anemone: anemones demand target feeding with pieces of crustacean flesh or silversides at least once or twice a week.

invertebrates. Some animals, such as small anemones that are attached to a moveable rock, feather duster worms, small basket stars, some soft corals, and barnacles, can be removed from the aquarium and placed in a bucket or small tank with a high concentration of newly hatched brine shrimp and good aeration. After several hours they will be well fed and can be replaced in the display tank.

### Anemones

Anemones are beautiful animals, but are often difficult to keep. They require the highest quality water and intense, full-spectrum lighting to keep them in good condition. Anemones of the genera *Stichodactyla*, *Heteractis*, and *Entacmaea* (the easiest to keep by far), the typical clownfish anemones, trap and feed on larger invertebrates and fishes as well as planktonic creatures in nature, so they relish a piece of shrimp or fish once or twice a week. If a clownfish is kept with the anemone, it can often be persuaded to feed its companion. Try giving the clownfish a morsel of food too big for it to swallow, and it will usually carry the food to the anemone and obligingly thrust it deeply into the anemone's tentacles. Fine-tentacled anemones also take small planktonic food, so it is good to give them an occasional feeding of live baby brine shrimp. Anemones, like their cousins the corals, also obtain nourishment a third way. Their tissues contain living algal cells called *Zooxanthellae*; and in exchange for a protected place to live, these algal cells produce food through photosynthesis in excess of their own needs and supply it to the anemone.

Lighting must be intense and close to full-spectrum to provide the algal cells buried in the anemone's tissues with enough light for photosynthesis. The good reef aquarist understands this and provides his or her anemones with adequate lighting of the right type so they remain in good health. Once an anemone has turned completely white or cream-colored, all the algal cells are gone and the anemone is on a downhill ride that is almost impossible to reverse. It may live another six months or so, but will lose condition, get very much smaller, and eventually die. This is why anemones often fail to live very long in captivity. The only remedy is to ensure adequate light while the anemone is still in good condition.

Under the right conditions, the reproduction of anemones by splitting and/or egg production can occur regularly in hobbyists' tanks. Even with intense light, however, be sure your anemones are routinely fed.

## Corals

While reef aquarists once believed that the path to success with corals lay in providing intense illumination and starving the aquarium, it is now understood that many corals need to be fed to thrive, grow, and reproduce. Most corals are equipped with extensible feeding tentacles that they put to good use in the wild, catching passing plankton and other food items, such as marine snow, and directing them to the mouth. (Marine "snow" consists of complex globs of organic detritus, dead or dying planktonic items, phytoplankton, animal wastes, and more, all held together by a mucus generated by bacteria.)

When selecting a new fish specimen, be sure it is responsive when offered food.

Many substitutes for wild plankton and marine snow are now commercially available, including frozen and liquid coral rations, live phytoplankton, CYCLOP-EEZE®, oyster eggs, rotifers, *Artemia* nauplii, and a growing array of copepods and other zooplankton, both live and preserved.

Corals with large, fleshy polyps will be healthier and grow faster if target-fed with meaty foods such as mysid shrimp, krill, minced crustacean flesh, squid, and other high-protein foods of marine origin. Although many of these animals are naturally nocturnal, extending their feeding tentacles after dark, they can be trained to open while the lights are on once they learn that food is present.

The once very-hard-to-keep non-photosynthetic corals, such as Sun Corals (*Tubastrea* spp.), gorgonians, and some challenging soft corals, are now being successfully maintained with feedings of tiny planktonic items, including rotifers, live phytoplankton, CYCLOP-EEZE®, newly hatched brine shrimp, smaller *Mysis* shrimp, and myriad other experimental foods.

## Summary

A marine aquarist can now buy good quality marine flake foods, formulated frozen food, marine pelleted food for bottom feeders, and many types of dried marine macroalgae for fish with herbivorous leanings—and this will keep most marine fish and invertebrates reasonably happy. As long as feeding is fairly regular, not too much food is given at one time, and you include as much variety as possible, the tank's inhabitants will be quite satisfied and will not resort to buying groceries on the black market from the dog and the canary (OK, think Disney movie and that comment might make some sense).

An aquarist can also grow or buy live marine macroalgae (*Gracilaria*, *Sargassum*, and *Ulva* spp.) for herbivorous fish, culture amphipods and copepods in a refugium, make up a shrimp-based food mix with vitamins B and C every month, add a little iodine and minerals to the food mix, perhaps add some color-enhancing CYCLOP-EEZE®, and feed live brine shrimp grown out in a green microalgae culture every two or three days— and really have happy fish.

I have tried to avoid getting too academic in this chapter, so I haven't discussed such things as the various amino-acid building blocks of proteins and which of these are essential (i.e., can't be made by the fish themselves) and which aren't (i.e., the fish can make them from other amino acids); ash residue; proximate analysis of various food organisms; undigestible fiber; the essential w3 series of fatty acids required by all fish, and those not needed by marine fish; protein quality; and many, many more topics of essential interest to marine fish culturists and nutritionists. The average marine aquarist doesn't use this kind of information, at least not directly.

I have tried to talk about things that will help a marine aquarist to understand and supply the basic nutritional needs of marine tropical fish. So it seems fitting that I close this chapter with a list of comments and ideas on foods and feeding, most just common sense, that will help you to meet the needs of your finny aquatic friends. Note that in my book, *The Marine Aquarium Reference: Systems and Invertebrates*, there is an extensive chapter on food and feeding of marine invertebrates.

1. Strive for variety in foodstuffs. Avoid feeding one food item exclusively over a long period of time. Don't use rancid fats or oils, and don't feed seafood items that smell decayed.

2. Avoid too much fat; most marine tropical fish should have 10% or less fat in their diets. High-fat foods include squid, oily fish, and worms.

3. Avoid foods compounded for freshwater and cold water fish, especially trout and salmon—too much fat.

4. Avoid feeding large amounts of carbohydrates to carnivorous and omnivorous fish. Carbohydrates should constitute less than 5% of the diet of most marine tropical fish. Most marine fish do not need much fiber, either. About 5%, or even less, seems to be enough for most marine fish.

5. Feed high protein foods. The diet of most marine tropical fish should be 40–60% protein. Feed protein from various marine animal sources to include all the essential amino acids needed by all the different species that are in the tank. (Yeah, I know, 10% fat, 5% carbohydrate, 5% fiber, and 60% protein is only 80%. Don't worry about the other 20% of the diet, the fish will take care of that themselves. These are only rough guidelines, but they should give you some idea of the direction to go in providing food for marine tropical fish.)

6. Supplement the water-soluble vitamins C and the B group, especially C. The oil-soluble vitamins A, D, E, and K are less important to supplement if a good variety of fresh foods are fed. A little brewer's yeast in the food mix is a good source of B vitamins. (Today, many high-quality flake and frozen rations are supplemented with vitamins and color enhancers.)

7. Iodine is often lacking in the diet of marine tropical fish, and a constant lack of iodine can cause goiter. Supplement iodine if fresh foods are rarely fed.

8. Fish colors, especially yellow, orange, and red, are greatly enhanced by the addition of certain pigments to the diet. The most effective pigments are the carotenoids canthaxanthin and astaxanthin. Beta carotene

is probably the only carotenoid most aquarists can find, and it is slightly better than none, but fish generally cannot use beta carotene effectively. Astaxanthin, on the other hand, with the proper lighting, will brighten up yellow, red, and orange fish remarkably. Look for foods that list canthaxanthin and/or astaxanthin as ingredients. Note that some foods designed to enhance color in freshwater fish contain the male hormone testosterone. This is ineffective in enhancing the marine fish colors that are not

**Captive-bred Ocellaris Clownfish at feeding time in a large reef aquarium.**

Harlequin Filefish eating live polyps from a colony of "feeder coral," a captive-propagated colony of *Acropora yongei*—a fast-growing species known as Bali Green Staghorn. Some obligate corallivores can be weaned off live corals and trained to eat substitute prepared foods applied to dead coral branches. (See page 261.)

breeding colors. A good dose of testosterone, however, will quickly take the wind out of the sails of a breeding female of any fish species.

9. Breeding marine fish requires great attention to diet. Find and supply the natural diet for the species that is to be bred, or a good natural (fresh or frozen) substitute.

10. Raw foods of marine origin provide the best mix of essential nutrients, but also carry the greatest risk of disease and parasite introduction. Feed raw marine foods, but be very careful and select only foods from fresh and healthy sources. Freezing preserves the nutrition of marine foods better than cooking, but it is not as sure a control of disease contamination as is cooking.

11. Use a turkey baster to squirt small particulate foods or small live foods directly at specific invertebrates or in the vicinity of small fish.

12. Use a feeding stick or long-handled tweezers to target-feed individual polyps of large-polyped stony corals with large *Mysis* shrimp, krill, or pieces of of marine fish or crustacean flesh.

Feeding marine fishes and invertebrates has never been easier, given the choices of foods available, but as the diversity of animals in your marine aquarium grows, so, too, does the need to satisfy all the different appetites you have brought into your care. Feed them well and they will reward you with years of good health, growth, brilliant colors, and perhaps the chance to see reproductive behaviors in action.

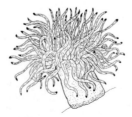

# Breeding Marine Fish

## *The Basic Process and Easiest Species*

THIS CHAPTER WAS ORIGINALLY PUBLISHED IN 1982 AND WAS REVISED AND expanded for the second edition in 1992. For all of the '80s and most of the '90s, this chapter was pretty much the most comprehensive work on breeding tropical marine fish available to marine hobbyists. At the end of the '90s, several new books on rearing marine tropical fish were published that greatly expanded the marine aquarist's base of knowledge and stimulated rapid growth of this intriguing and difficult branch of the marine aquarium hobby. Frank Hoff published his book, *Conditioning, Spawning, and Rearing of Fish with Emphasis on Marine Clownfish,* in 1996. My book, *Breeding the Orchid Dottyback: an Aquarist's Journal,* followed in 1997. Joyce Wilkerson's remarkable tome, *Clownfishes: A Guide to Their Captive Care, Breeding and Natural History,* closed out the '90s in 1998. Then there was a long wait until 2007, when Matthew Wittenrich completed his magnum opus, *The Complete Illustrated Breeder's Guide to Marine Aquarium Fishes.*

Breeders of marine fish and invertebrates were not idle between the publications of these books. The phenomenon of the Internet changed the face of communication among marine aquarists. Online magazines, aquarist forums, informational websites, and the instant communication of e-mail all gave aquarists rapid and extensive access to worlds of information, opinions, and advertising, some good and some bad. Now

Young Green Mandarinfish, *Synchiropus splendidus*, captive-bred by Matthew Wittenrich, author of *The Complete Illustrated Breeder's Guide to Marine Aquarium Fishes.*

one can have instant access to mind-boggling amounts of information, of both a scientific and popular nature, on breeding marine fish and the reproductive biology of marine organisms. Although this is a boon to those who seek knowledge, it takes a while to sift through the information that is available, discarding that which is inaccurate and filling in the gaps between casual observations and scientific treatises. The Internet is almost always the first place to begin a search. But still, there's nothing like a book from a good author that allows the reader to learn and effectively use the author's knowledge and vision of a broad subject.

This chapter won't answer all your questions if you are strongly interested in breeding marine fish. It is a good place to start, however, and it will give you the fundamentals of the process. It is probably less expensive in terms of money and equipment (but not time) to breed the easier species of marine fish than it is to set up a good coral-reef aquarium. I'm fond of saying, "Biology does not change, but technology does." The technology that I used back in 1972 was primitive compared to the knowledge and equipment now available, but it was adequate then to rear considerable numbers of many species of marine fish, and the same homemade equipment and techniques can be successful today in the quest to rear clownfish, gobies, and other species.

Now, as before, clownfish are the best species for beginners. They are popular, will spawn in a small environment, and have large eggs that are easily seen. The larvae are large, have a short larval period, and are relatively easy to rear. (The Banggai Cardinalfish may be the easiest fish to breed, but its mouthbrooding habits deliver fully developed juvenile fish, and rearing them teaches little that can be applied to the majority of marine fishes.) By rearing clownfish, you will learn the essentials of conditioning, spawning, larval rearing, metamorphosis, and juvenile grow-out.

**EASY SPECIES:**

Now, as before, clownfish are the best species for beginners in marine breeding.

❖

This chapter will tell you all you absolutely need to know to rear clownfish. However, there is an extensive body of literature out there, along with online hobbyist forums, that will greatly help the first-time (or second- or third-time) fish breeder to succeed. There are now many other species with which a breeder of marine fish can work. The Marine

Above: Yellow Watchman Gobies, captive-bred by Amy Drehmel. These gobies pair off and spawn readily, and larvae can be fed S-strain rotifers as a first food. Next page: Matt Wittenrich's study of *Amphiprion* clownfish species and color morphs.

Ornamental Fish & Invert Breeders' Association (MOFIB) has an on-line forum that pretty well covers most current hobbyist breeding activity, and the Breeder's Registry has a library of reports on breeding both fish and invertebrates. These sources will tell you what species are being bred by hobbyists and, to some degree, how to work with many species of marine fish and invertebrates. And there are other forums, as well, that have sections for breeders of many organisms. Matthew Wittenrich's book, mentioned above, will also be a very useful resource to both new and experienced marine fish breeders. So, although this chapter is a good basic resource for the aspiring breeder, there is now much more information available for guidance.

When I first began rearing clownfish in 1972, there were only a few species commonly available. *Amphiprion ocellaris*, the False Clown Anemonefish, or Ocellaris Clown, which I first started breeding, was by far the most common clownfish available. It probably still is, although there are now many other species that are not uncommon in the trade but were

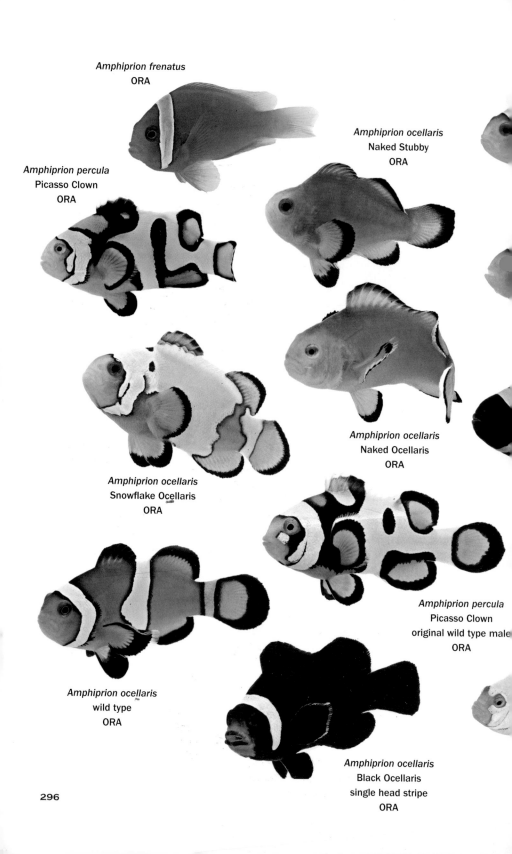

*Amphiprion frenatus*
ORA

*Amphiprion percula*
Picasso Clown
ORA

*Amphiprion ocellaris*
Naked Stubby
ORA

*Amphiprion ocellaris*
Snowflake Ocellaris
ORA

*Amphiprion ocellaris*
Naked Ocellaris
ORA

*Amphiprion percula*
Picasso Clown
original wild type male
ORA

*Amphiprion ocellaris*
wild type
ORA

*Amphiprion ocellaris*
Black Ocellaris
single head stripe
ORA

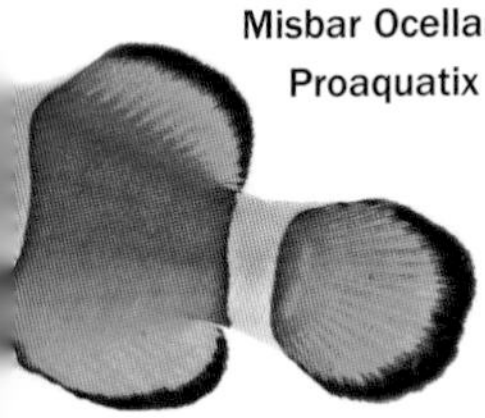

Amphiprion ocellaris
Misbar Ocellaris
Proaquatix

Amphiprion percula
Solomon Islands
wild type

Amphiprion percula
Onyx Percula
Solomon Islands
wild type

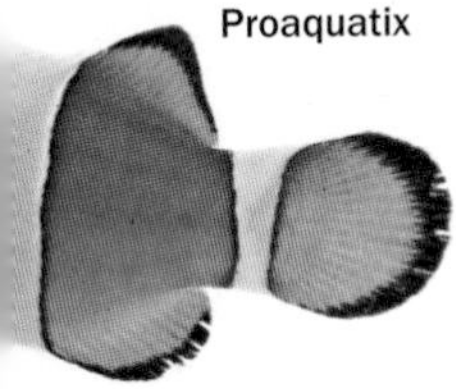

Amphiprion ocellaris
Proaquatix

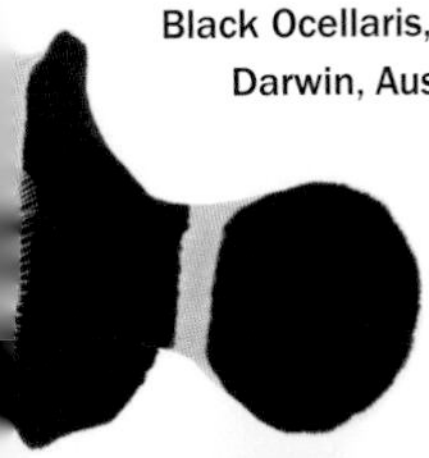

Amphiprion ocellaris
Black Ocellaris, wild type
Darwin, Australia

Amphiprion percula
Solomon Islands
wild type

Premnas biaculeatus
wild type

Amphiprion clarkii
ORA

Amphiprion percula
Platinum Percula
ORA

Amphiprion ocellaris
Wyoming White Ocellaris
C-Quest Hatcheries

Captive-bred Percula Clownfish juveniles with a distinctive "misbar" color pattern.

only pictures in books back in the '70s. The company I started in 1973, Aqualife Research Corporation, reared about 10 species of clownfish over the 23 years or so of its existence. Now, in the first decade of the twenty-first century, I think almost all of the 28 named species of clownfish have been reared. Some are quite a bit easier than others to rear in captivity.

The most interesting and amazing thing to me is that so many variations, some apparently with a genetic basis, are developing in the captive genotypes of the Percula and Ocellaris Clownfish. When I first bred Ocellaris and Percula Clowns back in 1972, I wondered if variations in color and form would appear and be set by breeders of the future. I thought that in 50 or 100 years we might see new strains of clownfish that were far different from the wild-caught species. After all, I reasoned, it did take the Chinese many centuries to change the common carp into goldfish and eventually koi—although we do have the advantage of advanced technology and biological knowledge, so it might not take as long. How genotypes of marine fish might adapt through selective breeding was an unknown. And wow! After fewer than 30 years, there are many relatively well established, stable color variations of Percula and Ocellaris Clownfish. Black, white, red, solid orange, and variable patterns of these colors now exist, and hobbyists and commercial producers are working with the different strains to set them into established "breeds" and create new strains as well. Most of these color morphs appeared in the mid-1990s. In her 1998 book, Wilkerson mentions four different color variations of Percula Clowns that were just becoming available at that time. Today, only about a decade later, many interesting names are applied to these color morphs—sometimes to distinguish very subtle variations in color shades and patterns. It is amazing to see the development of so many variations in a species that was totally wild such a short time ago. I'm glad I've lived to see the early development of domestication in species that I helped to bring into the fold of captive cultivation.

## Captive breeding: a brief look back

Not so very long ago, as late as the early 1970s, it was possible to find authoritative quotes in the aquarium literature stating that marine tropical fish could not be successfully reared in commercial numbers because the particular conditions required by the delicate larvae could not be consistently maintained. This was certainly true up until the late '60s, but at that time increased interest and experimentation in the propagation of marine food fish stimulated development of new techniques that could be transferred, with a few modifications, to the culture of some marine tropical fish. Propagation of pompano, the gourmet fish of our subtropical waters, was the subject of intense and highly competitive efforts by several commercial firms and government laboratories. These efforts, some biologically successful and some not, have all been dropped or redirected due to financial, economic, and technical difficulties. Some individuals involved in these projects, however, have shifted their knowledge and talents to the propagation of marine tropical fish. Although it developed slowly at first, the farming of marine tropical fish now has a strong toehold and should continue to expand.

**GAINING MOMENTUM:**
Marine breeding started slowly, with many failures, but is now gaining momentum, producing new species every year.

It was soon apparent that the most immediate financial rewards did not come from food-fish culture, although the market was vast (as was the initial capital investment). The propagation of marine tropical fish promised a better and faster return, for even though the market was much smaller than that for food fish, the price per unit was far higher. In late 1972 and early 1973, I began to work at home in my garage on the problems of rearing marine tropical fish, and in early 1973 succeeded in rearing thousands of juvenile "False Percula," or Common Clownfish, *Amphiprion ocellaris*, from two spawning pairs. The early part of this work was reported in the March-April 1973 issue (Vol. 9, No. 2 ) of *Salt Water Aquarium* magazine, published by the late Robert P. L. Straughan. Mr. Straughan contributed greatly to the development of the marine aquarium hobby and was always optimistic about the possibility of rearing marine tropical fish on a grand scale. It seemed appropriate that the first account of rearing large numbers of a marine tropical fish should appear in his publication.

Since that time there has been much activity and many published articles centered on marine tropical fish propagation, and many species have been reared through the larval stage, although only a few in commercial numbers. Aqualife Research first marketed tank-reared Ocellaris Clownfish and Neon Gobies in 1973, and since then, many other companies have begun rearing clownfishes and other species commercially.

With the important contributions of such pioneering companies as Bill & Katy Addison's C-Quest in Puerto Rico, Frank Baensch's Reef Culture Technologies in Hawaii, and Oceans, Reefs & Aquariums and Proaquatix in Florida, there is now a good selection of tank-reared marine tropicals on the market, and more suppliers are sure to spring up as demand grows. Although many aquarists have expanded their hobby in the last decade to include home-based "garage" hatcheries that provide local hobbyists with high-quality marine fish and corals, the demand for "CB" (captive-bred) stock cannot always be met.

The number of species of marine ornamental tropical fish that have been spawned and reared is growing by leaps and bounds, with more added every year. The list provided on the next page gives an idea of the range of families that include species successfully bred in captivity. (A hobbyist organization, The Breeder's Registry, listed in the back pages, keeps an up-to-date listing of marine organisms bred by hobbyists and commercial ventures.)

Many other species have been spawned and reared for only a few days

# Marine fish families bred in captivity

Antennariidae (Frogfishes)
Apogonidae (Cardinalfishes)
Batrachoididae (Toadfishes)
Blenniidae (Blennies)
Callionymidae (Mandarinfishes)
Carangidae (Jacks, Pompanos, Lookdowns)
Diodontidae (Porcupinefishes)
Ephippidae (Spadefishes)
Gobiesocidae (Clingfishes)
Gobiidae (Gobies)
Grammidae (Grammas & Basslets)
Labridae (Wrasses)
Monacanthidae (Filefishes)
Monodactylidae (Moonfishes)

Opistognathidae (Jawfishes)
Ostraciidae (Boxfishes)
Plesiopidae (Comets)
Plotosidae (Eeltail Catfishes)
Pomacentridae (Damselfishes)
Pomacanthidae (Angelfishes)
Pseudochromidae (Dottybacks)
Pseudomugilidae (Blue-eyes)
Sciaenidae (Drums)
Serranidae (Groupers)
Siganidae (Rabbitfishes)
Syngnathidae (Seahorses & Seadragons)
Tetraodontidae (Puffers)
Tripterygiidae (Threefin Blennies)

**Among the Holy Grail species for captive breeders are the many marine angelfishes.**

into the larval stage, and a number of others have been reared from wild spawned eggs or larvae taken in plankton tows. A number of food and bait species from tropical and subtropical waters have also been reared very successfully. On the invertebrate side of things, ornamental shrimps, giant clams (*Tridacna* spp.), and numerous corals of all types are being captive-propagated.

Thus, the basic technology exists to breed and raise many important marine aquarium species, and tank-reared fish and invertebrates will, no doubt, be a significant part of the marine aquarium hobby's future.

## Modes of reproduction

The propagation of marine tropical fish progressed slowly for years. There were many reasons for this, but perhaps the most important of them was the lack of understanding of—and the difficulty of creating—the pelagic environment essential for larval survival. Since widespread marine aquarium–keeping is a relatively recent development, most aquarists' basic concepts of aquatic life are based on their knowledge of freshwater fish.

Freshwater fish reproduction involves processes we can understand, which fit in well with our preconceived ideas of terrestrial animal reproduction—things like nest-making, live birth, baby fish that can be easily seen with the naked eye and that swim in schools, parental care of eggs, and parental protection of baby fish—all of the above taking place in a bottom-oriented (benthic) environment. It is natural to retain these concepts when we think about marine aquariums.

Unfortunately, these freshwater concepts about the nature of the watery world can cause a number of misconceptions about what we see in the marine environment. Most marine fish do not care for their young once they have hatched. In fact, since most marine fish spend their larval period as a part of the plankton, many plankton-feeding fish quickly eat their own young if they happen to drift by. During their time in the plankton, larval fish are totally dependent on planktonic microorganisms for food, and although they can move about within the space of a few feet, at most, major movement is dependent on ocean currents during their early larval life.

The modes of reproduction of marine fish can be put in four basic categories:

1. The most common is release of tiny, transparent, free-floating (pe-

lagic) eggs with complete absence of parental care. Angelfish, butterflyfish, tangs, groupers, snappers, wrasses, grunts, drums, and parrotfishes are among those that employ this type of reproductive style. These are the most challenging fishes for would-be aquaculturists.

2. The second most common mode is attachment of the eggs to a secure substrate, usually near the bottom, in a type of nesting behavior. These are termed demersal eggs (in contrast to free-floating pelagic eggs), and the resulting larvae may be large, as with clownfish, or quite small, as with damselfish. Gobies, blennies, damselfish, and clownfish are common nest-building marine tropical fish.

3. A variation on the demersal theme is oral incubation of eggs, or mouthbrooding. Instead of attaching the eggs to the bottom, the male retains them in his oral cavity during the period of incubation. Jawfish and cardinalfish are mouthbrooders. (Most famous is the Banggai Cardinalfish, *Pterapogon kauderni*, introduced to the marine aquarium hobby in 1995, which has a most unusual characteristic for marine fish: the eggs and young are brooded in the mouth of the male to juvenile competency, bypassing a pelagic stage completely. Because of this unusual reproductive characteristic, this species suffers from great popularity in the marine aquarium hobby and very limited reproductive capacity in nature, which results in a restricted range and small populations. Thus, this species is easy to breed but extraordinarily susceptible to overfishing, and is now in danger of severe population reduction in many areas of its natural habitat.)

4. A very few marine species, such as seahorses and livebearing Brotulas, give birth to well-developed live young.

Livebearers, mouthbrooders, and those fish that lay demersal eggs produce far fewer eggs than do fish that spawn pelagic eggs. These species aer-

**SPAWN SIZES:**
Fishes that release pelagic eggs into the plankton produce much larger spawns than do demersal spawners and mouthbrooders.

❖

ate and protect their eggs from predators during early development, attaining an economy of reproductive energy in exchange for a period of parental care. Nesting and mouthbrooding species incubate their eggs from three to ten (or more) days, depending on the species, and the young are hatched with a small residual yolk sac, fully developed eyes and mouth

Tiny prolarva of a captive-bred Harlequin Filefish in a drop of water, with bright green yolk sac, floating above its own shadow.

parts, and the ability to swim with purpose and direction. Some settle immediately on the reef where they were hatched, while others may still pass some time as creatures of the plankton, but the helpless egg and prolarval stages of a pelagic egg are avoided and the total larval period is usually shortened.

The spawn of species that protect their eggs varies in number from a low of 50–100 to a high of 10,000–15,000, whereas those species that spawn pelagic eggs can produce well over 200,000 eggs per spawn and may spawn on almost a daily basis during the height of the spawning season. Of course, small species, such as pygmy angelfish, spawn fewer eggs—only 300 to 500 per spawn—but these spawns can also occur on a daily basis.

The larvae that hatch from pelagic eggs are completely helpless. They carry a large yolk sac and have not yet formed pigmented eyes, a functional gut, or mouth parts, and the paired fins are still mere buds. Another 72 hours must pass before these larvae develop to the point that the yolk sac is consumed and they can swim and feed on their own.

The popular aquarium literature in recent years has published numerous articles and several very good books on rearing marine tropical fish, and most have been helpful to aspiring culturists. However, the successful

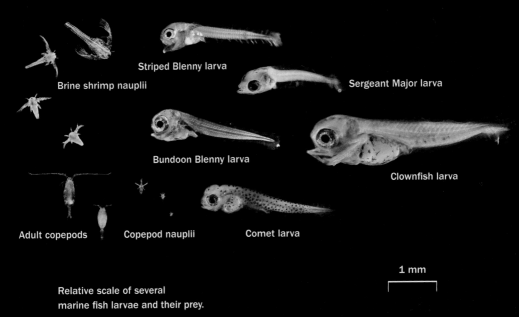

Brine shrimp nauplii

Striped Blenny larva

Sergeant Major larva

Bundoon Blenny larva

Clownfish larva

Adult copepods    Copepod nauplii    Comet larva

1 mm

Relative scale of several
marine fish larvae and their prey.

rearing of marine fish requires consistent care, detailed observation, basic knowledge, and a good bit of experience. The printed page cannot supply the dedication and actual experience, but it can give basic information and some suggestions on technique. In this chapter, I will try to summarize this information and present a basic guide to rearing clownfish, since they are among the easiest of all marine tropical fish to rear and will give the amateur marine fish breeder the best chance to succeed.

There are a number of other species that the amateur marine breeder may be able to rear as the quintessence of the marine fish–keeping experience: Banggai Cardinalfishes, Neon Gobies and other species of gobies and blennies, seahorses, Royal Grammas, jawfishes, and dottybacks. Some of these fish are more difficult to rear than clownfish, but are definite possibilities for the dedicated beginner.

## Spawning

Marine tropical fish are not unlike all other creatures of the earth that depend on sexual reproduction to continue their species. The drive to reproduce is extremely strong, and they will spawn, providing—and this is crucial—that the environment and the physical condition of the fish

**Maldives Clownfish (*Amphiprion nigripes*) pair with eggs spawned near large anemone.**

meet the species' minimum requirements for reproduction. The problem, therefore, is to identify and provide the necessary conditions for each species that is to be spawned. There are four basic criteria:

1. Adult fish in good health
2. Proper nutrition—quality and quantity
3. Suitable physical environment—light, temperature, and surroundings
4. Proper chemical environment—water quality

Obviously, all the proper conditions exist in nature during the spawning season, so we must look to the wild to find clues to the conditions that must be created. The following discussion is specifically about the Common or Ocellaris Clownfish, *Amphiprion ocellaris*, but can apply in principle to other species.

The fish must be adult, that is, of the proper size and age for spawning activity, and must be in good physical condition. There must be male and female fish present; in the case of clownfish, one of each sex is all that is necessary. In fact, unless the aquarium is quite large, a mated pair will seldom allow others of their species to survive within the tank. (Other species, however, such as wrasses and damsels, may need to aggregate in small groups before spawning behavior is stimulated.) I have found no distinct color markings on Ocellaris Clownfish that differentiate male and female, but there are size and shape differences between adults. The female is larger and more robust than the male, and when the gonads are active, the abdomen is quite rotund. The adult male is perhaps half to three-quarters the size of the full grown female and is slim, without the heavy belly of the female. Given a population of adult fish, these size and shape characteristics are sufficient to select sexes with about 90% accuracy. Immature fish and young adults cannot be accurately sexed on appearance—indeed, when young, they are probably all immature males.

Sex reversal has recently been demonstrated in seven species of clownfish. The sex change is protanderous, from male to female, and is apparently stimulated by changes in the social structure of the group. In the wild, one dominant female, an adult male, and a variable group of subadult fish inhabit the same general area around a host anemone. The smaller fish are repressed in sexual development by the presence of the active pair. They do not mature sexually or grow large in size. If the adult male is lost to a predator, the largest of the immature male fish rapidly matures and becomes the female's mate. If the female is lost, the active male changes relatively quickly into a female and mates with the now-maturing young male. Nature thus assures that every host anemone will have a functional pair of clownfish without regard to any predetermined genetic sex distinction.

Depending on where you live, it can be difficult to find adult fish in good condition, and it is usually best to grow your own clownfish broodstock. (Mated pairs are best found via your local aquarium shop, marine society, or online breeders' forums.) It takes a little patience—6 to 18 months depending on their size when you begin—but there is the advantage of often winding up with more than one pair. Start with a good, established tank of at least 20 gallons (40 is better), and then purchase 8 to 12 healthy young clownfish. Statistically, you need a minimum of six fish to assure that at least one of each sex is present, assuming an equal distribution of sexes and no artificial selection in choice of fish. Statistics also do not allow for sex change, but this phenomenon works to the advantage of the aquarist in the case of clownfish, unless one begins with sexually mature fish.

If you begin with juvenile fish, tank-reared clowns are good for the initial breeding stock because they haven't been exposed to treatment or collection chemicals, but wild-caught fish should do just as well if they are in good condition. Depending on their age and size, the fish will coexist peacefully for a while until they begin to pair. An anemone, preferably a Bubbletip Anemone (*Entacmaea quadricolor*), will promote natural behavior patterns and thus is an aid to pairing and spawning. However, an anemone is not necessary, and most serious clownfish breeders do not keep anemones with their broodstock.

When a pair forms, the two fish become protective of a territory around the anemone and prevent any other fish of the same or closely related species from entering their area. The territorial imperative is so intense that a strong pair will destroy the hapless fish that cannot flee their boundaries.

The new pair, or the other fish, must be removed soon after aggressiveness is first displayed, to prevent loss of the unpaired fish. The unpaired fish may form another pair after the first pair is removed. The tank may be partitioned to house separate pairs, but the partition should be opaque so the pairs do not visually impinge on each other's territories.

After pairing, the fish are prepared for spawning by maintaining an optimum environment in the aquarium, as per the previous chapters, and providing the best possible nutrition. The daily duration of light and the tank temperature are also important. The pituitary gland, which sends hormones that activate the gonads, is stimulated to do so by constant summer day length and warm temperatures. The aquarium light should be set to provide 14 hours of light per day, and the temperature should be a constant 80°F (26.6°C). Also, provide rocks, flower pots, slates, tiles, or other hard surfaces near the anemone to give the fish a spawn site. All that is needed from this point on is good aquarium management and patience. The fish will do what comes naturally when they mature.

The behavior of the pair usually gives an indication of impending spawning. The female is the dominant member of the pair, since she is larger and seems to be chiefly responsible for defense of the territory. She is

Pair of Neon Gobies (*Elacatinus oceanops*). Female, at left, has a fuller form.

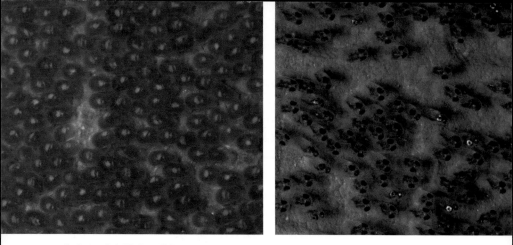

Left: newly laid clownfish eggs on a clay tile. Right: 7-day-old clownfish eggs.

the one that attacks the fish, net, or hand that dares to invade their protectorate. The male, on the other hand, guards and nurtures the eggs and seems to be constantly appeasing the female so she will suffer his presence. Evidently there is a behavioral conflict in the female. On the one hand, she has a built-in desire to drive the male from the territory as she does with other members of her species, but on the other she must keep him near her to reproduce. Obviously, there must be a frequent exchange of information between them to remind both of their respective functions.

When the female attacks the male, he turns the attack away by head shaking and "chattering" directly in front of the female, a sort of submissive behavior. Just as the female must not actually attack the male, he must not actually flee from her, or reproduction will not succeed. As the attack is turned away, the male, and often the female as well, engages in cleaning activity on any nearby hard surface. This is a displacement activity that diverts the female away from attack and the male from flee behavior. To the casual anthropomorphic eye, the fish appear to be "playing tag" and "showing off;" however, these are actually ritualized behavior patterns that strengthen the pair bond and prepare the fish for spawning.

Unless you observe the fish carefully and critically each day, the first spawn will probably come as a surprise. As the time for spawning approaches, the fish may display heightened chasing activity and increased substrate biting. The female also becomes notably full in the abdomen. These conditions may persist for several days, especially with a first spawn, and you may think that the fish just don't know what to do. Take heart, though, for it will eventually occur.

Common Clownfish almost always spawn in late afternoon or early evening. The female's ovipositor extends early on the day of spawning, and her fullness is quite pronounced. The male's organ is small and almost transparent and appears only shortly before the spawn occurs. The pair select a spawn site an hour or two before the first eggs are laid and begin to clean the site by biting at the substrate while jerking their heads from side to side. This activity becomes very intense as spawning approaches. At the end of the cleaning activity, the female begins to make passes over the cleaned area with her ovipositor lightly touching the hard surface. After several "dry" passes, the first bright orange eggs appear. They slip individually from the ovipositor, touch the substrate at one end, and instantly adhere. A mass of very sticky, microscopic filaments attach the egg to the nest site. This is a flexible attachment and allows the eggs great side-to-side movement. The female leaves behind a single straight line of eggs across the nest site at each pass. Any eggs that do not adhere are quickly eaten by either parent. The female continues to lay a line of eggs at each pass until the patch of tightly packed eggs covers an area 1-4 inches (2–10 cm) in diameter. The female pauses after every few passes and allows the male to fertilize the eggs she has just laid down. The male's motions are more rapid and fluttery than the female's, and he seems to cover most of the enlarging patch of eggs each time he is active.

The male is the chief caretaker of the developing eggs. He frequently fans them with his pectoral and caudal fins, which aerates them and stimulates the developing embryos by movement. He also "mouths" the eggs, which consists of gentle biting at the egg patch. Although the parents are said to remove dead and diseased eggs this way, I have never seen them actually select and remove a dead egg. Eggs that die quickly decompose and are swept off the nest by the general care patterns of the male. Any fallen eggs are usually consumed by one of the parents. The female also takes care of the nest in the same manner as the male, but her attentions are much less frequent.

Complete development to hatching takes place in 6–12 days, depending primarily on temperature. The average time is 7–8 days at the typical temperature of 80°F (26.6°C). Temperatures below 75°F (24°C) greatly delay development and hatching. The bright orange of the new eggs becomes dark brown in about three days as the tissues of the developing embryo envelop the yolk. The dark pigment of the eyes becomes noticeable at about day 4 and turn silvery at day 5 or 6, when the light-reflecting pig-

Courtship display seen in a breeding pair of Sharpnose Puffers, *Canthigaster rostrata.*

ment forms. On the day of hatching, the embryo develops a light violet sheen and the egg almost seems to bulge a little.

## Hatching

Normal hatching always occurs at night, within two hours of first dark. Usually all the eggs in the nest hatch very quickly, within 15 or 20 minutes. If any eggs do not hatch at this time, chances are that they will wait for the following night to hatch.

Night hatching effectively reduces predation on the newly hatched larvae when they are near the bottom and are most vulnerable to bottom-dwelling plankton predators, including their own parents. The adults will seek out and consume every larva at first light if they remain together in the breeding tank. The clownfish larva is doubled up in the egg at hatching, with the tail tucked in just below the head at the tip of the egg. For maximum reproductive economy, the eggs must be small and numerous; but for maximum survival, the larvae must be as large as possible at first feeding. Various species have different methods of resolving these conflicting demands. Most pelagic spawning species carry a large yolk sac in a small egg and hatch very early into an only partly developed prolarval stage. The prolarva then continues development to a significantly larger first-feeding larva outside the physical constraints of a small egg.

Pelagic eggs get no parental care, so they are subject to many predators and environmental hazards during their early development. Such species depend on the production of vast numbers of eggs for survival. The egg in the mouthbrooding jawfish is also small, about a millimeter in diameter, but the larva that hatches is comparatively large, about 4 millimeters long, and its head is almost 1 millimeter in diameter. This economy of space is achieved by wrapping the body of the larva about the head during development. At hatching, after 5–7 days of incubation, the body unwinds from the head and, despite development in a small egg, the larva is a respectable size and is ready to begin feeding almost immediately.

The clownfish egg is one of the largest of marine fish eggs at 1 mm in diameter and about 2 mm in length. Most larval fish hatch from their eggs by dissolving the egg shells with a proteolytic enzyme and then thrusting themselves head-first out of their egg cases with tail and body movements. Clownfish are different, however. At hatching, the egg case ruptures at the tail just below the top of the egg. The tail and lower body then fall free, and the larva pulls itself from the egg (which is still attached to the substrate) with a few rapid jerks of the tail and body. If the egg does not remain attached to the substrate, the larva is unable to easily free its head from the tip of the egg case, and swims about pushing the egg case in front of it. This is usually fatal to the larval fish, for it can neither respire normally nor remove its egg-case cap. Therefore, clownfish eggs should not be removed from the substrate before hatching.

### Larval rearing

Clownfish spend the first two to three weeks of their lives as pelagic larvae. In nature, this period is spent in the upper reaches of the sea, feeding on the tiny animals that surround them in the plankton. Juvenile coloration develops as early as 8 days and as late as 20 days, and shortly after this metamorphosis they begin life on the bottom. The period of greatest concern to the marine fish breeder is the first two weeks, for this is the stage that is most difficult to maintain and feed.

Since the larvae are immediately pelagic at hatching, the first task is to set up a rearing tank that substitutes for the pelagic environment, and to have it ready when the larvae hatch. This is relatively simple for a small-scale operation. An adequate rearing environment can be prepared with a bare (filterless), high-sided tank; one or two fine-bubble air releasers; and good lighting directly over the tank. Black plastic wrapped around the tank excludes side light and helps the larval fish find the pelagic food organisms. With careful management, about 100 fish can be taken through the larval stage (to about ⅜-inch long) in a 10-gallon tank, but a 20–50-gallon tank will yield greater success.

The first major challenge is recovering the larvae, since they must be moved from the breeding tank to the rearing tank. There are three basic methods for achieving this transfer.

The first method consists of removing the part of the substrate containing the nest and transferring it to the larval rearing tank, and artificially hatching the eggs. The eggs can be kept in good condition until hatching with an even curtain of bubbles gently rolling over the entire nest. Darkening the tank at the proper time causes the eggs to hatch.

Second, and perhaps most feasible for the amateur marine breeder, is to remove the newly hatched larvae from the breeding tank with a siphon or container. The larvae are strongly attracted to a light source after hatching, probably an adaptation to ensure their movement into the upper water strata. Because of this trait, it is easy to concentrate them in one corner of the aquarium by shining a flashlight on that corner. Darkening the tank a few hours early on the day of hatch will hasten the event and, hopefully, prevent late-night activity on the part of the aquarist. When the larvae have accumulated in one area of the tank, they can be removed for transfer to the rearing tank either by siphoning them from the tank into a bucket or by capturing them with a cup or glass. The cup method is more time-consuming and frustrating, but there is less chance of injury than there is with the siphon. A net should never be used—the larvae cannot withstand the physical abrasion it would cause at this early age.

The third method requires a more elaborate setup, with the breeding tank mounted directly over the larval tank and a constant water flow between the two. This way, the hatched larvae are automatically siphoned down to the rearing tanks and the two water masses (breeding and rearing) do not differ in quality. The intake from the rearing tank to the pumped return to the breeding tank must be well protected by a large surface area of fine-mesh screen to prevent loss of larvae, and the flow must be discontinued or greatly diminished when the young fish begin to feed to prevent loss of the larval fish food. Only those amateur breeders strongly inclined toward systems engineering will find it necessary to build such a unit.

## Diagram of a breeding system for marine organisms

with reproductive modes that include colonial proliferation, benthic eggs
and/or larvae, fission, budding, and short-term pelagic larvae.

### Basic schematic

Organisms in rearing trays may be moved from one tray
to the other to allow each tray to be cleaned and sterilized
as necessary. More than two rearing trays or tanks may
be included.

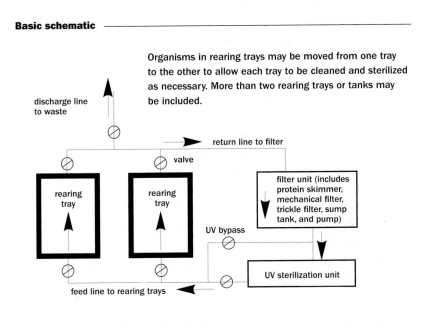

discharge line
to waste

return line to filter

valve

rearing
tray

rearing
tray

filter unit (includes
protein skimmer,
mechanical filter,
trickle filter, sump
tank, and pump)

UV bypass

UV sterilization unit

feed line to rearing trays

### Side view

Proper lighting for photosynthesis required.
May be either fluorescent or metal halide.

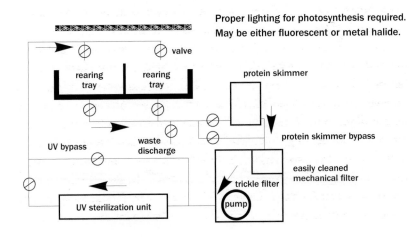

valve

rearing
tray

rearing
tray

protein skimmer

protein skimmer bypass

UV bypass

waste
discharge

easily cleaned
mechanical filter

trickle filter

UV sterilization unit

pump

Once the larvae have been transferred from the breeding tank to water of the same temperature and pH in the rearing tank, the hard part begins—providing the proper type and abundance of food organisms (usually rotifers) for the larval fish. There is a good reason for the fantastic reproductive potential of most marine fish: very few, one out of millions, survive the larval and juvenile stages in nature. Thus, a great many lives must be launched to assure the survival of a few and the continuance of the species.

These tiny larvae have little stored food and must begin feeding very soon after their systems are mature enough to capture food organisms. The available food organisms must be both compatible with the larvae's nutritional and behavioral requirements and abundant enough to provide energy for both movement and growth. Most attempts at rearing marine fish larvae fail for one or more of three reasons:

1. Improper physical and/or chemical environment
2. Lack of an acceptable first food organism
3. Lack of sufficient numbers of food organisms

The proper physical and chemical rearing environment has already been discussed, and it remains only to say that the tank bottom must be cleaned every day or two, and if possible, a partial water change done at the same time. One water change of 50–80% once a week for the two- to three-week rearing period is all that is really necessary, if a 10–20% change

Tiny rotifers (greatly magnified) raised in greenwater (phytoplankton) are the ideal first food for many marine fish larvae, which are too small to take baby brine shrimp.

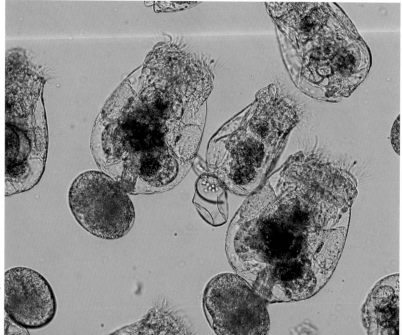

is not accomplished every two days. The more larvae that are reared in the tank, of course, the more important water changes become. Bottom cleaning is best done with a small siphon that picks up sediment without endangering larvae higher in the water column.

Don't be alarmed if a green algal bloom develops in the rearing tank. This is actually good for the rearing environment, as it provides nutrition for the food organisms present and takes up some of the metabolites produced by the animals in the tank. (Author Matt Wittenrich recommends adding live phytoplankton to the rearing tank water, to both feed the rotifers and help the larvae spot their prey more easily.) A white bloom, however, may be caused by bacteria and is usually detrimental to the larvae. Too many larvae, too many food organisms, lack of bottom cleaning, too much turbulence, and introduction of too much scuzzy water (scientific terminology) from the food-organism rearing tanks can all contribute to conditions that foster excessive bacterial growth. A thorough cleaning and water change, with subsequent restocking of food organisms, may save the larvae if a bacterial bloom is caught in the early stages. It is important to note that it is possible to rear limited numbers of clownfish in small tanks without any significant water changes over a three-week period if care is taken to keep food organism populations at just the right levels.

Marine fish can be reared scientifically, using precise measurement of water quality and food organism density, which is the best way to achieve reproducible results; or the aquarist can develop a "feel" for the requirements of the larvae and know from trial and error what will and what will not work. In actual practice, a blending of the two approaches seems to produce the best results. Perhaps the most important consideration—aside from the basics of tank, water, air, and light—is to have the proper abundance of an acceptable food organism, usually rotifers or wild plankton. Three to eight food organisms per ml is a good level, although clownfish can survive on less, especially if there are only a few larvae to feed. If you can't make an actual count of the number of food organisms by looking at a prepared sample in a counting chamber under a microscope, you'll have to use simpler techniques or even just go by visual estimate. With a little experience, it's possible to get to the point of looking into the tank and immediately knowing if the food levels are adequate.

Five food organisms per ml translates to about 150 per ounce, so a shot glass of rearing-tank water should contain over 150 food organisms.

At this level there are 25 to 30 food organisms per teaspoon, an easy enough number to count. The best way to get an estimate of the actual level of food organisms in the tank is to count the number in each of four or five sample teaspoons, and when the average count is between 25 and 30, there will be enough food organisms for good larval survival. Placing the sample in a shallow glass dish and examining it over a black background with a low-power hand lens will facilitate the count. Maintaining the food organisms at this level will assure survival of most of the larvae.

Even though clownfish are about the largest and best-developed of marine fish larvae when they begin feeding, newly hatched brine shrimp are still too large to be used as a first food. Of all the possible first foods that the aquarist can work with, there are four that give a good chance of success:

1. Wild plankton
2. Cultured marine rotifers
3. Fresh-frozen rotifers
4. Cultured marine ciliates

Other organisms and methods may also be successful, but these are ones that have been tested and proven. It may also be possible to rear a few clownfish with pulverized dry foods as a first offering and then quickly switch to new hatch brine shrimp as soon as the larvae are large enough to take them. This latter method would require frequent tank cleanings and water changes, and would be worth trying if the only other thing available was determination. A good quality dry flake food pulverized in a mortar and pestle, dry egg yolk, and freshwater fish-fry food are all possible dead food particles. (Aquaculture specialty suppliers now sell very fine powdered foods for larval feeding.) If dry, pulverized food is used, the water turbulence controlled by the air release should be kept at a high level to keep the food in suspension as long as possible. It should not be so high, however, that the larvae cannot control their own movements. Feeding should also be very frequent to keep food levels in the tank high enough, and for a long enough time, for the larval fish to get adequate nutrition. This also necessitates frequent siphoning of the tank bottom.

For those aquarists living near the coast, one of the easiest larval foods to obtain will be wild plankton. The relative ease or difficulty of collecting wild plankton every day for 10 to 15 days will determine, for each individual case, whether to culture a food organism or rely on plankton

The author dipping for plankton off a pier near his home in the Florida Keys.

collection. The very smallest zooplankters are not needed by the relatively large clownfish larvae, so it is possible to get by with a homemade
plankton net if you have access to the tidal flow of ocean or bay. Wild
plankton, although it is an excellent food for larval fish, has a couple of
drawbacks: there is great variability in quality, and there is the possibility
of the introduction of planktonic predators and parasites, primarily *Amyloodinium*. These problems, however, can be controlled by straining the
plankton before feeding to eliminate organisms larger than 300 microns,
and through the judicious use of light copper treatment. A light copper
treatment (0.05–0.1 ppm) placed in the collected plankton for half an
hour before feeding (and then removed when the plankton is sieved) will
kill *Amyloodinium,* which would otherwise infect the larval fish in a week

Small setup for breeding pelagic-spawning species employs deep vessels with snagging devices near the surface to catch floating eggs or larvae. Larvae of most pelagic-spawning species are tiny and may require microplanktonic items as first foods.

or two, and jellyfish or hydroid medusae and arrow worms, which will kill larval fish that are very small.

A half-meter plankton net of a 50–75-micron mesh can be purchased at most oceanic research supply houses and will do nicely to collect the necessary wild plankton. Professional plankton nets are expensive, so a handy aquarist may wish to make one instead. Finding a material that will catch the smaller zooplankter and still let enough water pass through is the most difficult part of the project. A worn bed sheet may do the trick, but some experimentation is going to be required. Depending on the situation (quality of plankton, size of the rearing tank, and number of larvae), one collection of plankton per day for the first three or four days may be adequate, but two may make for better success.

Most wild plankton can survive for several hours in a bucket under light aeration, so feeding from one collection can be spread out. The best chance of success will be had by combining wild plankton with cultured rotifers, although either one alone is adequate. Observe the larval fish carefully to make sure that they are feeding. An actively feeding larva frequently flexes its body into an S-shaped curve and then snaps forward suddenly to capture the prey immediately before it. The gut area will also become rounded with ingested food and take on a whitish color from plankton or rotifers. It is important to get the larvae feeding on new hatch brine shrimp as soon as possible, for this will enhance their growth rate considerably. Add new hatch brine shrimp early, but in small quantities. Three to four days after feeding begins is about right. The color of the gut will change from whitish to a pink or orange color when they begin to take the baby brine shrimp.

Post-larval clownfish seem reluctant to take non-living foods until after they take on adult coloration. At this point, somewhere between 10 and 20 days out, they will take blended shrimp or scallop and pulverized dry flake food. Go easy on the dry flake food, for it can cause the gut of young fish to bloat if it is overfed. Also, keep the tank bottom clean once the switch to dry foods has begun. In fact, in a small rearing situation it is best to move the young fish to a tank with an established biological filter (live rock, trickle, or undergravel) as soon as all have taken on adult coloration and begin to stay near the tank side or bottom.

Be careful not to overfeed baby brine shrimp at this point. The small fish don't seem to have any mechanism that tells them to stop feeding when they've eaten enough, and they can continue to feed on brine shrimp until they look like little footballs—and then fall to the bottom and die.

**WILD PLANKTON:**

Aquarists with access to the shore can harvest wild plankton that includes prey items in many sizes, an easy way to feed larval fish.

❧

### Rotifer culture

Marine fish culturists have looked long and hard for a good first food organism for marine fish larvae. Baby brine shrimp, although an excellent and readily available food, were seen as having limited value because they were just too large for most marine fish larvae. What was needed was a small organism, about half the size (or less) of baby brine shrimp, that was easy to culture in large numbers and would be readily taken by the fish larvae and provide their first nutritional needs. The National Marine Fisheries Service at the Fishery-Oceanography Center in La Jolla, California, working on the culture of the Northern Anchovy and the Gulf Croaker in 1969 and 1970, reported good success using cultures of the marine rotifer *Brachionus plicatilis*. A starter culture of this organism was sent to our Florida pompano culture program in December of 1970 and proved to be a successful first food for pompano, Spotfin Pinfish, seatrout, redfish, and other species at our laboratory. This organism is now widely used in fish culture throughout the world and is available from many fish culture laboratories and several private companies. It was a short hop from food fish to tropical fish culture, and *B. plicatilis* is probably used to some extent in all marine tropical fish culture operations.

*B. plicatilis* is not difficult to culture, but it does require daily care by the aquarist. The strongest and most nutritive rotifer cultures are those fed on one-celled marine algae (phytoplankton). The best algae to use are *Dunaliella*, *Isochrysis*, *Monochrysis*, and *Chlorella*, as these are easy for the rotifers to eat and provide good nutrition. The algae should be grown under conditions of constant illumination in 1- to 5-gallon containers and at temperatures of 75 to 80°F. There should be no way that rotifers can get back to the algae cultures, for these hungry little beasts will quickly wipe out the algae if they do. Feed the algae with a basic nutrient mix: saltwater enriched with nitrate, phosphate, and iron. A liquid "all-purpose" houseplant food will fill the bill. Algae and rotifer culture requires frequent replacement of the saltwater or great economy and reuse of a well filtered reservoir stock.

Small cultures of algae and rotifers are dynamic—they reproduce and grow fiercely when excellent conditions are provided—and when the limits of growth are reached, they crash quickly into death and decay. Therefore, each culture has to be harvested and renewed regularly to keep it constantly in the growth phase. The growth of the rotifer cultures can be controlled somewhat by the amount of algae fed. Feeding can be increased several days before a hatch is due, thus stepping up production of rotifers for the time when they are most needed. The rotifers are harvested by passing the culture through a fine screen (25–50 microns) and collecting the concentrated rotifers on top of the screen for feeding to the rearing tank.

It is also possible—not better, but possible—to rear rotifers for larval fish without the problems of algae culture. Dry activated yeast, the kind used in baking bread, can be fed in light suspension to rotifer cultures, resulting in good growth. Yeast suspensions have been used for decades to feed small aquatic organisms. This is best done outside under sunlight,

**Diagram of a small-scale larval food culture system**

air lines with valves for each bottle

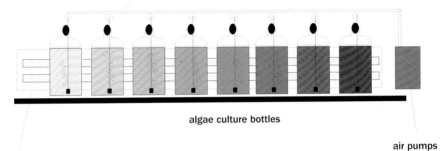

algae culture bottles

air pumps

fluorescent lighting

rotifer cultures

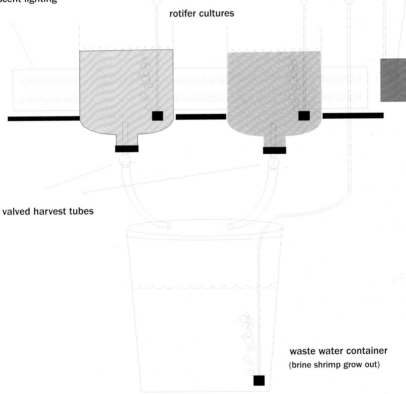

valved harvest tubes

waste water container
(brine shrimp grow out)

since the yeast method encourages bacterial growth and sunlight helps control it. Using this method, rotifers can be grown in small volumes— 15 to 40 gallons—but they do better in larger volumes of 90 to 200 gallons. A plastic kiddie pool about 1 foot deep and 5 feet across in partial shade, with several airstones for turbulence, makes a very good culture vessel. Low temperatures, below 70°F, depress rotifer reproduction, so accommodation must be made for winter conditions.

The yeast for feeding to the rotifers is prepared by dissolving about 1 tablespoon of the dry yeast in a pint of warm water. The resulting milky suspension can be kept in the refrigerator for several days and fed to the cultures as required. The rotifer cultures should be fed the yeast solution once a day for maintenance and a low harvest rate, or twice a day for maximum harvest. The bottom of small-volume cultures should be siphoned every day and any water loss made up with clean saltwater. The proper amount of the yeast suspension to feed is that amount which keeps the culture water slightly milky for a few hours after feeding. It is wise to have several such cultures, for yeast-fed rotifer cultures are far more precarious than algae-fed cultures. Note that without culturing rotifers in some volume, there is no way to develop the numbers necessary for even a small clownfish-rearing experiment.

Yeast is acceptable and easy to feed, but it is not the best nutritionally for rotifers or larval fish. Other easy rotifer foods are now available. Several commercial firms produce a refrigerated, very concentrated algae paste that provides a natural food at a reasonable price. This product is a more nutritional food and results in a cleaner, more stable rotifer culture. Concentrated live phytoplankton in refrigerated packets are also available, but they cost more. Other possibilities: a vegetable juice–based rotifer food (described in my book, *Breeding the Orchid Dottyback: An Aquarist's Journal*), and, best of all, basic algae culture, which is not too difficult for the determined rotifer culturist to grow.

It is also possible to rear clownfish larvae solely on commercially grown and preserved rotifers as a first food. The rotifers are taken from dense cultures, strained and washed, and then frozen in saltwater in small blocks or preserved in a liquid suspension. The frozen blocks are thawed in a cup or two of saltwater just before feeding, and then fed to the rearing tank. The rotifers are dead, of course, but if tank turbulence is adequate, they do not immediately settle out. They remain in the water column long enough for

Placing a batch of clownfish eggs spawned on a tile into a rearing tub, where they will be kept gently aerated until hatching. Small-scale breeders find such tubs, with black sides and no corners, ideal for feeding and raising larval fish through metamorphosis.

the clownfish larvae to obtain adequate food. They do settle fairly quickly, however, and the bottom must be siphoned daily if frozen rotifers are used. Also, more than one feeding per day is necessary because the rotifers are not continuously available to the larval fish. Two, and perhaps three, feedings a day are necessary, depending on tank conditions. When frozen rotifers are used as a first larval food, newly hatched brine shrimp must be provided as soon as possible for best success.

Marine ciliates in the genus *Euplotes* have been used successfully to rear limited numbers of clownfish larvae at the Wilhelma Aquarium in Stuttgart, Germany. However, the most successful trials with *Euplotes* also included a low density of various other zooplankters produced by a tank rich in invertebrate populations. *Euplotes* are smaller and apparently less nutritious for larval fish than rotifers, but they can bridge the gap from first feeding to baby brine shrimp for some larvae. Living *Euplotes* cultures can be obtained from some scientific supply houses and can be cultured

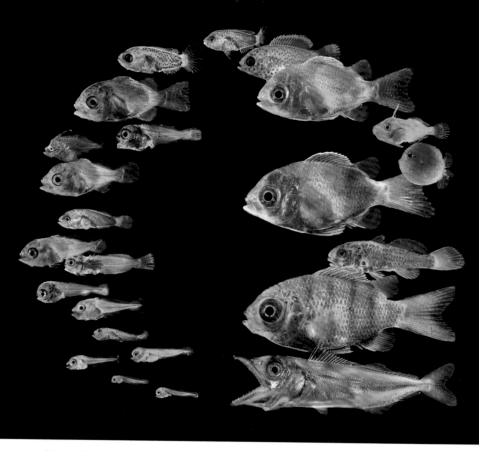

Marine fish larvae vary greatly in size and form, as illustrated by this assemblage from coastal Florida waters, ranging from just-hatched to month-old near-juveniles.

with yeast suspensions as described for rotifers. Potato water, algal cultures, and decomposing meat can also create rich cultures of *Euplotes*.

### Juvenile growth

When the young clownfish are fully colored and about ¼ to ½ inch long, they should be moved to a tank with an established filter. They will grow faster and stronger in a benthic (bottom) environment after this stage of development is attained. Gradually wean them from dependence on baby brine shrimp to standard marine tropical fish foods.

### Other species

The amateur marine fish breeder must concentrate on those species that will reproduce readily in the aquarium and have hardy eggs and/or early larvae that allow recovery. The Neon Goby and the Royal Gramma are two species that fulfill these requirements. Both species can be paired using the same method as described for clownfish, for a mated pair will not tolerate other individuals in their tank space. Despite this similarity, there are many biological differences between them. The male is usually the larger of the pair in both Neon Gobies and Royal Grammas, and the abdominal fullness of the active female is the prominent sexual difference.

Neon Gobies, *Elacatinus oceanops*, attach their eggs to the substrate very much like clownfish, but their nests are more secretive. They place their eggs under shells and rocks, and the presence of the nest is seldom known until the tank is suddenly filled with tiny, transparent hatchlings. Hatching usually takes place at night, but it is not uncommon for a nest to hatch in the daytime. The male is in charge of the nest and spends much time working over the eggs. The presence of a nest can be suspected if the male is observed entering and leaving the same small opening with great frequency.

Royal Grammas, *Gramma loreto*, have been spawned and reared successfully by quite a number of marine hobbyists. Their reproductive mode had been little known for years, and because their relatives, the sea basses, produce planktonic eggs, it was thought that the grammas might also release free-floating eggs. Tank spawns, however, demonstrated that Royal Grammas are secretive nest-builders. The male selects a nest site hidden deep in some crevice or under a rock. He actively cleans this hidden area of stones and shells until the nest site meets his specifications. He then brings algal strands into the nest area until it appears filled, with only a small entry hole visible. The female is enticed into the nest at about this point, the male also enters, and up to 30 minutes may pass before either of them emerge. During this period, the female lays from 20 to 100 eggs with numerous long, sticky filaments extending from their surface that serve to bind the eggs to each other and to the surrounding algal mass.

The eggs are relatively large, about 1 millimeter in diameter, and have six or more small oil droplets. They have a yellowish, translucent appearance. The female may enter the nest every day or two for a month or more and repeat the performance each time. The male cares for the eggs in the nest periodically, but the eggs do not seem to require the nearly constant care a male clownfish gives to his nest. The eggs develop slowly (5 to 7 days from fertilization to hatching) and hatch in the same daily sequence in which they were laid. Thus, only a few are ready to hatch each night.

Royal Gramma (*Gramma loreto*) pair, with larger male at front, prior to spawning in an aquarium cave.

The constant daily hatch of larvae throughout the spawning season may be an adaptation to take advantage of conditions favorable for survival whenever they may occur. The larvae are relatively large and hardy, but in the aquarium, recovery is complicated by the hatch and release of only a few per night. They somehow find their way out of the nest site and into the upper water column after hatching. Hatching always takes place within a few hours after dark, as it does with clownfish hatching. The male is in the nest at hatching, but does not seem to aid the hatchlings in their journey to the plankton-rich upper water levels. The small, transparent larvae are ready to feed on the day after hatching and grow very fast under the right conditions.

Dottybacks are also nest-builders and make good, not-too-difficult breeding subjects. Among the mouthbrooders, the Yellowhead Jawfish (*Opistognathus aurifrons*) is a great fish for home breeders, as is the Bang-gai Cardinalfish, which deserves to be captive-bred by more hobbyists. The Marine Betta, or Comet, (*Calloplesiops altivelis*) produces large, easy-to-feed larvae, but needs special coaxing to induce spawning.

Marine Bettas, or Comets, are reluctant spawners but produce large, easy-to-rear young.

The gains being made in the captive breeding of marine fishes are quite startling, given that we actually know relatively little of the biology of many of the creatures that find their way into our marine aquariums. Success by amateurs, as well as professional aquaculturists, is a sign of the changes in this developing hobby and an indication of its new direction. Reports of observations and breeding attempts by amateur marine aquarists, even those published in local society newsletters, add much to our knowledge, understanding, and enjoyment of the ocean life within our homes. So be encouraged to observe, think, and share your findings with fellow marine aquarists.

## Invertebrate culture

Over the last few years, marine aquarists have learned to keep a great many species of invertebrates that are capable of a variety of reproductive modes in addition to the production of microscopic, free-floating eggs and long-lived pelagic larvae. Just a few short years ago, keeping hard and soft corals and other animals that depend on symbiotic algal cells within their tissues was considered almost impossible. Even anemones seldom survived long in the typical marine aquarium. Now, an advanced marine aquarist can not only keep many of these animals alive and healthy, but can also breed many species naturally in good reef tank systems.

The Porifera (the sponges), the Cnidaria (the corals and anemones), and some of the Annelida (the polychaete worms) are the animals that are most easy to propagate naturally in reef systems. The Mollusca (clams, oysters, snails, and octopus), Arthropoda (mainly the crustaceans—crabs, lobsters, and shrimp), and Echinodermata (starfish, sea urchins, brittle stars, and sea cucumbers) are more difficult, since most of these reproduce with pelagic larvae and require great care during the tiny, pelagic larval stage. Some of these difficult-to-rear invertebrates are almost impossible.

Take the spiny lobster, for example. We worked for several years try-ing to rear the Caribbean Spiny Lobster, *Panulirus argus*, in our laborato-ry in the Florida Keys. The period of larval life in nature is 6 to 9 months long, and the tiny larvae go through about 11 different larval stages. We managed to bring them through seven stages in 81 days, but were not able to rear them completely though the larval stage. More recently, Japa-nese biologists have been able to rear a few specimens of the Japanese Spiny Lobster, *Panulirus japonicus*, through to the juvenile stage, but this

Matt Pedersen's broodstock Harlequin Filefish pair spawning in a patch of macroalgae.

Development of first successful captive-bred Harlequin Filefish: newly laid eggs, top; just-hatched prolarva, right; 18 days post-hatch, with erect dorsal spike, bottom; 54 days post-hatch, pre-settlement larva, left.

required 340 to 403 days in the larval stages. Detailed accounts of our rearing experiments are included in my book, *Lobsters: Florida, Bahamas, the Caribbean,* and these would be helpful to an aquarist interested in rearing crustaceans.

Most of these invertebrate organisms require low-nutrient water, high-intensity lighting of the proper spectral quality, oxygen levels at or near saturation, control of dissolved carbon dioxide, low levels of dissolved organics, proper management of trace elements, and active water flows. Given these environmental conditions, many invertebrates can reproduce through colonial proliferation (new polyps forming in a stony, colonial

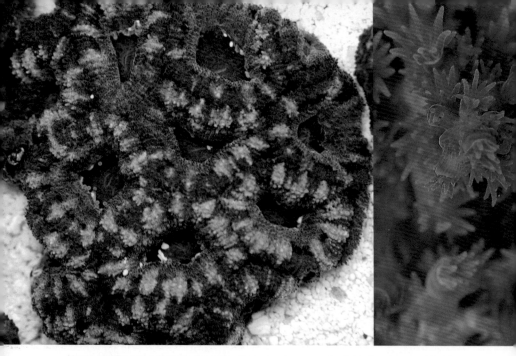

Above, highly prized *Acanthastrea* spp. stony corals are easily divided and propagated by cutting the skeleton between polyps and growing them in optimum reef conditions.

matrix), fission (splitting apart), budding (small polyps forming at the base of a large single animal), actual physical separation of healthy colonies, production of benthic eggs and larvae, and/or production of short-term pelagic larvae. These are all reproductive modes that may adapt to a "set it up and let it run" production system. A marine aquarist may be able to reproduce certain marine organisms in such systems on a care and maintenance schedule that allows for dinner out and a movie once a week or so, and maybe even a free Saturday afternoon once a month. Fragmentation of stony corals, of course, has come into its own, and there is now an international cottage industry producing asexually propagated clones of *Acropora, Montipora, Pocillopora, Seriatopora, Acanthastrea,* and many other genera of corals. One needs a healthy mother colony that can withstand being pruned, a cutting tool, some underwater epoxy or instant glue, and some bits of hard substrate or coral propagation plugs. Each fragment is affixed to a new base and allowed to recover and grow. With the faster-growing species, an attractive new colony can develop within a period of months.

Similarly, soft corals and gorgonians can be easy subjects for division into new colonies. Typically a sharp, sterilized scalpel or razor blade is used to slice pieces from a healthy parent coral, and each cutting is glued to a

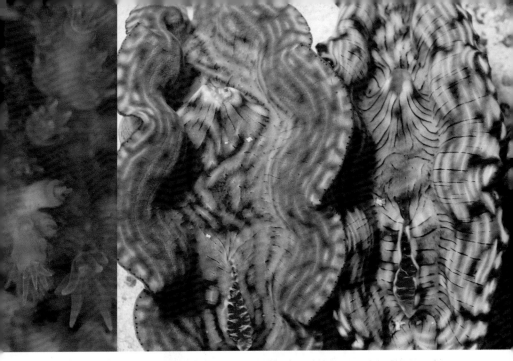

Left, captive-grown *Acropora* colony at Oceans, Reefs & Aquariums. Right, ORA captive-bred *Tridacna derasa* clams displaying colors enhanced by selective breeding.

small piece of coral rubble or a cement disk. Commonly propagated genera include *Sinularia, Sarcophyton, Capnella,* and others. Some soft corals, such as *Xenia,* simply spread on their own, expanding on adjacent substrate and even climbing the aquarium walls when conditions are right.

As time goes on, I think we will see more than a few marine aquarists producing some species of shrimps, sponges, marine worms, and mollusks for their own satisfaction and for small, localized markets. These invertebrates may reproduce from their own spawns, controlled and reared by the aquarist, or by the physical separation of the colonial organisms by the aquarist.

### CORAL FARMERS

Many soft and stony corals are easily propagated using asexual means, growing new clones from cuttings and fragments.

❖

## Mariculture

Marine aquarists can also count on seeing more and more farm-raised fishes, corals, giant clams, and other invertebrates coming from the ocean itself in a process called mariculture. An increasing range of species is being raised in marine bays and lagoons, in pens or on sunken structures

Panther Groupers (*Cromileptes altivelis*) are now captive-bred in Asian facilities—primarily to supply food markets, but with solid sales into the aquarium trade.

(in the case of maricultured corals), or in pools or raceways supplied with water from the sea.

Mariculture is a major source of edible finfish, such as salmon and cod; shellfish, such as prawns and mussels; and edible or commercially valuable seaweeds and pearls. Through the efforts of such pioneers as Gerald Heslinga, Walt Smith, Dave Palmer, Daniel Knop, and others, a number of tropical islands that are home to coral reefs have become important suppliers of maricultured *Tridacna* clams, stony and soft corals, grazing snails, and even live foods for marine aquarists, such as macroalgae and amphipods.

An interesting new development is the raising of post-larval reef fish in mariculture and aquaculture facilities, in the tropics or even in the developed nations where most marine aquarists live. Small juvenile fishes are netted or trapped and, with methods still being perfected, raised to a salable size in captive or semi-open systems and conditioned to eat prepared rations. Proponents of this approach claim their fish are better adapted to captive life than wild-caught mature fish. They also argue that capturing small juveniles places less fishing pressure on the reefs than harvesting adult specimens does.

Finally, part of the lure of breeding and propagating marine fishes and invertebrates is that the ultimate book on how to do so has not been written. In fact, it may be several human lifetimes before we sort out all of the challenges of breeding the tens of thousands of marine organisms that one might consider worth propagating. My best advice is to learn from the work of published aquarists, listen to the success and failure stories of your peers, and be ready to experiment. Be ready to fail, and fail again, and if you succeed with a new species, by all means, share your findings with the rest of us. Modern marine aquarium husbandry has been able to evolve so rapidly over the past few decades for two simple reasons: people have been willing to experiment and try radical techniques, and they've been willing to generously share their secrets when they've met with success.

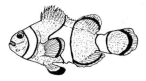

# Index

# Selected References

This is by no means a complete listing, but the books listed below have been of value and interest to me and they should also benefit other marine aquarists.

I have included a few highly technical academic publications because an advanced aquarist may wish to consult these foundation works, but for the most part, the list is composed of popular or general works that the average marine aquarist will find informative and useful. Collecting and reading a variety of books makes a good marine aquarist a better marine aquarist.

Most of these books are available at libraries, bookstores, and aquarium shops. Aquarium societies often have excellent collections and may allow members to borrow from them. I have also listed some out-of-print books, which are often available from libraries and society collections. The popular aquarium magazines and many aquarium society newsletters are also excellent sources of topical information. Internet websites, online forums, and videos can also yield valuable information.

Adey, W.H. and K. Loveland. 1991. *Dynamic Aquaria*. Academic Press, San Diego, CA.

Allen, G.R. 1975. *The Anemonefishes: Their Classification and Biology* (2nd Ed.). TFH Publications, Neptune City, NJ.

—. 1980. *Anemonefishes of the World: Species, Care, and Breeding*. Aquarium Systems, Mentor, OH.

Allen, G.R. and R. Steene. 1994. *Indo-Pacific Coral Reef Field Guide*. Tropical Reef Research, Singapore.

Allen, G.R. 2000. *Marine Fishes of Tropical Australia and South-east Asia*. Western Australian Museum, Perth.

Andrews, C., A. Exell, and N. Carrington. 1988. *The Manual of Fish Health*. Tetra Press, Blacksburg, VA.

Axelrod, H.F., W.E. Burgess, and R. Hunziker. 1990. *Dr. Burgess's Atlas of Marine Aquarium Fishes.* TFH Publications, Inc., Neptune City, NJ.

Baensch, H.A. and H. Debelius. 1994. *Marine Atlas, Vol. 1.* Mergus, Melle, Germany.

Bassleer, G. 1996. *Diseases in Marine Aquarium Fish, Causes—Symptoms—Treatment.* Bassleer Biofish, with English translation by Global Communications, Lannoo Drukkerij, Belgium.

—. 2003. *The New Illustrated Guide to Fish Diseases in Ornamental Tropical and Pond Fish.* Bassleer Biofish, Westmeerbeek, Belgium.

Borneman, Eric H. 2001. *Aquarium Corals.* Microcosm/TFH Publications, Neptune City, NJ.

Breder, C.M., Jr. and D.E. Rosen. 1966. *Modes of Reproduction in Fishes.* TFH Publications, Neptune City, NJ.

Burgess, W., H.R. Axelrod, and R.E. Hunziker III. 2000. *Dr. Burgess's Atlas of Marine Aquarium Fishes, Third Edition.* TFH Publications, Neptune City, NJ.

Byatt, A., A. Fothergill, and M. Holmes. 2001. *The Blue Planet.* BBC Worldwide Ltd., London.

Cannon, L. and M. Goyen. 1989. *Exploring Australia's Great Barrier Reef—a World Heritage Site.* The Watermark Press, Surry Hills, NSW, Australia.

Cato, J.C. and C.L. Brown, eds. 2003. *Marine Ornamental Species: Collection, Culture, and Conservation.* Wiley-Blackwell, Ames, IA.

Chaplin, C.C. 1972. *Fishwatchers Guide to West Atlantic Coral Reefs.* Livingston Publishing Co., Wynnewood, PA.

Clifton, R. 1993. *Marine Fish—the Recognition and Treatment of Diseases.* Peregrine Publishing, McKinney, TX.

Colin, P.L. 1975. *The Neon Gobies.* TFH Publications, Neptune City, NJ.

—. 1978. *Caribbean Reef Invertebrates and Plants.* TFH Publications, Neptune City, NJ.

Colin, P.L. and C. Arneson. 1995. *Tropical Pacific Invertebrates.* Coral Reef Press, CA.

Cushing, D.H. 1975. *Marine Ecology and Fisheries.* Cambridge University Press, Cambridge.

—. 1981. *Fisheries Biology, a Study in Population Dynamics.* University of Wisconsin Press, Madison, WI.

Dakin, N. 1992. *The Book of the Marine Aquarium.* Tetra Press, Blacksburg, VA.

Davidson, O.G. 1998. *The Enchanted Braid: Coming to Terms with Nature on the Coral Reef.* John Wiley & Sons, Inc., New York.

Dawes, C.J. 1981. *Marine Botany.* John Wiley & Sons, Inc., New York.

Dawson, E.Y. 1956. *How to Know the Seaweeds.* William C. Brown Co., Dubuque, IA.

de Graaf, F. 1973. *Marine Aquarium Guide* (English translation, Dr. J. Spiekerman). Pet Library, Harrison, NJ.

Debelius, H. 1989. *Fishes for the Invertebrate Aquarium* (3rd ed., English). Aquarium Systems, Mentor, OH.

Delbeek, J.C. and J. Sprung. 1994. *The Reef Aquarium: A Comprehensive Guide to the Identification and Care of Tropical Marine Invertebrates (Vol. 1)*. Ricordea Publishing, Coconut Grove, FL.

—. 1997. *The Reef Aquarium: A Comprehensive Guide to the Identification and Care of Tropical Marine Invertebrates (Vol 2)*. Two Little Fishies, Coconut Grove, FL.

—. 2005. *The Reef Aquarium: Science, Art, and Technology (Vol. 3)*. Ricordea Publishing, Coconut Grove, FL.

DelFavero, C. 2005. *Aquarium Keeping & Rescue*. Microcosm/TFH Publishing, Neptune City, NJ.

Dewey, D., ed. 1986. *For What It's Worth, Vol. 1*. FAMA Anthology Library Series. RC Modeler Corp., Sierra Madre, CA.

Dubinsky, Z., ed. 1990. *Coral Reefs: Ecosystems of the World, Vol. 25*. Elsevier Science, New York.

Fenner, R.M. 2008. *The Conscientious Marine Aquarist, Revised and Updated Second Edition*. Microcosm/TFH Publications, Neptune City, NJ.

Florida Aqua Farms. 1987. *Plankton Culture Manual*. Florida Aqua Farms, Dade City, FL.

Fosså, S.A. and A.J. Nilsen. 1996. *The Modern Coral Reef Aquarium, Vol. 1*. Birgit Schmettkamp Verlag, Bornheim, Germany.

—. 2000. *The Modern Coral Reef Aquarium, Vol. 3*. Birgit Schmettkamp Verlag, Bornheim, Germany.

—. 2002. *The Modern Coral Reef Aquarium, Vol. 4*. Birgit Schmettkamp Verlag, Bornheim, Germany.

Friese, U.E. 1972. *Sea Anemones*. TFH Publications, Neptune City, NJ.

Goemans, B. and Ichinotsubo, L. 2008. *The Marine Fish Health and Feeding Handbook*. Microcosm/TFH Publications, Neptune City, NJ.

Gosliner, T.M., D.W. Behrens, and G.C. Williams. 1996. *Coral Reef Animals of the Indo-Pacific*. Sea Challengers, Monterey, CA.

Gratzek, J.B., R.E. Wolke, E.B. Shotts, Jr., D. Dawe, and G. Blasiola. 1992. *Fish Diseases and Water Chemistry*. Tetra Press, Morris Plains, NJ.

Gratzek, J.B., ed. 1992. *Aquariology: The Science of Fish Health Management*. Tetra Press, Morris Plains, NJ.

Gray, W. 1993. *Coral Reefs & Islands: The Natural History of a Threatened Paradise*. David & Charles, Devon, UK.

Green, E. 2003. *Marine Ornamental Species: Collection, Culture, and Conservation*. Iowa State Press, Ames, IA.

Halver, J.E., ed. 1989. *Fish Nutrition*. Academic Press, London.

Halver, J.E. and R.W. Hardy. 2002. *Fish Nutrition (3rd Ed.)*. Academic Press, Inc., San Diego, CA.

Herwig, N. 1979. *Handbook of Drugs and Chemicals Used in the Treatment of Fish Diseases.* Charles C. Thomas, Publishers, Springfield, IL.

Hemdal, Jay F. 2006. *Advanced Marine Aquarium Techniques: Guide to Successful Professional Marine Aquarium Systems.* TFH Publications, Neptune City, NJ.

Hoff, Frank H. 1996. *Conditioning, spawning and rearing of fish with emphasis on marine clownfish.* Florida Aqua Farms, Dade City, FL.

Hoff, F. and T. Snell. 2007. *Plankton Culture Manual, 6th Edition.* Florida Aqua Farms, Dade City, FL.

Holliday, L. 1989. *Coral Reefs.* Salamander Books, Ltd., London.

Humann, P. 2002. *The Reef Set: Reef Fish, Reef Creature, Reef Coral.* New World Publications, Jacksonville, FL.

Kaplan, E.G. 1982. *A Field Guide to Coral Reefs, Caribbean and Florida.* Houghton Mifflin Co., Boston.

—. 1988. *A Field Guide to Southeastern and Caribbean Seashores.* Houghton Mifflin Co., Boston.

Keenleyside, M.H.A. 1979. *Diversity and Adaptation in Fish Behavior.* Springer-Verlag, New York.

Lieske, E. and R. Myers. 2001. *Coral Reef Fishes.* Princeton University Press, Princeton, NJ.

Littler, D.S., M. Littler, K.E. Bucher, and J.N. Norris. 1989. *Marine Plants of the Caribbean.* Smithsonian Institution Press, Washington, DC.

Mather, P. and I. Bennett. 1993. *A Coral Reef Handbook (3rd ed).* Surrey Beatty & Sons Pty., Ltd., Chipping Northon, NSW, Australia.

Michael, Scott W. 1999. *Marine Fishes: A PocketExpert Guide.* Microcosm/TFH Publications, Neptune City, NJ.

—. 2001. *Reef Fishes, Vol. 1.* Microcosm/TFH Publications, Neptune City, NJ.

—. 2004. *Reef Fishes, Vol. 2: Basslets, Dottybacks & Hawkfishes.* Microcosm/TFH Publications, Neptune City, NJ.

—. 2004. *Reef Fishes, Vol. 3: Angelfishes & Butterflyfishes.* Microcosm/TFH Publications, Neptune City, NJ.

—. 2005. *Reef Aquarium Fishes: A PocketExpert Guide.* Microcosm/TFH Publications, Neptune City, NJ.

—. 2007. *Adventurous Aquarist Guide: The 101 Best Saltwater Fishes.* Microcosm/TFH Publications, Neptune City, NJ.

—. 2007. *Adventurous Aquarist: The 101 Best Marine Invertebrates.* Microcosm/TFH Publications, Neptune City, NJ.

—. 2008. *Reef Fishes, Vol. 4: Damselfishes & Anemonefishes.* Microcosm/TFH Publications, Neptune City, NJ.

—. 2009. *Reef Fishes, Vol. 5: Wrasses & Parrotfishes.* Microcosm/TFH Publications, Neptune City, NJ.

Mills, D. 1987. *Tetra Encyclopedia of the Marine Aquarium.* Tetra Press, Blacksburg, VA.

Miner, R.W. 1950. *Field Book of Seashore Life.* G. P. Putnam's Sons, New York.

Moe, Martin A., Jr. 1989 (revised 1992). *The Marine Aquarium Reference: Systems and Invertebrates.* Green Turtle Publications, Islamorada, FL.

—. 1997. *Breeding the Orchid Dottyback.* Green Turtle Publications, Plantation, FL.

Moe, Martin A., Jr. and B. Moe. 2000. *The Marine Aquarist's Quiz Book.* Green Turtle Publications, Plantation, FL.

Nilsen, A.J. and S. Fosså. 2003. *Reef Secrets.* Microcosm/TFH Publications, Neptune City, NJ.

Noga, E.J. 2000. *Fish Disease, Diagnosis and Treatment.* Iowa State Press, Ames, IA.

Norman, J.R. 1958. *A History of Fishes.* Hill and Wang, New York.

Nybakken, J.W. 1982. *Marine Biology—an Ecological Approach.* Harper & Row Publishers, Inc., New York.

Ostrowski, A.C. and C.W. Laidley. 2001. Application of marine foodfish techniques in ornamental aquaculture: reproduction and larval first feeding. *Aquar Sci Cons* 3:191-204.

Paletta, M.S. 2001. *The New Marine Aquarium.* Microcosm/TFH Publications, Neptune City, NJ.

—. 2003. *Ultimate Marine Aquariums.* Microcosm/TFH Publications, Neptune City, NJ.

Palko, B.J. 1981. *A Balanced Marine Aquarium.* NOAA Technical Memorandum, NMFSSEFC—59 (out of print), pp. 1–25.

Post, G. 1987. *Textbook of Fish Health: Revised and Expanded Edition.* TFH Publications, Neptune City, NJ.

Quick, J.A., Jr. 1977. *Marine Disease Primer: Book One, A guide to disease prevention in aquarium fishes and invertebrates* (out of print). Marine Hobbyist News Publications, Bloomington, IL.

Randall, J.E. and B.P. Bishop. 1965. *Food Habits of Reef Fishes of the West Indies.* In: *Stud Trop Oceanogr* 5: 665–840.

Randall, J.E. 1968. *Caribbean Reef Fishes.* TFH Publications, Neptune City, NJ.

Reichenbach-Klinke, H.H. 1972. *Fish Pathology.* English translation, Christa Ahrens. TFH Publications, Neptune City, NJ.

Robins, C.R., G.C. Ray, J. Douglass, and E. Freund. 1986. *A Field Guide to the Atlantic Coast Fishes of North America.* Houghton Mifflin Co., Boston.

Schubert, G. 1987. *Fish Disease—a Complete Introduction.* TFH Publications, Neptune City, NJ.

Sefton, N. and S.K. Webster. 1986. *Caribbean Reef Invertebrates.* Sea Challengers, Monterey, CA.

Shimek, R.L. 2004. *Marine Invertebrates: A PocketExpert Guide.* Microcosm/TFH Publications, Neptune City, NJ.

Sorokin, Y.I. 1995. *Coral Reef Ecology.* Springer Verlag, Berlin, Germany.

Spotte, S. 1970. *Fish and Invertebrate Culture: Water Management in Closed Systems.* John Wiley & Sons, Inc., New York.

—. 1973. *Marine Aquarium Keeping.* John Wiley & Sons, Inc., New York.

—. 1979. *Seawater Aquariums, The Captive Environment.* John Wiley & Sons, Inc., New York.

—. 1992. *Captive Seawater Fishes: Science and Technology.* John Wiley & Sons, Inc., New York.

Steene, R. 1990. *Coral Reefs: Nature's Richest Realm.* Mallard Press, New York.

Sterrer, W. 1986, ed. *Marine Fauna and Flora of Bermuda. A Systematic Guide to the Identification of Marine Organisms.* John Wiley & Sons, Inc., New York.

Steene, R.C. 1979. *Butterfly and Angelfishes of the World, Vol. 1: Australia.* John Wiley & Sons, Inc., New York.

Steene. R.C., G.R. Allen, and H.A. Baensch. 1980. *Butterfly and Angelfishes of the World, Vol. 2: Atlantic Ocean, Caribbean Sea, Red Sea, Indo-Pacific.* John Wiley & Sons, Inc., New York.

Straughan, R.P.L. 1970. *The Salt Water Aquarium in the Home* (out of print). A. S. Barnes and Company, Cranbury, NJ.

Tackett, D.N. and L.Tackett. 2002. *Reef Life.* Microcosm/TFH Publications, Neptune City, NJ.

Thresher, Ronald E. 1980. *Reef Fish: Behavior and Ecology on the Reef and in the Aquarium* (out of print). Palmetto Publishing Company, St. Petersburg, FL.

Thresher, Ronald E. 1984. *Reproduction in Reef Fishes.* TFH Publications, Neptune City, NJ.

Tullock, John H. 1997. *Natural Reef Aquariums.* Microcosm/TFH Publications, Neptune City, NJ.

Untergasser, D. 1989. *Handbook of Fish Diseases.* TFH Publications, Neptune City, NJ.

Veron, J.E.N. 2000. *Corals of the World.* Australian Institute of Marine Science, Townsville, QLD, Australia.

Voss, G.L. 1976. *Seashore Life of Florida and the Caribbean.* Banyan Books, Inc., Miami, FL.

Voss, G.L. 1988. *Coral Reefs of Florida.* Pineapple Press, Sarasota, FL.

Walls, J.G. 1975. *Fishes of the Northern Gulf of Mexico.* TFH Publications, Neptune City, NJ.

Walls, J.G., ed. 1982. *Encyclopedia of Marine Invertebrates.* TFH Publications, Neptune City, NJ.

Wilkens, P. 1973. *The Saltwater Aquarium for Tropical Marine Invertebrates.* 2nd Extended Edition (English Translation). Engelbert Pfriem, Wuppertal-Elberfeld, Germany.

Wilkerson, Joyce D. 1998. *Clownfishes: A Guide to Their Captive Care, Breeding and Natural History.* Microcosm/TFH Publications, Neptune City, NJ.

Wood, E.M. 1983. *Reef Corals of the World: Biology and Field Guide.* TFH Publications, Neptune City, NJ.

Wood, R. 1999. *Reef Evolution.* Oxford University Press, NY.

## Aquarium Societies

**Marine Aquarium Societies
of North America (MASNA)**
http://www.masna.org

Check your local aquarium shop for the names and addresses of local aquarium societies and clubs. Individual societies often have speakers, programs, tank shows, auctions, field trips, weekend workshops, conferences, and other events for local aquarists, as well as providing a forum for the exchange of ideas, experiences, equipment, fish, invertebrates, and plants.

There are also many scheduled conferences and events sponsored by one or more marine aquarium clubs and societies.

**MACNA**
Marine Aquarium Conference of North America (MASNA)
http://www.macnaxxi.com

**IMAC WEST**
International Marine Aquarium Conference (West)
http://www.imacwest.com

## Marine Aquarium Magazines

*Aquarium Fish International*
http://www.fishchannel.com/affc_portal.aspx

*CORAL Magazine*
http://www.coralmagazine.com/

*Freshwater and Marine Aquarium*
http://www.fishchannel.com/fama_portal.aspx

*Practical Fishkeeping* (UK)
http://www.practicalfishkeeping.co.uk

*ReefLife*
http://reeflifemagazine.com

*Tropical Fish Hobbyist*
http://www.tfhmagazine.com/

*UltraMarine* (UK)
http://www.ultramarinemagazine.co.uk

## Marine Breeding & Captive Propagation

**The Breeder's Registry**
http://www.breedersregistry.org/

**Marine Ornamental Fish & Invertebrate Breeders (MOFIB)**
http://www.marinebreeder.org/

**MASNA Breeding Forums**
http://www.masna.org/forums.aspx

# Photo Credits

*All images by*
## Matthew L. Wittenrich
(AquaticPixels.net)
*except those noted below.*

**Scott W. Michael** (coralrealm.com): 182–183, 184–185, 186–187, 310

**Alf Jacob Nilsen** (BioPhoto.net): 18–19, 52, 60, 73, 88, 101, 111, 140, 148, 152, 187, 275, 329

**Denise Nielsen Tackett** & **Larry Tackett** (tackettproductions.com): 46, 58, 128, 284, 123, 306, 312

**Matt Pedersen:** 28, 277, 290, 304, 305, 330, 331

**AquaticLife LLC** (AquaticLife.com): 130, 131, 132, 133

**Scott Cohen** (SeaDwelling.com): 65, 97

**J. Charles Delbeek:** 196

**Suk Choo Kim | CPR Aquatics** (CPRUSA.com): 72

**Vince Suh** (uniquecorals.com): 332 (left)

*Special thanks* to **Jeffrey A. Turner** (Reef Aquaria Design), designer of the systems on these pages: 21, 26, 40, 90, 112, 157, 254

*All illustrations* by the **author.**

# About the Author

MARTIN ANDREAS MOE, JR. HAS BEEN AROUND FOR A LONG TIME. HE holds a master's degree from the University of South Florida and his scientific and popular articles and books date back to 1962, when he began his career as a marine biologist for the State of Florida. He entered the private sector and developed the basic technology for breeding Florida pompano in 1970. He accomplished the first commercial culture of marine tropical fish (Ocellaris Clownfish and Neon Gobies) in a garage in 1972, and over the years has reared more than 30 species of marine tropical fish, including spawning, rearing, and even hybridizing French and Grey Angelfish. He founded the first commercial marine fish hatchery, Aqualife Research Corporation, in 1973 to produce tropical marine aquarium fish, and Green Turtle Publications in 1982 to write and publish books on the marine aquarium hobby. Moe is the author of a definitive book on tropical Atlantic lobsters, *Lobsters: Florida, the Bahamas, the Caribbean*, as well as his popular and best-selling marine aquarium books, *Marine Aquarium Handbook: Beginner to Breeder* and *The Marine Aquarium Reference: Systems and Invertebrates*. Other books he authored are *Breeding the Orchid Dottyback: An Aquarist's Journal* and (with his wife, Barbara) *The Marine Aquarists' Quiz Book*. He and Barbara now live in the Florida Keys and have come full circle—they have set up a small experimental marine culture laboratory in a spare room. Recently, after three years of work developing the technology for large-scale breeding of the Long-spined Sea Urchin, *Diadema antillarum*, Moe has been successful, and this technology may be instrumental in future coral reef restoration efforts in the tropical western Atlantic and Caribbean.